This book is to be returned on
or before the date stamped below

26. MAR. 1999

20. MAR. 99

CANCELLED

COMPANY LAW

European Community Law Series
Series Editor: Professor D Lasok, QC (University of Exeter)

European Community Law will have an important impact upon the law of the United Kingdom and other countries concerned with EC legislation. This new series will provide authoritative and up-to-date accounts of specific topics and areas. The volumes are addressed to legal practitioners, in-house lawyers, businessmen and to all those who need to communicate with lawyers in this field.

Volumes will include:

Peter Stone, *Copyright Law in the United Kingdom and the European Community*

Rosa Greaves, *Transport Law of the European Community*

Friedl Weiss, *Public Supply and Public Works Contracts in European Community Law*

Philippe Bourin, *The European Investment Bank*

David Freestone, *Environmental Protection in the European Community*

S K Chatterjee, *Legal Aspects of Drug Control and Treatment within the European Community*

European Community Law Series

COMPANY LAW
in the United Kingdom and the
European Community:
Its Harmonization and Unification

Frank Wooldridge

THE ATHLONE PRESS
London & Atlantic Highlands, NJ

First published 1991 by The Athlone Press Ltd
1 Park Drive, London NW11 7SG and
171 First Avenue, Atlantic Highlands, NJ 07716

© Frank Wooldridge 1991

British Library Cataloguing in Publication Data
Wooldridge, Frank
  Company law in the United Kingdom and the European
  Community: its harmonisation and unification.
  1. European Community countries. Companies. Law
  I. Title
  342.666094

  ISBN 0–485–70003–4

Library of Congress Cataloging-in-Publication Data
Wooldridge, Frank.
    Company law in the UK and the EC: its harmonisation and
  unification / Frank Wooldridge.
      p.   cm. — (European Community law series)
    Includes bibliographical references and index.
    ISBN 0–485–70003–4 (cl.)
      1. Corporation law—European Economic Community countries.
  2. Corporation law—Great Britain. I. Title. II. Series.
  KJE2448.W66   1991
  346.4'066—dc20
  [344.0666]

Typeset by J&L Composition Ltd, Filey, North Yorkshire
Printed in Great Britain by Billings and Sons Ltd, Worcester

Contents

Series Preface

West European integration has become an irreversible and ever-expanding process affecting directly not only the Member States of the European Community but also business interests and individuals in all walks of life. The prediction that, in time, 80 per cent of the national legislation will eventually emanate from Brussels may not be accurate but the volume of regulations and directives so far produced in the Community has already assumed formidable dimensions. Consequently textbooks, commentaries and source publications have grown in size to the point of being too voluminous to be handled by anyone interested in a particular area. Moreover, in view of the abundance of material, large publications cannot always do justice to every topic which merits a treatment in depth.

In response to this challenge, The Athlone Press has launched a European Community Law Series addressed mainly to legal practice and the business world and also to students of law. The Series consists of concise and relatively short monographs designed to break new ground and fill the gaps in the existing literature. In monographs unencumbered with general information but still within the context of the integrative process, the Series offers guidance to the practitioner and businessman.

Volumes in the Series will take more or less self-contained subjects, and the Series will eventually compose a specialist library.

D Lasok

Series Editor

Volume Preface

The present work attempts to give a succinct but fairly comprehensive account of the harmonization and unification of company law in the European Economic Community. Although the impetus towards such harmonization may have slackened somewhat in recent years, there has been some revival of the activities of the Community institutions in this field. Thus the Eleventh Company Law Directive, which is concerned with disclosure requirements in respect of branches established by a foreign company in a Member State, and the Twelfth Company Law Directive, which is concerned with single-member private companies, were enacted by the Council of Ministers in December 1989. In addition, a new draft Statute for the European Company, to which the Commission attaches considerable importance, was published in October 1989.

Although the topic of the harmonization of company law has been somewhat neglected by English writers in comparison with such topics as Community competition or intellectual property law, and despite the fact that a number of criticisms have been made concerning the Commission's approach to harmonization, the importance of this topic should amply justify the completion of a new work on it. This appears specifically true when one remembers the very significant impact of such harmonization on the legal system of the Member States.

The present work examines the different Treaty bases for such harmonization, and existing controversies about the constitutionality of certain proposed bases. It also deals with the problems to which harmonization has given rise. It includes an account of the existing harmonizing directives and draft directives in the field of company law. Consideration has also been given to the impact of certain of the harmonizing directives in the legal systems of some Member States, in particular the United Kingdom, France and

Germany. In addition, an account has been provided of the Regulation on the European Economic Interest Grouping, and of the draft Statute for European Companies, which it is envisaged will also take the form of a Regulation. Despite the fact that this instrument has a number of defects and is unlikely to come into force, the work also considers the Convention on the Mutual Recognition of Companies and Firms for the sake of completeness.

Although an endeavour has been made to place emphasis on simplicity and clarity throughout the book, the author has sometimes attempted to deal with certain detailed questions, relating to such matters as company accounts. It is hoped that the book will prove useful to all who are interested in European company law, including practitioners, teachers, students and company officers.

Frank Wooldridge
London

1

Introduction: An Outline of the Work of the Community to Date

Topics to be covered

The present work will attempt to give a short account of the harmonization and unification of company law by the institutions of the European Communities. It will thus be principally concerned with the harmonization and unification of company law through the medium of Directives enacted by the Council of Ministers of the European Communities. The account given of such harmonization will necessarily include considerations of the proposals contained in the draft Tenth Directive on cross-border mergers of public limited companies.[1] It was formerly intended that such mergers, which may be anticipated to have beneficial economic effects, would be governed by a draft Convention;[2] indeed, this was expressly provided for in Article 220 of the Treaty of Rome. However, the proposal was converted into the above-mentioned draft Directive, based to a considerable extent on the Third Directive, which deals with national mergers of public limited companies.[3]

The book will also contain a chapter on the mutual recognition of companies, which is also of importance for the development of a Community company law, and is provided for in Article 220 of the Treaty of Rome, as well as in the Convention for the Mutual Recognition of Companies and Legal Persons, based on its afore-mentioned article. This Convention was signed by the six original Member States on 20 February 1968. Furthermore, an account will be given of two instruments providing for the establishment of bodies governed wholly or partly by a supranational system of law, i.e. Community law. These instruments are the Council Regulation of 25 July 1985 on the European Economic Interest Grouping[4] and the amended proposal for a Council Regulation on the Statute for European Companies.[5] The EEIG is a new form of undertaking largely governed by directly applicable rules of

Community law. The European Company, which would sometimes form a satisfactory alternative to an international merger, is intended as an instrument for the concentration of enterprises in the Common Market, and at present is designed as a company governed in part by a detailed Statute, which would not, however, be identical in all Member States.

The present work will not concern itself with the rapidly developing field of securities law concerned with the issue, holding of, and dealings in securities, and related matters, in which a number of measures have been adopted or proposed by the Community.[6] This field is rapidly coming to be recognized as a discipline separate from company law. It will also not contain any special detailed treatment of the directives applicable to the accounts of banks and financial institutions.

The Impact of the EEC Treaty Provisions on Freedom of Establishment

The European Economic Community is stated in Article 2 of the Rome Treaty to have as its task – by establishing a common market and by progressively approximating the economic policies of the Member States – the promotion throughout the Community of a harmonious development of economic activities, a continuous and balanced expansion, an increase in stability, and an accelerated increase in the standard of living. In furtherance of this task, Article 52 provides for the abolition of restrictions on the freedom of establishment of nationals of Member States. Article 58(1) accords similar treatment to companies and firms within the meaning of Article 58(2) which are formed in accordance with the law of a Member State, and have their registered office, central administration, or principal place of business within the Community.

The definition of companies and firms contained in Article 58(2) includes all enterprises which are profit-making. It would appear that the phrase 'profit-making' means that they have as their object, under their constitutions, the making of a profit, whether they actually succeed in making one or not. The definition thus includes partnerships, limited or unlimited companies, co-operative societies, building societies, mutual assurance clubs, and legal entities governed by public law which pursue the objective of making a profit, such as nationalized industries. A British[7] limited company which is exempted from the requirement of using the word 'limited' as the last word of its name in accordance with sections 30 and 31 of the Companies Act 1985 does not fall outside the definition in Article 58(2) because, by section 30, such a company is not prevented from making profits but only from distributing them. It would seem that charities and social clubs which do not take the form of limited companies, and trade-union organizations, fall outside Article 58(2).[8]

According to most textwriters, the right of establishment conferred by the EEC Treaty can manifest itself in two different ways. On the one hand, subsidiaries, branches or agencies may be set up. This is known as secondary establishment. In *Re Insurance Services, EC Commission v. Germany*[9] the European Court of Justice held that an undertaking is established in a Member State as soon as it has a permanent presence there, even if that presence consists merely of

> an office managed by the undertaking's own staff or by a person who is independent but authorized to act on a permanent basis for the undertaking, as would be the case with an agency.

The view has also been expressed that establishment may take the form of participation in the setting up of a new company, or the transfer of the central management and control of a company, often called its real head office.[10] However, in so far as the latter matter is concerned, the court pointed out in the *Daily Mail* case, the conditions under which a company may transfer its central management and control from one Member State to another are still governed by the national law of the State in which it is incorporated, and that to which it wishes to move. For the latter reason, the court found that in the present state of Community law, Articles 52 and 58 of the Treaty did not confer any such right of transfer upon a company incorporated under the law of a Member State. It is submitted that it was open to the court to come to a different conclusion in the special circumstances of the *Daily Mail* case, because both English law and the law of the Netherlands permitted such a transfer.[11]

A controversy exists as to whether companies and firms which merely have a registered office in a Member State benefit from freedom of establishment. According to the private international law doctrines followed by the majority of Member States, the law governing a company's affairs is that of the *siège réel* (central administration), and it would thus be possible for a company to be registered in a Member State but to have its central administration outside the Community, and in consequence for its legal existence not to be recognized in the other Member States. The General Programme for the Removal of Restrictions on the Right of Establishment[12] takes account of the *siège réel* doctrine, and somewhat controversially requires that before a company may benefit from the right of establishment it must have a continuous and effective link with the economy of one of the Member States.

Methods of Harmonization and Unification of Company Law Provided for in the Treaty

The Directives

Differences in national company laws may clearly have an effect on the freedom of establishment provided for in the Treaty. Article 54(3)(g) provides that measures should be taken by the Community to secure freedom of establishment by:

> co-ordinating to the necessary extent the safeguards which, for the protection of the interests of members and others, are required by Member States of companies and firms within the meaning of the second paragraph of Article 58 with a view to making such safeguards equivalent throughout the Comunity.

The wording of Article 54(3)(g) is unclear in some respects. It is unclear whether 'co-ordinating' has a different meaning from approximation or harmonization: however, this appears not to be the case.[13] Furthermore, there is some lack of clarity about the object of the harmonization; one may legitimately pose the question as to which provisions of company law are not safeguards for shareholders and third parties of the kind envisaged.[14] This question is rendered particularly difficult by reason of the interdependence between provisions of national company laws. Furthermore, it will often prove very difficult to determine whether provisions of national company laws are in fact equivalent.[15]

Article 54(2) empowers the Council to issue Directives to carry out its tasks under that Article, including those under Article 54(3)(g). Although, as already pointed out, the Council's tasks under that Article are limited to measures for the protection of shareholders and third parties, the Community institutions have placed a wide construction on Article 54(3)(g). It is noteworthy that the distinguished French lawyer R. Houin has argued that there are in fact no limitations on a Directive made under Article 54(3)(g).[16] The Commission has indeed adopted the view that the harmonization of national company laws and the creation of a common market for companies is necessary for the proper functioning of the Common Market.

Directives are stated in Article 189 of the Rome Treaty to be binding as to the result to be achieved, but to leave to the national authorities the choice of form and matter. It is sometimes argued that the company law Directives leave too many options open to the Member State. However, many of the provisions of the company law Directives leave little discretion to the Member States in respect of their implementation.[17] Such provisions may have direct effect in the Member States once the time for their implementation has elapsed. They will thus prevail over any contrary provisions of national law, and be capable of being invoked by natural or legal persons in the Member States.[18] It should also be noted that once a Member State has enacted legislation conforming with the requirements of a Directive, it will not be able to amend this legislation effectively in a manner which conflicts with these requirements. This effect of a Directive is sometimes referred to as its blocking or congealing effect. Sometimes the meaning of certain provisions in a Directive is unclear, and thus results in difficulties for national legislators. National courts are required to interpret the legislation adopted for the implementation of a Directive in conformity with the requirements of Community law, in so far as they are given discretion to be so under national law.[19]

The Council of Ministers of the European Communities has so far enacted twelve harmonizing company law Directives under Article 54(3)(g), which now requires a qualified majority vote in co-operation with the European Parliament. The complex co-operation procedure introduced by Article 7 of the Single European Act gives the European Parliament a considerable measure of influence over the content of European legislation, because it is able to exercise some control over the manner in which the Council must vote to adopt a proposal. Thus, for example, if

Parliament rejects the common position which must first of all be reached in the Council, the Council may still adopt the proposal within a maximum period of four months, provided that it does so by unanimous vote. The more general provisions of Article 100 have been invoked for the purpose of harmonizing securities law, but they have not yet been invoked for the purposes of harmonization of company law. Article 100 requires a unanimous vote in the Council, and empowers the harmonization of legislative and administrative provisions directly affecting the establishment and functioning of the Common Market. It is now apparent that company law harmonization may take place under Article 100A, which was inserted in the Rome Treaty by the Single European Act.[20] This text permits such harmonization by means of a qualified majority.

The harmonization Directives which have so far been enacted in the field of company law are:

1. First Council Directive of 9 March 1968 (18/151/EEC) concerning the capacity of the company and its directors, and questions of publicity and nullity of the company.[21]
2. Second Council Directive of 13 December 1976 (72/91/EEC) on the formation of public limited companies and the maintenance and alteration of their capital.[22]
3. Third Council Directive of 9 October 1978 (78/855/EEC) concerning mergers of public limited liability companies.[23]
4. Fourth Council Directive of 25 July 1978 (78/660/EEC) on the annual accounts of certain types of companies.[24]
4a. Council Directive of 27 November 1984 (84/569/EEC) revising the amounts expressed in ECU in Directive 78.660. EEC.[25]
5. Sixth Council Directive of 17 December 1982 (82.891.EEC) concerning the division of public limited companies.[26]
6. Seventh Council Directive of 13 June 1983 (83.349.EEC) on consolidated accounts.[27]
7. Eighth Council Directive of 10 April 1984 (84/258/EEC) on the approval of persons responsible for carrying out statutory audits of accounting documents.[28]
8. Council Directive of 8 December 1986 (86/635/EEC) on the annual accounts and consolidated accounts of banks and other financial institutions.[29]

9. Council Directive on the obligations of branches established in a Member State by credit institutions and financial institutions having their head office outside that Member State regarding the publication of annual accounting documents.[30]
10. Eleventh Council Directive of 30 December 1989 on disclosure requirements in respect of branches opened in a Member State by companies governed by the law of another Member State.[31]
11. Twelfth Council Directive of 30 December 1989 concerning single-member private limited companies.[32]

In addition to the above instruments, a number of Commission proposals for harmonizing Directives exist which have not yet been enacted by the Council of Ministers. These proposals are:

1. Amended proposal for a Fifth Council Directive on the structure of public limited companies, and the powers and obligation of their organs.[33]
2. Amended proposal for a Council Directive on procedures for consulting and informing employees of undertakings with complex structures (draft 'Vredeling').[34]
3. Proposal for a Tenth Council Directive on cross-border mergers of public limited companies.[35]
4. Proposal for a Council Directive amending Directive 78/660/EEC on annual accounts and Directives 83/349/EEC on consolidated accounts as regards the scope of those Directives.[36]
5. Proposal for a Council Directive on the annual accounts and consolidated accounts of insurance undertakings.[37]

Further proposals for the harmonization of European company law may well be introduced in the near future. It is likely that these will include a draft Ninth Directive on the conduct of Groups; preliminary drafts of such a Directive have already been published.[38]

The Conventions

Article 220 is also of importance for the development of Community company law. It provides that Member States shall, so far as necessary, enter into negotiations with each other with a view to ensuring for the benefit of their nations:

– the mutual recognition of firms or companies as defined in Article 58(2), the maintenance of legal personality in the event of transfer of registered office from one country to another, and the possibility of mergers between firms and companies which are subject to different domestic laws.

The six original Member States signed the Convention for the Mutual Recognition of Companies and Legal Persons in furtherance of this provision on 29 February 1968. It never came into force because the Netherlands failed to ratify it. The United Kingdom agreed to accede to it by the Act of Accession of 1972, but was empowered to enter into negotiations for the making of necessary adjustments thereto. The Convention was at one time under reconsideration by an *ad hoc* working group. However, the value of the Convention has been doubted by many authorities,[39] and no further meetings of the working group are anticipated in the near future. The Convention has been supplemented by a protocol, signed on 3 June 1971, giving the European Court of Justice competence to make preliminary rulings on the interpretation of the Convention, in the same way as Article 177 of the Rome Treaty does in the case of the EEC Treaty.

The transfer of the seat (registered office) from one Member State to another gives rise to problems which come about as a result of the differences between the company laws of the Members. The transfer of the registered office to another country is legally impossible in a number of Member States, including Germany, Belgium, the UK, Ireland, Denmark and the Netherlands. In these countries, a transfer of seat implies liquidation, and the taxation of the hidden reserves.[40] Such a transfer is permitted under French and Italian law, under certain conditions.[41] If these are complied with, French or Italian companies may leave their state of residence without being wound up, but they may still incur significant tax liabilities. Problems also arise in connection with the transfer of the central administration (real seat) of a company from one Member State to another. It was held by the European Court of Justice in the *Daily Mail* case[42] that the problem of the transfer of the registered office or real seat of a company from one Member State to another could not be solved by the rules concerning the right of establishment, but were to be dealt with in future legislation or Conventions.

No such legislation or Convention has been enacted, but a considerable amount of preliminary work has been done on cross-frontier mergers. Such mergers are either prohibited or rendered unsurmountably difficult under legislation and case law in most of the Member States at present.[43] Thus, for example, German doctrine treats mergers between a German company and a foreign company as excluded by law, whether the German company is acquired or being acquired, or is the new company or one of those ceasing to exist. In addition to the strict legal position, cross-frontier mergers would also attract heavy tax liabilities in respect of hidden reserves in many Member States.

As has already been pointed out, it is now intended that such mergers will be permitted by a harmonizing Directive, but it is understood that the proposal has encountered a situation of deadlock in the European Parliament, because of the approach taken in it to worker participation.

The regulations
Council Regulation (EEC) No. 213/85 of 25 July 1985 on the European Economic Interest Grouping[44] (EEIG) is based upon Article 235 EEC. Article 235, which has been made very considerable use of as a basis for European legislation, enables the Community to extend its activities, subject to certain safeguards. It provides:

> Where action by the Community appears necessary to achieve, in the course of the operation at the Common Market, one of the objections of the Community, and where this Treaty has not provided the necessary powers of action, the Council shall, by unanimous decision, on a proposal from the Commission and after the Assembly has been consulted, take the appropriate steps.

Although the Council Regulation on the EEIG contains a number of directly applicable provisions, it requires Member States to enact supplementary legislation in a number of different areas.

It is now proposed that the Statute for a European Company shall take the form of a Regulation under Article 100A EEC, and that it shall be complemented by a Directive on employee participation.[45] The constitutional basis of this proposal has given rise to controversy.

9

Policies Pursued by the Community Institutions

As has already been indicated, the Community has engaged in an ambitious programme of company law harmonization, and the Council and Commission have assumed very wide powers under Article 54(3)(g). The Commission has recently defined its harmonization policy on the ground that, for the proper functioning of the internal market, it is desirable that all those who deal with public companies in the Community (shareholders, creditors and workers) can trust they are dealing with broadly the same legal structure, and have roughly the same rights.[46]

The Community has sometimes been accused of pursuing a policy of harmonization for its own sake in the field of company law as well as in other fields.[47] Furthermore, it has sometimes been questioned whether certain proposals, such as the provisions of the amended draft Fifth Directive concerning worker participation and preliminary versions of the draft Ninth Directive on the Conduct of Groups of Companies, are properly based on Article 54(3)(g).[48] It should be apparent from the above defence of the Commission's harmonization policy that harmonization of company law has sometimes been treated by the Community Institutions as a political instrument aimed at the creation of a Common Market.[49] It now appears to be the case, however, that the movement towards such harmonization is somewhat losing its momentum at present.

Certain of the harmonizing directives impose very detailed obligations upon Member States, and their implementation should have resulted in the practical unification of European company law in a number of different fields. This would seem to be true in particular of the First, Second and Third Directives, which contain comparatively few optional provisions. However, it has sometimes proved impossible to achieve such a detailed degree of harmonization because of differences between national laws and practices, as well as between national attitudes and policies. Such policy differences will often become manifest in the negotiations in the Council of Ministers.

The latter factors should explain why Community legislation in the field of company law sometimes takes a long time to enact, and why certain of the relevant instruments, such as the Fourth and Seventh Directive, provide for a number of options and alternatives. They also explain why certain draft Directives, such as the draft

Fifth and Tenth Directives, have not yet been adopted. Similar difficulties explain why it has so far not been possible to adopt the draft Statute for European Companies, the original version of which dates from 1970.[50]

Apart from objections based upon the very wide interpretation given to Article 54(3)(g) by the Community Institutions, there have been a number of other objections to the Community's approach to the harmonization of company law. The sheer volume of Community legislation has caused hardship to government departments called upon to implement different directives within a short time period. Thus, only two years was given for the implementation of the complex and far-reaching provisions of the Second Directive. The granting of such a short time period resulted in enforcement proceedings under Article 169 being taken against a number of Member States. It is noteworthy that certain later instruments granted a longer period for their implementation: thus the Seventh Directive on consolidated accounts gave a period of four and a half years. An additional example is provided by the Regulation on the EEIG, which did not become applicable until 1 July 1989. Four years after the publication of the instrument, Member States were required to enact implementing legislation. Exception is often taken to the piecemeal 'salami' tactics of harmonization adopted by the Community: thus, for example, three related Directives were made on the subject of accounts and auditors at different times, and it proved difficult for Member States to implement the Fourth Directive on individual company accounts, which was the first of the Directives to be enacted, in the absence of provisions on group accounts and the qualifications of auditors, which were dealt with in the Seventh and Eighth Directives, enacted some years later.[51] It is noteworthy that Germany implemented all three Directives by one piece of legislation, the *Bilanzrichtliniengesetz* of 19 December 1985.[52]

There have been a number of cogent criticisms about the methods by which harmonizing Directives have been adopted. Certain of the original proposals have not been accompanied by an adequate explanatory memorandum. It has often been the case that when harmonizing Directives are finally enacted, insufficient attention is paid to the opinions of the European Parliament, or the Economic and Social Committee, or of textwriters. Futhermore, negotiations within the Council are secret, and in the past have often led to the adoption of a text differing substantially from the latest published draft.[53] It appears unlikely that the difficulties mentioned in the last two sentences will be entirely removed as a result of the new co-operation procedure.

Considerable efforts are likely to be made in the near future to adopt the new proposals already mentioned concerning the European Company. It is felt by the Commission that making a European company form available to enterprises would meet a need that is growing increasingly pressing as the 1992 single market deadline approaches. Cross-frontier co-operation in the Community would appear to be not only an essential aspect of the creation of an effective common market , but also to be absolutely vital if the Community's national industries in major industrial sectors are to maintain and improve a competitive position both at home and in the world at large.[54] It is hoped that if a company of a European type were available, it would prove to be a valuable instrument of cross-frontier co-operation. The chief obstacle to such introduction which has so far been encountered has consisted of the inability to reach a satisfactory compromise which would bridge the gap between different national attitudes on worker participation. It is possible that progress on the draft Regulation for European Companies might have a favourable influence on the progress of some Directives involving the harmonization of company law, and in particular that of the draft Tenth Directive on Cross-Frontier mergers.[55]

Some Contributions Made by National Systems of Law

The nature of the negotiating process in the Council of Ministers necessarily implies that many of the provisions of the harmonizing Directives will represent a compromise between the approaches to the relevant problem taken by the Member States. However, such provisions may sometimes have their own original features, or display the influence of one or more particular systems of law. Thus, for example, although the provisions of Article 11 of the First Directive concerning the nullity of companies represent a compromise, those of Article 9, which govern the power of the organs of a company to bind it as against third parties, are clearly more influenced by German law than by the laws of the five other original Member States.[56] This system of law had a considerable influence on many of the detailed provisions of the Second

Directive. The Third Directive is influenced to a considerable extent by the provisions of French, German and Italian law governing the merger of companies. Article 2(3) of the Fourth Directive, which requires the annual accounts to give a true and fair view of the company's assets, liabilities, financial position and profit or loss, is clearly influenced by English and Irish law: however, despite the importance given to the true and fair value, this Directive remains to a large extent based on prescriptive codification as it is known in France and Germany, where the use of national accounting models [*Kontorahmen* and *plans comptables*] is common practice. The mandatory and permissive conditions for the preparation of consolidated accounts provided for by Article 1 of the Seventh Directive display the influence of British, Irish, French and German law. As already pointed out, this Directive is to a large extent a compromise measure, which endeavours to leave much of the law and practice of each Member State intact.

The amended proposal for a Fifth Directive, which has proved very controversial and has not yet been enacted by the Council of Ministers, provides that Member States may choose to apply one of five alternative systems of employee participation to companies having 1,000 or more employees. One of these proposed systems, involving a two-tier structure of management and supervisory boards with employees electing between one-third and one-half of the supervisory board,[57] is derived directly from German law. Another, under which there would be a unitary board of directors with employees electing between one-third and one-half of the non-executive directors,[58] is adapted from German law. The proposed system by which there would be a two-tier or unitary structure of management and supervisory boards, with employees' representatives being entitled to veto nominations for the supervisory board,[59] is derived from the Dutch system of co-optation. The fourth alternative, according to which there would be a consultative council combined with either a two-tier board or a unitary board,[60] is derived from the system of works councils familiar in France and other Member States. The final alternative, under which there would be collective agreements guaranteeing a measure of employee participation with either a two-tier board or a one-tier board,[61] is derived from Italian law. Despite the breadth of choice given, the United Kingdom remains opposed to the compulsory participation of workers in company decision-making. However, the amended proposal for a Council Regulation on the Statute for European Companies published in October 1989 (which is likely to be further amended) is influenced by all the alternative schemes of participation which have been mentioned above.

The failure of the Commission to make much progress with the preliminary drafts which it has published for a Ninth Directive on Groups of Companies is probably explained by the fact that these drafts have been based to too great an extent on German *Konzernrecht*, and proposals for its reform, and that insufficient attention has been paid to the recognized defects of this legal regime, and to the view of interest groups such as UNICE and the CBI, which have argued that no general regulation of groups is necessary. The provisions of the 1975 version of the draft Statute for European Companies on groups of companies was also based largely upon German law, and has also proved controversial. It is not, of course, suggested that a rule, regime or institution belonging to the legal system of only one or two Member States cannot sometimes provide a valuable inspiration for the development of European company law in particular circumstances. Thus, the French *groupement d'intérêt économique* (GIE) provided useful inspiration for the creation of the EEIG, which may enjoy some success as a vehicle for co-operation between undertakings.[62]

Progress Achieved so far and Impediments thereto
As should already be evident, the harmonizing Directives enacted so far cover a very wide field. It is unfortunate that it has hitherto been impossible to adopt the amended Fifth Directive owing to opposition from certain Member States,[63] and to enact the draft Tenth Directive owing to the situation of deadlock in the European Parliament. The reasons for the protracted failure to enact the draft Statute for European Companies are largely concerned with the differing approaches to worker participation in the different Member States. Unfortunately, it may prove difficult to reach satisfactory compromise on this matter in the near future.

The degree of harmonization achieved so far in the Member States may well be exaggerated. The First Company Law Directive, for example, has been implemented in quite disparate ways in certain Member States. Furthermore, it must be remembered that the Fourth and Seventh Directives contain a number of optional provisions; thus, for example, Germany now makes provision for merger accounting,[64] but France does not. Because of the existence of so many options in these instruments, comparability between sets of accounts emanating from different Member States has not been achieved. A large number of other relevant examples of the kinds already mentioned might be cited.

2

The First and Second Council Directives

THE FIRST DIRECTIVE

Enactment and Scope of the First Directive

The full titles of the First and Second Directives make it clear that both instruments are concerned with the co-ordination of the safeguards for the protection of the interests of Members and others required by Member States. The provisions of the First Directive are, in general, less detailed and complex than those of the Second Directive, but certain of them require more fundamental doctrinal innovations in the Member States than do the provisions of the latter Directive. The provisions of both instruments often leave little discretion as to the manner of their implementation. The enactment of the First Directive represented the Council of Ministers' first venture into the harmonization of commercial, company or civil law.[1] This Directive was first proposed in draft form by the Commission in February 1964.[2] It was then referred to the Economic and Social Committee, after which the European Parliament had it under consideration for nearly two years. The revised draft Directive which was then submitted to the Council of Ministers in October 1966 reflected some of the changes suggested by the latter two bodies.[3] The final form of the Directive was enacted by the Council on 9 March 1964.[4] The Directive has subsequently undergone minor textual amendments of no substantive importance to take account of the accession of new Member States. It deals with three topics: disclosure, the validity of obligations entered into by a company, and the nullity of a company.[5] It is applicable to public and private limited companies and partnerships limited by shares in the Member States,[6] but does not apply to companies having a variable capital. The latter type of entity is used by co-operative societies and investment companies in France.

16

Disclosure Provisions of the First Directive

Member States are required by Article 2(1) of the Directive to secure the disclosure of at least the following documents and particulars:

1. the instrument of constitution and statutes and any amendments to them, including any extension of the duration of the company;[7]
2. after every such amendment, the complex text of the amended document;[8]
3. the appointment, termination of office and particulars of the persons who either as a body constituted pursuant to law or as members of any such body: (a) are authorized to represent the company in dealings with third persons and in legal proceedings; (b) take part in its administration, supervision or control;[9]
4. at least once a year, the amount of capital subscribed in the case of a company having an authorized capital, unless any increase in the subscribed capital requires an amendment of the statutes; [10]
5. the balance sheet and profit and loss account for each financial year, together with details of the persons who are required by law to certify the balance sheet;[11]
6. any transfer of the seat of the company;[12]
7. the winding up of the company,[13] any declaration of nullity of the company by the courts,[14] the appointment of liquidators, their particulars and powers (unless such powers are exclusively derived from law or the statutes of the company),[15] the termination of the liquidation and, in Member States where striking off entails legal consequences, the fact of any such striking off.[16]

Companies in Great Britain are required to report the above matters (where relevant) to the Registrar of Companies,[17] who is required to publish them in the *London* or *Edinburgh Gazette*.[18]

By Articles 3(1) and (2), the documents and information to be disclosed may be deposited in a file which in each Member State is opened at a central register, register of commerce or register of companies. Such documents and information may instead be transcribed in the register. The three possible methods of filing are explained by the fact that not all Member States make use of the principle of centralized registration adopted by the United Kingdom.[19] The documents and information must also be published in the national gazette indicated for the purpose by the Member State concerned, either in full or in summary, or by means of an announcement that the document has either been added to the relevant file or entered in the register.[20]

Article 3(5) of the Directive has clearly been influenced by Article 15(2) of the German Commercial Code [*Handelsgesetzbuch*]. It provides that the documents and information may be relied on by the company as against third parties only after they have been published in accordance with paragraph 4, unless the company proves that third parties had knowledge thereof. The documents and information may not be relied upon with regard to transactions taking place before the sixteenth day following the publication as against parties who prove that it was impossible for them to have knowledge thereof.[21]

Member States are obliged by Article 4 to require that a company's letters and order forms should give particulars of the register in which the file mentioned in Article 3 is kept, together with the number of the company in that register. They must also give particulars of the legal form of the company, the location of its seat, and the fact that it is being wound up. Where in these documents mention is made of the capital of the company, the reference must be to the capital subscribed and paid up. The meaning of the phrase 'order forms' is somewhat unclear, and it is uncertain whether it embraces only orders on standardized forms emanating from the company and addressed to its suppliers, or whether it also includes purchase forms of a standardized nature which the company issues to the purchasers of its goods.[22]

Validity of the Obligations Entered into by the Company

Pre-incorporation contracts
Article 7 of the First Directive provides that if, before a company being formed has acquired legal personality, action has been carried out in its name and the company does not assume the obligations arising from such action, the persons who acted shall, without limit, be jointly and severally liable thereon, unless otherwise agreed. Article 7 would seem to have been inspired by German[23] and Italian law.[24] The meaning of the last three words thereof would seem to be far from clear.[25] It is perhaps surprising

that Article 7 does not deal with the question of the ratification of pre-incorporation contracts.

Contracts entered into by a company already in existence
Article 9(1) of the First Directive stipulates that acts done by the organs of the company shall be binding on it even if these acts are not within the objects of the company, unless such acts exeed the powers which the law confers, or allows to be conferred, on those organs. It continues by stating that Member States may provide that the company shall not be bound where such acts are outside the objects of the company, if it proves that the third party knew that the act was outside those objects or could not, in view of the circumstances, have been unaware of it; disclosure of the statutes shall not of itself be sufficient proof thereof. The provisions of Article 9(1) represent a compromise between the legal provisions which governed the present matter in the five original Member States which accepted the principle of *spécialité statutaire* (which is comparable with the British and Irish doctrine of *ultra vires*), according to which a company may not perform legal transactions outside the scope of its objects, and those which were operative in Germany, according to which limitations placed on these authority conferred by the statutes might be disregarded, provided that the organ which act on behalf of the company had the necessary authority to bind it. According to German law, a legal person has an unlimited capacity to act through its organs.[26] German law conceives that a company's will is formed through the acts of will of these organs.[27] The other original Member States accepted the mandate theory deprived from Roman law, and enshrined in the Napoleonic Codes, according to which the relationship between a company and the person or body which deals on its behalf with a third party was conceived as being in essence that between a principal and an agent. The traditional view is that, in such a relationship, the scope of the agent's authority to enter into binding contracts is determined by the mandate given to the principal. In recent times, French law has moved away from the mandate theory towards a more Germanic approach, according to which a specific statutory definition is provided of the powers of management and representation of the *conseil d'administration* and the *président* of a *société anonyme* where the traditional board structure is adopted,[28] and also of those of the *directoire* and its

19

chairman where a *société anonyme* adopts an optional two-tier structure.[29]

The term organ has no precise meaning under United Kingdom law and, perhaps somewhat unfortunately, it has not been used in the Companies Act 1989. It seems that the term is used in the Directive to refer to the body which normally has the power to represent the company. In the United Kingdom and the Republic of Ireland, this is the board of directors: managing directors would not seem to be organs for the present purposes, but possibly to come within the provisions of Article 9(3), which is discussed below. It appears that Article 9(1) apply *inter alia* to the situation familiar to some small English companies, where the company has only one director, and to board meetings where one director constitutes a quorum under the company's Articles.[30] The usual method of representation in German companies is by the board of directors [*Vorstand*] in accordance with Article 78(1) of the *Aktiengesetz* of 1965 but, if the Articles so provide, some companies may be represented by a single director, two or more directors acting together, or by a director acting together with a commercial agent called a *Prokurist*, who has extensive powers by virtue of Articles 49–53 of the Commercial Code. Private companies are also represented in similar ways. Thus German company law knows many kinds of representative organs, but not all of them appear to be treated as organs for the purposes of Article 9(1) which, as already indicated, appears to be referring to the organ which normally has the power to represent the company. This seems to follow from Article 9(3) which contains certain legal provisions governing the effect of norms of national law derogating from the legal rules generally operative concerning the authority to represent the company.

It appears that there are some defects in the wording of Article 9(1) of the First Directive, and it is well known that the implementing legislation in Great Britain[31] has given rise to some problems.[32] Thus it is not clear what was meant by good faith for the purposes of the old section 35 of the Companies Act 1985.[33] Further difficulties also arose as to whether the old Section 35 applied only to persons dealing with the company for valuable consideration, and whether this section applied to transactions with single directors in all circumstances.[34]

The law in Great Britain has recently been changed by the

enactment of sections 35–35B and 322A of the Companies Act 1985, which were incorporated therein by sections 108 and 109 of the Companies Act 1989. These new sections were influenced by the recommendations contained in the Prentice Report, which suggested the abolition of the *ultra vires* rule as between the company and third parties. The new provisions are rather complex and still appear to have some unsatisfactory features. Section 35(1), which goes further than is required by Article 9(1) of the Directive, provides that the validity of an act done by a company shall not be called into question on the ground of lack of capacity, or by reason of anything in the company's memorandum. The provisions of section 35(2) are so worded that it is likely that a shareholder will be able to sue personally to prevent an *ultra vires* transaction only in very limited circumstances.[35] Section 35A(1), which corresponds to the old section 35 of the Companies Act 1985, still uses the phrase good faith and the presumptions regarding good faith may well be too favourable to the third party.[36] It is clear from the wording of sections 35(1) and 35A(2) that these sections are applicable to acts done by a company, including transactions to which it is a party, and thus should be treated as applicable to persons who deal with the company otherwise than for valuable consideration.

The new section 35A, unlike paragraph 6(1) of the Irish European Communities (Companies) Regulations,[37] fails to make use of the concept of organs. It allows for the board of directors to act along with anyone ostensibly, impliedly or expressly authorized by it. The wording of section 35(A)(1), which provides that in favour of a person dealing with a company in good faith, the power of the directors to bind the company shall be deemed to be free of any limitation under the company's constitution, may perhaps be unfortunate, as such a limitation is capable of being treated as referring *inter alia* to a provision in the Articles prescribing the size of the quorum.[38]

The complex provisions of section 322A of the Companies Act 1985 stipulate that certain transactions involving directors are voidable at the instance of the company. Although this section has a wide ambit, it seems possible to reconcile it with Article 9 of the First Directive on the ground that in so far as it fails to confer the power on the corporate organ, the board of directors, of entering into binding transactions with directors and other stated persons, the imposition of such a legal limitation is compatible with the first sentence of Article 9(1). The alternative argument that, where the other party to a transaction with the company was a director of the company, or of its holding company, or was a person connected or associated with such a director in accordance with the terms of section 322A, he was not a third party in the sense of the Directive, may not, however, be sustainable.

Acording to Article 9(2) of the First Directive, the limits of the powers of the organs of a company arising from the statutes or from a decision of the competent organs, may never be relied on against third parties, even if they have been disclosed. The provision appears to have been influenced by the German theory concerning the power of representation of the company's organs. It was originally thought unnecessary to implement Article 9(2) in Great Britain, probably because the rule in *Royal British Bank v. Turquand*[39] and the doctrine of ostensible authority vest extensive power in the directors to bind the company in relation to persons dealing with it. However, sections 35A(3) of the Companies Act 1985 would appear to take acount of Article 9(2). This provision stipulates that the references made to limitations under the company's constitution include limitations deriving from a resolution of the general meeting or any class meeting of the shareholders or from any agreement between the members of the company or any class of shareholders.

Article 9(3), which represents a compromise, stipulates that if the national law provides that authority to represent a company may, in derogation from the legal rules governing the subject, be conferred by the statutes on a single person or on several persons acting jointly, that law may provide that such a provision in the statutes may be relied on against third parties, on condition that it applies to the general power of representation. This provision also states that the question whether it can be relied upon against third parties is governed by Article 3. Although Article 9(3) has been implemented, for example, in the Netherlands, it has not been implemented in Great Britain. However, although the new provisions described above have some unsatisfactory features, they would seem to comply with the requirements of the First Directive more faithfully than that of the old ones.

Nullity of the Company

The possibility that a company may be declared void as from its inception is a clear threat to its shareholders, creditors and employees. Although provisions of national law concerning the nullity of companies in existence before the First Directive came into effect did much to mitigate the possible effects of nullity, the possibility that discontented shareholders might bring an action for the nullity of the company based upon contractual grounds – as in France, where the theory that the company is a contract has persisted until recently,[40] or on the basis of formal defects in the constitution, as in Germany and Italy – still remained. Articles 10–12 of the First Directive seek to co-ordinate national legal provisions concerning nullity, and to limit severely the grounds on which it can be declared. Article 10 of the Directive, which is intended to prevent the defective constitution of companies, represents a compromise between the legal provisions of the original Member States having this aim in view. Article 11 provides that the nullity of a company can be ordered only by a decision of a court on six carefully defined grounds.[41] Article 121(1) provides that persons who contract with a company which has been annulled under the impression that it was validly incorporated receive the same protection in accordance with the provisions of Article 3 governing publicity as if the company had acted *ultra vires*. The nullity of a company entails its winding up, but does not affect the validity of any commitments entered into with it.[42]

The view is generally taken that the question of the nullity of companies does not arise under British law. This is because s.13(3) and (4) of the Companies Act 1985 provide that a company comes into existence and becomes capable of exercising all the functions of an incorporated company as from the date of incorporation mentioned in the certificate of incorporation; furthermore, this certificate is stated by section 13(7)(a) to be conclusive evidence that the requirements of the Act in respect of registration and matters precedent and incidental thereto have been complied with, and that the association is a company authorized to be registered and is duly registered under the Act. It is thus in principle not possible to call in question matters which occurred prior to and contemporaneously with the registration, as is the case in many other Member States. It is therefore clear why the

European Communities Act 1972 and the Companies Act 1985 contained no provisions implementing Articles 10–12.

Implementation in the Member States

As already pointed out, the First Directive was implemented in Great Britain by section 9 of the European Communities Act 1972. This section was repealed by Schedule 1 to the Companies Consolidation (Consequential Provisions) Act 1985. It was then replaced by sections 18, 35, 36(4), 42, 351, 711 of, and Schedule 12 to, the Companies Act 1985. The defects of implementation in Great Britain have been considered above. As already pointed out, section 35 has been replaced by sections 35–35B of the Companies Act 1988, which were incorporated therein by the Companies Act 1989. The latter Act, like its forerunners, applies to England and Wales and to Scotland but is in principle inapplicable in Northern Ireland.[43] The Directive was implemented in France by Ordonnance no. 69–1176 of 20 December 1969, amending the law of 24 July 1966 concerning commercial companies, and also by Decree no. 69–1177 of 24 December 1969, amending Decree no. 66–236 of March 1967 on commercial companies and Decree 66–237 of 23 March 1967 relating to the commercial registry.[44] The implementing law was passed in the Netherlands on 29 April 1971.[45] Implementation also occurred rather late in Belgium, by means of a law passed on 6 March 1973.[46]

In the Republic of Ireland, pre-incorporation contracts and *ultra vires* transactions are governed respectively by section 37 and section 8(1) of the Companies Act 1963, which were enacted in anticipation of the First Directive. There are, not surprisingly, significant differences between important phrases in the Directive and these sections. It would thus seem desirable for account to be taken of the wording of the First Directive in interpreting these sections. However, Keane J. failed to adopt such an approach in the case of *Northern Bank Finance Corporation v. Quinn.*[47] Further provisions of the First Directive were implemented in Ireland by the Statutory Instrument No. 163 of 1973 (the European Communities (Companies) Regulation 1973). The most important matters governed by this instrument would seem to be the publication of notices, and organs authorized to bind the company.[48] In Italy, implementation took place by Presidential Decree no. 127 of 21 December 1969, which made a number of amendments to the Civil Code.[49]

Germany was the only original Member to implement the Directive within the time limit provided for therein. This implementation took place by the so-called *Koordinierungsgesetz* of 15 August 1969.[50] Implementation took place in Luxembourg by the law of 23 November 1972.[51] In Denmark it took place first of all by Act no. 503 of 29 November 1972 and then by the Companies Acts nos 370 and 371 of 13 June 1973.[52] Greece was slow to implement the First Directive, but two Presidential Decrees were enacted with this object in view on 28 November 1986 and 10 December 1986, respectively. The first of these Decrees amended the law of 1920 governing public limited companies[53] whilst the second Decree amended the law of the same year governing private companies and partnerships limited by shares.[54] The Directive was implemented in Portugal by means of Decree Law 282/86 of 2 September 1986 and Decree Law 403/86 of 3 December 1986. It was implemented in Spain by Law 19/1989 of 25 July 1989.[55]

THE SECOND DIRECTIVE

Enactment and Scope of the Second Directive

The Commission's proposal for a Second Directive was submitted to the Council on 9 March 1970.[56] However, the Council failed to adopt it until 13 December 1976, and then only after amending it very radically.[57] One interrelationship between the two Directives consists of the fact that the Second Directive contains certain provisions on disclosure in its introductory part which supplement those of the First Directive. Furthermore, as already pointed out, the full titles of both instruments are in similar terms. The Second Directive is principally concerned with the formation of public companies, and the maintenance and alteration of their capital.[58] Member States may decide not to apply the Directive to investment companies with a variable capital and to co-operatives incorporated as public companies.[59] In Great Britain, many of the provisions of the Second Directive have been made applicable to private companies. There is a fairly abundant literature on the Directive,[60] which instrument unfortunately contains no subheadings.

Description of the Company

The enactment of the Directive makes it necessary for Member States to distinguish between public and private companies. Thus, in Great Britain a public company is one which satisfies certain rather complex requirements.[61] Article 1 of the Second Directive requires that public companies be distinguished by name from private companies. This requirement is complied with in Great Britain by sections 25(1) and 27(4) of the Companies Act 1985, which require that the name of a public company shall end with the words 'public limited company', which may, however, be abbreviated to p.l.c.[62]

Disclosure Requirements

According to Article 2 of the Directive, the statutes[63] or the instrument of incorporation[64] must contain information concerning five matters. The name and type of the company must be disclosed, as also must the objects, the amount of the subscribed[65] and if, applicable, authorized capital,[66] and the duration of the company, if not indefinite. Article 2 also requires that the rules governing the number of and procedure for appointing members of the bodies responsible for representing the company with regard to third parties, administration, management, supervision or control of the company, and the allocation of powers among these bodies be disclosed, so long as they are not legally determined.[67]

Article 3 requires the disclosure of eleven matters (some of which are irrelevant for British purposes), in the statutes, or in the instrument of incorporation, or in a separate document of which official notification in accordance with Article 3 of the First Directive, as well as registration are required. Disclosure is thus required of the nominal value of shares subscribed for, and at least once a year, the number thereof, for each class of shares. Furthermore, disclosure must be made of the amount of subscribed capital paid up at the time of incorporation or commencement of business; the total amount of all the costs of formation and preparation for the commencement of business; and any special advantages given to a promoter. Disclosure in respect of the last two items is required in Great Britain by section 117(3)(c) and (d) of the Companies Act 1985 (as amended).

Responsibility for Liabilities Incurred during the Period before Authorization
The above matter is dealt with in Article 4, which provides that responsibility for liabilities incurred by or on behalf of the company during the period before any authorization to commence business is granted must be specified by law, apart from liabilities incurred under contracts which are conditional on the commencement of business.[68]

Dissolution of the Company
Article 5 is concerned with the winding up of the company if its membership falls below two. It provides that such an event does not lead to a dissolution *ipso jure*. Should a Member State's legislation provide for the dissolution of the company by order of the court under the latter circumstance, the company must be given time to regularize the situation. The Second Directive goes a considerable way towards recognizing one-man companies, which have long been permitted to exist in Germany and have also been introduced in Denmark, France, Belgium and the Netherlands in recent years.

Provisions Governing the Raising of Capital when the Company is Formed
Article 6 of the Directive provides that a public company may not be incorporated or be authorized to commence business, unless it has a minimum capital of at least 25,000 units of account.[69] Shares may not be issued at a price lower than their nominal value, and the subscribed capital may consist only of assets capable of economic assessment.[70] An undertaking to perform work or supply services may not form part of these assets.[71] Shares issued for a cash consideration must be paid up to the extent of 25 per cent of their nominal value at the time when the company is incorporated, or when it is authorized to do business.[72] Shares issued for a non-cash consideration at either of these times must be fully paid up within five years of the relevant time. Articles 10(1) and (2) require detailed reports by experts on the nature and value of the non-cash consideration. Article 10(3) requires publicity to be given to the experts' report. A number of exemptions from the requirements of Articles 10(1)–(3) are provided for by Article 10(4). The requirements of Article 19(1) and (2) have been

27

implemented in Great Britain by sections 103 and 108 of the Companies Act 1985 (as amended), which may be criticized on the grounds of their undue complexity.[73]

Article 11(1) is clearly influenced by the provisions of Article 52 of the *Aktiengesetz* concerning *Nachgründung*, or secondary foundation. It provides that, should the company acquire any asset from any subscriber of its memorandum (or, at the option of each Member State, any shareholder or other person) within not less than two years of the incorporation for a consideration of 10 per cent or more of the subscribed capital, the issue must be examined, published and approved by the general meeting. Article 11(2) contains certain exceptions to Article 11(1), one of which relates to acquisitions made in the ordinary course of business.[74] Subject to the provisions relating to the reduction of subscribed capital, the shareholders may not be released from their obligation to pay up their contributions.[75] The same safeguards as those which are provided for in Articles 2–12 must be operative in the event of the conversion of another type of company into a public company.[76]

Increase of Capital

By Article 25(1), any increase of capital may be decided on by the general meeting. However, Article 25(2) provides that the statutes, the instrument of incorporation, or the general meeting may provide for increase up to an authorized amount, decided upon by the authorized body. This provision shows the influence of the German provisions concerning *genehmigtes Kapital* (approved capital) contained in Articles 202 *et seq*. of the German *Aktiengesetz*. As in the Federal Republic, the authorized body may be empowered to issue shares for a maximum period of five years; this authority may be renewed on one or more occasions by the general meeting.[77] Article 25(3) requires meetings of every class of shareholders whose rights would be affected by the increase. The provisions already mentioned are said by Article 25(4) to apply to the issue of all securities which are convertible shares, or carry the right to subscribe for shares. Article 26 – which, like Article 9, made certain changes in British law necessary[78] – provides that shares assessed on an increase of subscribed capital must be paid up to the extent of 25 per cent of their nominal value, plus any premiums. The provisions of Article 27(1) and (2), which apply to contributions in kind made on an increase of capital, correspond with those of Articles 9(2) and 10(1)–(3), which are applicable to contributions in kind made at the time of the formation of the company. Member states are permitted to dispense with the valuation requirements contained in Article 27(2) in the event of a merger or public offer for the purchase or exchange of shares where the shareholders in the target company are paid with the shares issued.[79]

Article 29(1) requires new issues of shares for cash to be offered to the existing shareholders on a pre-emptive basis. Such pre-emptive rights have existed in French, German and Italian public companies for a considerable period of time,[80] are common in American jurisdictions, and now exist in English public companies.[81] Article 29(2) provides that pre-emptive rights need not be made applicable in the case of issues of preference shares and that, should there be different classes of shares, the right of pre-emption may initially be given to the members of the class issued.[82] By Article 29(6), pre-emptive rights apply to convertible securities but not on their conversion. It is provided by Article 29(3) that the compulsory rights issue must be published in the national gazette, except when all a company's shares are registered (as is still frequently the case in the United Kingdom), in which case the shareholders must be informed in writing. The right of pre-emption must be exercised within at least fourteen days from the date of publication of the offer, or the date of posting of the letters to the shareholders.[83]

Article 29(4) provides that the right of pre-emption may be excluded by the general meeting, on a written report of the administrative or management bodies. The general meeting must act by a majority of not less than two-thirds of the votes attached to the shares or to the subscribed capital represented, unless a simple majority would represent at least half the subscribed capital.[84] Registration and official notification of such a decision are required.[85] Furthermore, Article 29(5) provides that directors may be given the power to restrict or prevent a compulsory rights issue for up to five years, either in the company's statutes or instrument of incorporation, or by the general meeting acting at least by the majority indicated in Article 29(4).[86] According to Article 29(7), underwriting commission in the form of shares is not to be taken as exclusion of the pre-emptive right.

Maintenance of Capital

The provisions governing the maintenance of capital cover a member of rather disparate topics.[87] Article 15(1)(a) provides that no distribution may be made to shareholders if the net assets would then be lower than the subscribed capital and capital reserves.[88] Uncalled capital is not normally to be included in subscribed capital. In addition, Article 15(1) provides that the amount of a distribution to shareholders may not exceed the amount of the profits at the end of the last financial year plus any profit brought forward and sums drawn from reserves available for this purpose, less any losses brought forward and sums placed to reserve in accordance with the law or the statutes.[89] Member States may provide for certain derogations from the present rules for investment companies with a fixed capital complying with the requirements of Article 15(6). Article 15(2) contains special requirements governing the payment of interim dividends.[90] By Article 16, any distribution in contravention of Article 15 must be returned by shareholders who have received it and know of the irregularity, or could not have been unaware of it.[91] Furthermore, by Article 17, a general meeting must be called to consider whether the company should be wound up or other measures taken when a serious loss of the subscribed capital, at most one-half, occurs. This provision would seem to be influenced by French[92] and German[93] law, and has not been very satisfactorily implemented in Great Britain by section 142 of the Companies ACt 1985.[94]

Article 18 provides that a company may not subscribe for its own shares.[95] The acquisition by a company of its own shares by a Member State may be permitted subject to the stringent conditions mentioned in Article 19(1). Authorization must be given by the general meeting for a maximum period of eighteen months.[96] The nominal value of all the shares acquired by the company must not amount to more than 10 per cent of the subscribed capital.[97] The acquisitions must not have the effect of reducing the net assets below the amount of the subscribed capital and the distributable reserve.[98] Only fully paid shares may be purchased by the company.[99] Article 19(2) provides that the approval of the general meeting may be dispensed with when there is a need to prevent serious and imminent harm to the company. The phraseology used is reminiscent of Article 71(1) sentence 1 of the German

Aktiengesetz, which permits a company to purchase its shares in order to prevent serious harm [*schweren Schaden*] to it.[100] In addition, Article 19(3) provides that the company may dispense with the approval of the general meeting where shares are purchased for distribution to its employees, or to the employee of an associated company, within one year of acquisition. The two permissive exceptions contained in Article 19 have not been adopted under British legislation.

Article 20 makes provision for further permissive exceptions to Article 19. These comprise the redemption of redeemable shares,[101] the acquisition of shares on a reduction of capital; the acquisition of shares as a result of a universal transfer of assets; the issue of shares as underwriting commission; the purchase of shares as a result of a court order in order to protect minorities;[102] the forfeiture of fully paid shares;[103] the acquisition of shares to indemnify minority shareholders in associated companies; and other cases of less importance. Apart from redeemable shares or shares acquired on a reduction of capital,[104] shares acquired in accordance with Article 20 must be disposed of within three years, in so far as they exceed 10 per cent of the subscribed capital. If they have not been disposed of, they must be cancelled.[105] Shares acquired in contravention of Articles 19 and 20 must be disposed of within a year, or otherwise be cancelled.[106]

The voting rights in respect of the shares acquired by a company in itself are suspended in accordance with Article 22, and so they cannot be used to increase the directors' control.[107] If the shares are included among the assets shown in the balance sheet, a capital reserve of the same amount must be included among the liabilities. The company's annual report must give details of all such purchases. Subject to certain exceptions, a company may not advance funds, nor make loans nor provide security, with a view to the acquisition of its shares by a third party.[108] The acceptance of the company's own shares as security is subject to similar conditions to the acquisition thereof.[109] It is noteworthy that since the Second Directive is not concerned with groups of companies, it contains no general prohibition on a subsidiary purchasing shares in its holding company, which may be objectionable on similar grounds to the purchase by a company of its own shares. However, most Member States do in fact provide for such a prohibition and the omission, a necessary consequence of the 'salami' tactics of harmonization, is not an important one.

Reduction of Capital

By Article 30, a reduction in the subscribed capital must normally take place by a decision of a general meeting, taken at least by a majority of not less than two-thirds of the votes attaching to the securities and the subscribed capital represented. The notice convening the meeting must at least specify the purpose of the reduction, and the manner in which it is to be carried out. It follows from Articles 32 and 33 that the creditors have the right to protection if the reduction is due to over-capitalization, but not if it is to offset losses. This dichotomy is paralleled in the legal systems of Great Britain, France and Germany.[110] It is provided by Article 31 that reductions of capital which affect a particular class of shareholders shall require a separate vote by that class.[111] Article 33 may be applied by those Member States, such as Germany, that wish to allow a reduction of capital in order to transfer the money into a statutory reserve, which may be used only to offset losses.[112] Article 34 provides that the subscribed capital must not be reduced below the minimum permitted capital. The provisions of Article 35 would seem to relate to the *parts de jouissance* (reimbursed shares) known in France and Belgium. Those of Article 36 would seem to relate principally to the compulsory amortization [*Einziehung*] with a reduction of capital known to German law, according to which provision for such amortization may be made in the company's Articles.[113] In the United Kingdom, the forfeiture of shares is permissible only in the event of the non-payment of calls.[114] Articles 35 and 36 are both permissive provisions, and have not given rise to any changes in English law.

Final Provisions

Article 39 prescribes requirements for the redemption of redeemable shares; this provision is permissive in character, and seems to have been influenced by section 58 of the Companies Act 1948.[115] Unlike the latter provision, however, it is not restricted to the redemption of redeemable preference shares. The rules contained in Article 39 are somewhat complex; this would seem to explain the complexity of the provisions of sections 159 and 160 of the Companies Act 1985 relating to the redemption of shares. As already indicated, Article 40 is concerned with the majorities required for certain decisions. Article 41 provides for exemptions from certain Articles in order to facilitate employee participation. Article 42 provides that for the purposes of the implementation of the Directive, the laws of the Member States shall ensure equal treatment to all shareholders who are in the same position. Recognition of this principle of non-discrimination occurs in British company law, and by the City Code on Take-Overs and Mergers. A corresponding principle known as *Gleichsbehandlung* is recognized under German company law.[116]

Implementation

The Second Directive was implemented in Germany by a law passed on 13 December 1978.[117] The next Member State to implement the Directive was the United Kingdom. Implementation occurred through the enactment of the Companies Act 1980. The Companies Act 1981 made 48 amendments to this Act, and repealed 24 of its provisions, one year later. The latter Act has now been replaced by the consolidating Act of 1985.[118] Implementation took place in France by law no. 81–1162 of 30 December 1981.[119] In Denmark, law no. 262, which amended the law governing public companies so as to give effect to the Second Directive, was passed on 9 June 1982.[120] Implementation by a number of other Member States was also late. Thus in the Republic of Ireland it took place through the Companies (Amendment) Act 1983 of 5 June 1983. In Luxembourg, it occurred through the law of 24 April 1983,[121] whilst in Belgium the implementing statute was passed on 5 December 1984.[122] In Italy, implementation did not occur until the enactment of the Presidential Decree of 10 February 1986.[123] In Greece, it occurred through the medium of the enactment of the Presidential Decree no. 409/86,[124] whilst in Portugal it took place as the result of the passing of Decree Law no. 262/86 of 2 September 1986. Implementation in Spain took place as the result of the passing of Law 19/1989 of 25 July 1989 and Decree Law 1564/1989 of 22 December 1989, which have already been referred to in connection with the First Directive.

3

Mergers and Divisions

MERGERS OF COMPANIES WITHIN THE SAME STATE

History and Scope of the Third Directive

The first proposal for the Third Directive on Mergers was submitted to the Council on 16 June 1970.[1] The proposal was amended twice,[2] and the Directive was finally adopted on 9 October 1978. It was originally intended to cover divisions of companies as well; it was proposed that such operations should be regulated by reference to the provisions governing mergers. However, when the 'merger' Directive was adopted in October 1978, the Council took the view that further work on divisions was necessary, and the latter matter came to be regulated in a formally separate Directive which was adopted by the Council on 17 December 1982.[3] The Third Directive is concerned with mergers between public companies in the same Member State. Its provisions are much influenced by French, German and Italian law, and its scope is somewhat limited because it does not regulate takeovers, which are more common in certain Member States, such as the United Kingdom and the Netherlands,[4] than the types of merger envisaged by the Directive, which are explained below. Because of the limited scope of the Directive, a very detailed account of its provisions seems inappropriate.[5] The principal significance of the Directive may well be that its provisions will have a considerable influence on those of the forthcoming Tenth Directive on cross-frontier mergers. Like the Sixth Directive on divisions, with which it is closely linked, the Third Directive does not contain any provisions governing taxation.

Forms of Merger Covered by the Directive

The Third Directive requires all the Member States to lay down uniform rules in respect of three types of merger operations. These are the merger by acquisition,[6] the merger by the formation of a new company,[7] and the merger of a parent company with a subsidiary in which it holds all the shares.[8] In the case of a merger by acquisition, one or more companies are wound up without going into liquidation, and transfer all their assets or liabilities to another company in exchange for the issue to their shareholders of shares in the acquiring company. When a merger by formation takes place, several companies are wound up without going into liquidaton, and transfer to a company which they set up all their assets and liabilities in exchange for the issue to their shareholders of shares in the new company.

Under Article 3(1) and 4(1), that part of the consideration, if any, which amounts to a cash payment by the new or acquiring company is linked to 10 per cent of the nominal value of the issued shares. However, Article 30 permits the laws of Member States to admit a cash element in excess of 10 per cent; in such an event, most of the provisions of the Directive remain applicable.[9]

Mechanics of the Merger

The rules which relate to mergers by acquisition are contained in Chapter II of the Directive, whilst those which relate to mergers by the formation of a new company are contained in Chapter III thereof, and are basically the same as those which relate to mergers by acquisition.[10] The board of management of each of the merging companies is required to draw up draft terms of merger as well as a detailed report explaining such terms and setting out the legal and economic grounds for them and, in particular, the share exchange ratio.[11] The draft merger terms must be published in the manner prescribed by the law of each Member State, in accordance with Article 3 of the First Directive, in respect of each of the merging companies.[12] They must be examined by one or more independent experts who must draw up a written report to the shareholders, which must state at least the method or methods used to arrive at the share exchange ratio proposed; and also whether such method or methods are adequate in the case in question.[13] The merger proposals must be approved by general meetings of each of the merging companies and of each class of shareholder affected; these requirements may be dispensed with in the case of the acquiring company, provided that certain conditions are fulfilled.[14] The approval of the general meeting requires a majority of not less than two-thirds of the votes attending to the shares or to the share capital represented.[15]

Protection of Employee Rights

The adoption of the Third Directive was delayed as a result of controversy concerning the above matter. Article 12 of this Directive stipulates that the protection of the rights of employees at each of the merging companies shall be regulated in accordance with Directive 77/187/EEC.[16] This Directive was adopted in February 1973, and it safeguards employee rights in the event of transfer of undertakings, business or parts of business. It has now been implemented in a number of Member States.[17]

Protection of Creditors' Rights

The Third Directive does not make provision for the complete unification of the rules governing the protection of creditors which apply in the various Member States. Article 13(1) thereof provides that the laws of the Member States must provide for an adequate system of protection for the interests of creditors of the merging companies whose claims antedate the publication of the draft sums of merger. Article 13(2), which seems to have been inspired by Article 347 of the German *Aktiengesetz*, stipulates that the laws of the Member States must at least provide that such creditors shall be liable to obtain adequate security, where the situation of the merging companies makes such protection necessary and where those creditors do not already have such safeguards. By Article 13(3), such protection may be different for the creditors of the company being acquired, and for the acquiring company. It is clear that protection for the creditors of the former company is especially necessary. However, somewhat surprisingly, it remains true to say that British law still provides only for the consent of creditors of the transferor company.[18] By Article 14, the provisions relating to the protection of creditors are applicable also to debenture holders of the merging companies, except where the merger has been approved by a general meeting of such holders (if such a meeting is provided for under national laws) or where the merger is approved by such holders individually.[19] By Article 15, holders of securities other than shares (which may obviously include debenture holders) to which special rights are attached must be given rights equivalent to those they possessed in the company being acquired, unless the alteration of those rights has been approved by a meeting of the holders of such securities if such a meeting is provided for under national laws, or by the holders of those securities individually, or unless the holders are entitled to have the securities repurchased by the acquiring company.[20]

Publicity Requirements and Liability

A merger must be given publicity in accordance with the requirements of the First Directive[21] in respect of each of the participating companies. By Article 20, the laws of the Member States are required to lay down rules governing civil liability towards the shareholders of the company being acquired of the members of the management and board of that company in respect of misconduct on the part of those members in preparing and implementing the merger.[22]

Exceptions for Subsidiaries

Certain important exceptions to the above rules are provided for under Articles 24–26 where a company is acquired by another which holds all its shares. Furthermore, Articles 27–29 provide for certain exceptions where the acquiring company holds 90 per cent or more, but not all, of the shares in the company being acquired.[23]

Date and Consequences of the Merger

It is provided by Article 17 of the Directive that the laws of the Member States shall determine the date on which a merger takes effect.[24] In addition, Article 19(1) provides that a merger has the consequences, *ipso jure* and simultaneously, that the transfer of the whole of the assets and liabilities by the acquiring company has effect for all parties concerned; that the shareholders of the company being acquired become shareholders of the acquiring company; and that the company which is acquired ceases to exist. It is noteworthy, however, that a court order remains necessary for the transfer of the assets and liabilities of the transferor company to the transferee company or companies to take place under the law of Great Britain.[25] The court order fixes the date of such transfer, which is also the date of dissolution of the transferor company. However, it is noteworthy that British law still does not provide that shareholders in the transferor company become *ipso jure* shareholders in the acquiring company, or companies. An allotment remains necessary for this to happen. French and German law are more in accordance with the requirements of the Directive in the latter regard.[26]

Implementation
The period within which the Third Directive should have been incorporated into national law expired on 23 October 1981.[27] However, no Member State managed to comply with this deadline. The first three countries to enact implementing legislation were Germany,[28] Denmark[29] and the Netherlands.[30] Divisions are not permitted in any of those three countries, and the Sixth Directive is not applicable to them. The Commission was conscious of the fact that certain other Member States attached great importance to being able to implement the Third Directive and the Sixth Directive on divisions in a single law, by reason of the close links between these two instruments. It was therefore decided to suspend the infringement procedure under Article 169 against Member States which had failed to observe the time limits but had informed the Commission of their intention of implementing the two Directives simultaneously. The final date for implementation of the latter instrument is stated in Article 26(1) thereof to be 1 January 1986. At the time of writing, seven Member States have implemented the provisions of both Directives in a single enactment. These are Portugal,[31] Greece,[32] the United Kingdom,[33] France,[34] Luxembourg,[35] Ireland[36] and Spain.[37] As already pointed out, the types of operation covered by the mergers Directive are uncommon in the United Kingdom; one reason for this may well be that the national provisions governing the protection of creditors are too rigorous.[38] The Directive is likely to have only a marginal effect. Indeed, it appears that the procedure contained in the Directive is cumbersome and not entirely in accordance with business needs. Its long-run effect may well be to make take-over bids, which are especially common in the United Kingdom and the Netherlands, more common in other European countries.

DIVISION OF COMPANIES WITHIN THE SAME STATE

History and Scope of the Sixth Directive

It was originally intended that the provisions governing divisions should be incorporated into the mergers Directive, but it was found impossible to realize this aim, since it was believed that the division of a company gave rise to special problems. However, as is pointed out in the preamble to the Sixth Directive,[39] there are similarities between merger and division operations, and it was felt that the risk that the guarantees given with regard to mergers under the Third Directive might be circumvented could be avoided only if provision was made for equivalent protection in the event of division. The Sixth Directive is applicable where Member States permit public companies governed by their law to carry out division operations by acquisition, or by the formation of new companies, as defined in Articles 2 and 21 of the Directive.[40] Such operations involve the transfer of all the assets and liabilities of a public limited liability company to several companies in such a way that the company is wound up without going into liquidation, and ultimately dissolved, and the shareholders in the company being divided receive shares in the recipient companies and possibly a cash payment not exceeding 10 per cent of the nominal value of the shares allotted.[41] Where the merger takes place by acquisition, the acquiring companies are already in existence; where it takes place by the formation of new companies, this is obviously not the case. The divisions Directive also applies where, in the case of one of the two kinds of operations specified in Article 1, the laws of a Member State permit the cash payment to exceed 10 per cent.[42] It is also applicable where the laws of a Member State permit one of the operations specified in Article 1 without the company being divided ceasing to exist.[43]

Some Important Provisions of the Sixth Directive

Many of the provisions of the Sixth Directive are the same as those of the Third Directive. Thus the draft terms of the division must be published and officially notified, and a number of documents including the accounts and a detailed written report by the directors on the division must be made available for inspection by all shareholders.[44] As is the case with mergers, a report by an independent expert is usually required on each of the companies involved in the division.[45] Furthermore, as is true of mergers, subject to certain exceptions the division must be approved by the general meetings of the company being divided and the recipient companies.[46] The minimum majority for approval is that prescribed by the Third Directive. It follows from Articles 17(1)(a) and 22 that once the division is carried out it has the effect of transferring *ipso jure*, both as between the company being divided and the recipient companies and as regards third parties to the recipient companies, all the assets and liabilities of the company being divided.[47] By Article 11 of the Sixth Directive, which is very similar to Article 12 of the Third Directive, the protection of the rights of the employees of each of the companies involved is regulated in accordance with Directive 77/187 on the approximation of the laws of the Member States relating to the safeguarding of employees' rights in the event of the transfer of undertakings, business or parts of businesses.

Although – as should be clear from what has been discussed above – there are great similarities between the Third and the Sixth Directive, the latter instrument differs from the former in certain ways. Thus the divisions Directive contains special rules for operations carried out under the supervision of a judicial authority.[48] In the case of such operations, the preparation and making available for inspection of the directors' reports on the division and the report of the independent expert are required (as is true of mergers), but the court is empowered, under certain circumstances, to relieve the companies involved from the obligation to publish the draft terms of the division, and to impose less generous requirements concerning the period, form and manner of inspection than those contained in Article 9 of the Sixth Directive.[49] The recognition of a division under the supervision of a judicial authority was a partial concession to the British procedure under what is now section 425 of the Companies Act 1985. Another difference from the provisions of the mergers Directive is that the divisions Directive empowers Member States to provide that the recipient companies shall be jointly and severally liable for the obligations of the company being divided.[50] Joint and several liability is obligatory where a creditor of the company to which the obligation has been transferred has not obtained satisfaction. Member States may limit that liability to the net assets allocated to each of the recipient companies other than the one to which the obligation has been transferred. They need not apply this provision where the operation of the division is subject, as in Great Britain, to the supervision of the court and a majority of the creditors have agreed to forgo such joint and several liability in accordance with the provisions of the Directive.[51]

Implementation

The above matter has already been discussed in some detail above. It is noteworthy, however, that Article 26(3) of the Sixth Directive permits the United Kingdom and Ireland to extend the provisions of the Directives to unregistered companies, provided that they do so before 1 January 1991. Neither country has taken this step as yet. Divisions of the kind contemplated by the Directive would seem to be very uncommon in both States.

DRAFT TENTH DIRECTIVE ON CROSS-BORDER MERGERS

Background

As has been pointed out above, there are serious legal obstacles to cross-border mergers which derive from the laws of the Member States.[52] It has been thought for a long time that such mergers are desirable for economic reasons. This seems especially true at present, when the Community faces intensified competition from the United States and Japan. It will be remembered that the draft Tenth Directive commenced its existence as a draft Convention which was expressly provided for in Article 220 EEC. It became obvious in 1980 that further work on this draft was impossible because of German fears that it would be used to circumvent national laws governing worker participation. The Commission thus decided to convert the proposal into a draft Directive and to begin negotiations again, building on the agreement already reached on the Third Directive. The new proposal is based upon Article 54(3)(g)EEC and concerns cross-border mergers of public limited companies. Its progress has recently been impeded as the result of opposition encountered in the European Parliament. The draft Directive, like the Third Directive, is concerned with assets and mergers, and it often makes reference to the corresponding provisions of the Third Directive. It is limited to requirements additional to those of the latter instrument, or to those aspects of cross-border mergers which differ from national mergers.

Some Important Provisions of the Draft Tenth Directive

The difficult question of employee participation is dealt with in Article 1(3), which has the practical effect of giving a Member State a veto over a merger which would result in the end of employee participation in an undertaking. In such an event, a Member State may refuse to apply the Directive to the merger, which – bearing in mind the obstacles to international mergers which result from national legislation or case law – probably means that it will not take place. This approach is put forward as a temporary one ending the adoption of the Fifth Directive. So far, it has not proved acceptable to the European Parliament. Generally speaking, the preparatory steps will be carried out by the companies involved in accordance with the relevant national law. By Article 5(1) the item of information in the draft merger terms will be standardized to a greater extent than is the case with national mergers. Furthermore, under Article 6(2) the publicity requirements in respect of cross-border mergers will be greater in some circumstances than those applicable to national mergers. The draft Tenth Directive does not contain any provision determining which law governs each company; this matter may have to be resolved before the instrument is adopted by the Council.

The provisions of the draft Directive are, in general, easy to understand. The draft terms of a cross-border merger will be required by Article 5(2) to be drawn up and certified in due legal form if this is prescribed by the law of a Member State by which one or more of the companies involved in the merger is governed. The provisions relating to the approval of the general meeting contained in Article 7 and the report of the expert contained in Article 8 follow the same model as the Third Directive. The same is true of the provisions of Article 9 governing creditor protection. Article 12 provides that the publication of a cross-border merger must take place for the company or companies being acquired before publication for the acquiring company.[53]

It is doubtful whether, if the deadlock which at present exists owing to the attitude taken by the European Parliament is resolved and the draft Directive is eventually adopted, it will have much effect unless Community legislation is also enacted governing the taxation of cross-border mergers which will relieve such operations of some of the fiscal burdens at present attached to them. The implementation of the Directive would probably have little effect in the United Kingdom, because the type of merger contemplated by it is not in common use in this country, where the take-over bid is much more common. A brief account of the draft Thirteenth Directive concerning take-over bids and other general bids appears in the final chapter of this book.[54]

4

The Fourth and Seventh Directives: Individual Company Accounts and Consolidated Accounts

THE FOURTH DIRECTIVE

History and Scope

The Fourth Directive took a long time to adopt. As already indicated above, Article 2(1) (f) of the First Directive mentioned the enactment of a Directive governing the annual accounts of private companies, which was to have been adopted before 9 March 1970. However, the first draft of the Directive was not submitted to the Council until 10 November 1971.[1] The proposal was amended in 1974.[2] The Directive was adopted on 25 July 1978.[3] It aims at the establishment in the Community of maximum equivalent legal requirements as regards the extent of the financial information which should be made available to the public by companies which are in competition with each other. It should be noted, however, that by reason of the large number of options it provides for, it may not achieve this aim.[4] The Directive, which is concerned with the content, auditing and publication of the accounts of public and private limited companies and partnerships limited by shares, is perhaps more important than the four instruments considered above. Pending subsequent harmonization, Member States were not required to apply the provisions of the Directive to banks and financial institutions[5] and insurance companies.[6] The Fourth Directive shows the influence of British, Irish and Dutch company law in the predominance it gives to the true and fair view, but its emphasis on standard formats for annual accounts,[7] and on the rules which must be followed in preparing such accounts and in calculating the amounts to be shown against individual items included in them,[8] as well as on the minimum amount of detail to be given, displays the influence of French and German law.[9]

There is considerable literature on the Fourth Directive.[10] It will, however, be possible to discuss only the most important features of this instrument and of the Seventh Directive on consolidated accounts in brief outline in the present chapter. Furthermore, a detailed account of the implementation of these instruments in the laws of the Member States seems beyond the scope of the present work.[11] Proposals have been made fairly recently for the amendment of both Directives; these are referred to at the end of this chapter.[12]

Different Types of Companies Mentioned in the Directive

The method of classification employed in the Fourth Directive is not based upon the distinction between public and private limited companies.[13] The Directive distinguishes between small, medium-sized and large companies, irrespective of whether a company falling within one of these categories is a public or a private company. A small company is defined in Article 11 (as amended by Council Directive 84/569 Article 1)[14] as a company which, on its balance sheet, satisfies at least two of the three following criteria:

(a) the balance sheet total does not exceed 1,500,000 ECU (European Units of Account);
(b) the net turnover does not exceed 3,200,000 ECU;
(c) the average number of employees during the financial year does not exceed 50.[15]

A medium-sized company is defined in Article 27 (as amended by Council Directive 84/549, Article 1) as a company which, on its balance sheet, satisfies at least two of the three following criteria:

(a) the balance sheet total does not exceed 6,200,000 ECU;
(b) the net turnover does not exceed 12,800,000 ECU;
(c) the average number of employees during the financial year does not exceed 250.[16]

There are transition periods of two years before the balance sheet date at which the special rules applicable to small or medium-sized companies begin to apply, and two consecutive years after the balance sheet date at which the company has ceased to exceed two of these three criteria.[17] A large company is one which is neither a small nor a medium-sized company. As is shown below, the publicity requirements in relation to the three different categories of company are different. Member States are permitted by Article 5(1) to prescribe special layouts for the accounts of investment companies and financial holding companies,[18] as defined respectively in Article 5(2) and (3). Article 57 of the Directive authorizes Member States to exempt subsidiary companies from publishing annual accounts under certain rather stringent conditions, including the condition that the subsidiary company's accounts are consolidated in group accounts, and the parent undertaking has guaranteed the commitments of the subsidiary. Article 58 exempts parent companies from publishing their profit and loss account on certain conditions. Special rules are made applicable to accounting for participating interests in affiliated undertakings by Article 59.[19]

The Annual Accounts

Article 2 defines the annual accounts to which it refers as the balance sheet, profit and loss account, and notes on the accounts. These documents constitute a composite whole. Furthermore, provision is made for an annual report, the contents of which are prescribed.[20] Article 5(1) of the Directive contains a general requirement that the annual accounts of limited companies should be audited by qualified auditors.[21] However, Article 5(2) permits Member States to exempt small companies from this audit requirement. This provision is intended to assist those Member States, such as the Federal Republic of Germany, which have too few qualified accountants to undertake the audit of all small companies.[22]

As already indicated, one of the principal innovatory features of the Directive consists of the prescription of formats of a very detailed and comprehensive nature for the presentation of accounts. The Directive contains two balance sheet formats: Article 9 thereof provides for a horizontal presentation, whilst Article 10 provides for a vertical presentation. Articles 23–26 contain four profit and loss account formats comprising two vertical and two horizontal presentations. The laws of the Member States may adopt any or several of these formats: in the latter case, they may permit companies to choose any of the admissible formats.[23]

Different requirements apply to the annual accounts in accordance with the size of the company. In accordance with Articles 11, 27 and 44, a small company may be permitted to draw up an abridged balance sheet, an abridged profit and loss account and abridged notes on the accounts. Under the foregoing provisions, a medium-sized company may be permitted to draw up a full balance sheet, full notes on the accounts and an abridged profit and loss account. A large company will be required to issue a full balance sheet, a full profit and loss account and full notes on the accounts. Furthermore, small or medium-sized companies may benefit from certain relaxations of the normal publicity requirements.[24]

In Great Britain, public companies, banking, insurance and shipping companies and companies which are authorized persons under the Financial Services Act 1986, and members of any group which includes companies of these types, are ineligible to be treated as 'small companies' or 'medium-sized companies', whatever their size. Other companies and groups are entitled to be treated as 'small' if they satisfy, in respect of at least two of the last three financial years, at least two of the following three conditions:

(i) net turnover not in excess of £2,000,000;
(ii) total assets on the balance sheet did not exceed £975,000;
(iii) weekly average number of employees did not exceed 50.[25]

Eligible companies and groups in Great Britain are entitled to be treated as 'medium-sized' if they satisfy, in respect of at least two of the last three financial years, at least two of the following requirements:

(i) net turnover is not in excess of £8,000,000;
(ii) total assets on the balance sheet did not exceed £3,900,000;
(iii) weekly average number of employees did not exceed 250.[26]

Small companies in Great Britain complying with the above requirements may deliver to the Registrar a modified balance sheet. Furthermore, such a company need not file a copy of its profit and loss account, or of its directors' report, or (with certain exceptions) the notes to its accounts, and it is not required to furnish particulars of its directors' remuneration, or of that of its higher-paid employees.[27]

French commercial companies, having a separate legal personality which comply with at least two of the three following conditions, are entitled to draw up and publish simplified balance sheets and profit and loss accounts:[28]

(a) annual turnover not in excess of 3,000,000 francs;
(b) the balance sheet total does not exceed 1,500,000 francs;
(c) the average number of permanent employees during the financial year does not exceed 10.

In addition, such French companies which satisfy at least two of the three following conditions do not have to mention or publish certain matters in the notes on the accounts:[29]

(a) annual turnover not in excess of 20,000,000 francs;
(b) the balance sheet total does not exceed 10,000,000 francs;
(c) the average number of permanent employees during the financial year does not exceed 50.

Such companies lose these concessions if the requirements mentioned above fail to be fulfilled for two consecutive financial years.[30]

Small companies are defined in Article 267(1) of the German Commercial Code (as amended) as companies which comply with at least two of the three following conditions:

(a) annual turnover not in excess of 8,000,000 DM;
(b) the balance sheet total does not exceed 3,900,000 DM;
(c) the average number of employees during the financial year does not exceed 50.

Medium-sized companies are defined in Article 267(2) as companies which exceed at least two of the requirements applicable to small companies, but comply with at least two of the following conditions:

(a) Annual turnover not in excess of 32,000,000 DM;
(b) the balance sheet total does not exceed 15,500,000 DM;
(c) the average number of employees during the financial year does not exceed 250.

Large companies are defined in Article 267(3) as companies which exceed at least two of the characteristics set out in Article 267(2) and companies whose shares are listed on a stock exchange within the Community. By Article 267(4), the consequences which attach to being a small, medium-sized or large company become applicable only when the appropriate conditions have been fulfilled at the accounts date for two financial years. Small companies may draw up an abridged balance sheet,[31] and an abridged profit and loss account.[32] They are also permitted to exclude certain items from the notes on the accounts,[33] and benefit from certain relaxations of the publicity requirements in respect of their accounts.[34] Medium-sized companies are also permitted to draw up an abridged profit and loss account,[35] and also benefit from certain relaxations of the publicity requirements.[36]

All the German provisions mentioned in the present and foregoing paragraphs apply only to capital companies, i.e. to public and private limited companies and to partnerships limited by shares.

The Requirement of a True and Fair View

Article 2(3) of the Directive provides that the annual accounts of a company shall give a 'true and fair view of the company's assets, liabilities, financial position and profit and loss'. Article 2(4) provides that information must be added in order to give a true and fair view if compliance with a provision of the Directive would not be sufficient for this purpose. Article 2(5) provides that, in the exceptional case where compliance with the rules of the Directive would not give a true and fair view, they must be departed from, and a full explanation given in the notes to the accounts. The Member States may define the exceptional cases in question, and lay down the relevant special rules. The requirement of a true and fair view has necessitated a number of significant changes in the laws of Member States other than the United Kingdom[37] and the Netherlands, which already adhered to this requirement before the adoption of the Fourth Directive.[38]

It should be noted that in certain Member States such as Belgium, France and Italy, tax laws require that the annual accounts present items in the balance sheet and the profit and loss account in accordance with their treatment for tax purposes, rather than in accordance with generally accepted accounting principles. Thus certain fixed assets may be depreciated at accelerated rates over a period which is shorter than their esti-mated useful lives, thus causing a misstatement of profitability and assets. In order to mitigate the impairment of the true and fair view in such cases, Article 43(1) no. 10 provides that the effect of tax-based valuation rules must be disclosed in the notes to the accounts.

Certain Other Rules Relating to the Accounts
By Article 4(4) the accounts should, in principle, contain compara-tive figures for the preceding financial year. Member States may provide that where these figures are not compatible, the figure for the preceding financial year must be adjusted. In any event, non-compatibility and any adjustment of the figures must be disclosed in the notes on the accounts.[39] Furthermore, by Article 3, the layout of the accounts must not be changed from one financial year to the next. Departures from this principle are permitted only in exceptional cases, and any such departure must be disclosed in the notes on the accounts, together with an explanation of the reasons therefor.[40] Article 7 provides that no set-off between asset and liability items, or between income and expenditure items, is permissible.[41]

Difficulties have arisen in the past in determining what are fixed assets and what are current assets under British law.[42] The Directive provides that fixed assets shall comprise those assets which are intended for use on a continuing basis for the purpose of the undertaking's activities. The distinction between fixed and current assets has become of less importance in this country since the implementation of Article 35(1)(b) of the Directive by Sch. 4, para. 18 of the Companies Act 1985 (as amended) which requires provision to be made for the depreciation of fixed assets.[43]

It is noteworthy that Article 31(1)(c)(aa) provides that only profits made at the balance sheet date may be included in the profit and loss account. This is interpreted as meaning that profits should not be anticipated but (in accordance with the concept of prudence enshrined in Article 31(1)(c)) be so included only when earned and ascertained. The requirements of Article 31 have been taken into account in Sch. 4, para. 2 of the Companies Act 1985 (as amended), which provides that only profits realized at the balance sheet date shall be included in the profit and loss account and thus be distri-butable, in accordance within section 263(1) and 263(3) of that Act.

Valuation Rules

Articles 32 to 40 state the accounting conventions and bases of valuation to be adopted in determining the amounts at which fixed and current assets respectively (and to a minor extent, liabilities) are to be stated in company accounts. The convention which is generally adopted is that of historic cost, with the valuation of the assets being based upon purchase price or production cost. However, Article 33 contains separate provisions which allow Member States to permit or require alternative accounting conventions based on other than historic cost. These provisions are considered in the next section. Member States are required to ensure that the items shown in the annual accounts are valued in accordance with the general principles set out in Article 31(1). The valuation must be undertaken upon the assumption that the undertaking is a going concern.[44] The methods of valuation must be applied consistently from one financial year to another. Furthermore, the valuation must be made on a prudent basis.[45]

Article 35(1)(b) provides that the purchase price or production cost of fixed assets with a limited economic life must be reduced by depreciation provisions calculated to write off the value of the assets systematically over their useful economic life. In Great Britain, the directors must make provision for depreciation, and particulars thereof must be shown separately.[46]

The Directive contains provisions governing the accounting treatment of certain intangible assets. Thus, Article 37 provides that the costs of research and development and the value of goodwill shall, in principle, be written off within a maximum period of five years. The laws of the Member States may permit derogations from this rule in the case of research and development; Member States are also permitted to derogate from the principle that no distributions of profit may take place unless there will remain distributable profits at least equivalent to the amount of research and development costs not written off.[47] Furthermore, Member States may permit companies to write off goodwill over a systematic period exceeding five years provided that this period does not exceed the useful economic life of the asset, and is disclosed in the notes on the accounts together with the supporting reasons therefor.[48] In Great Britain development costs may be shown as a fixed asset in a company's balance sheet in exceptional circumstances only. If they are so shown, the notes to the accounts must give the reasons for so doing, and must also state the period over which it is proposed to write them off out of profits.[49] Furthermore, purchased goodwill may be shown in a company's balance sheet as an asset at its cost of acquisition, but this amount may be written off over a period not exceeding the useful economic life of the asset, and the reasons for showing it as an asset and the period over which it will be written off must be shown in the notes to the accounts.[50]

Inflation Accounting

The provisions of Article 33 gave rise to controversy in the negotiations. The Federal Republic of Germany was originally opposed to the enactment of legal provisions permitting or requiring inflation accounting in the annual accounts of companies. Article 33(1) contemplates three possible departures from strict historic cost accounting. These are: (a) replacement value accounting for tangible fixed assets with limited useful economic lives and for stocks; (b) the use of other accounting methods which are designed to take account of inflation; and (c) revaluation of tangible fixed assets and financial fixed assets.

The use of all three methods which depart from strict historic cost accounting is subject to conditions. National law is required to define the rules for applying the valuation methods allowed. The valuation methods used, the items concerned and the method of calculation must be disclosed in the notes to the accounts. Article 33(2) states certain rules and limitations on the use of revaluation surpluses which are of a mandatory character. The net surpluses which arise from the application of Article 33(1) must be put in a revaluation reserve. No part of such a reserve may be transferred to the profit and loss account unless it has either been realized or represents an amount previously charged to the profit and loss account. Article 33(2)(1) provides that no part of the revaluation reserve may be distributed, either directly or indirectly, unless it has already been revalued; this will not prevent the reserve from being capitalized, in whole or in part, by the issue of fully paid up bonus shares. It now appears that the revaluation reserve is unavailable for the write-off of goodwill.[51] When any one of the three special valuation methods permitted by Article 33(1) is used, Article 33(4) requires the disclosure of historical cost information as a separate item in the balance sheet or in the notes on the accounts. Current cost accounting has been used in recent years in Great Britain, and provision for it is made in paragraphs 29–34 of Schedule 4 to the Companies Act 1985 (as amended) which would seem to comply generally with the requirements of the Fourth Directive.[52] Current cost accounting is permitted in France,[53] but not in Germany.

It should be noted in conclusion that Article 33(5) of the Fourth Directive provides that the Council shall, on a proposal from the Commission and within seven years of the notification of the Directive, examine and, where necessary, amend Article 33 in the light of economic and monetary trends in the Community. No such amendment has taken place at the time of writing.

Implementation
The Fourth Directive was first implemented in Great Britain by the Companies Act 1981. The relevant implementing provisions are now to be found in the Companies Act 1985 (as amended) and in Schedule 4 thereto. Implementation in Northern Ireland is governed by the Companies (Northern Ireland) Order of 1986.[54] Implementation took place in Denmark by two laws: law no. 284 of 10 June 1981,[55] which is applicable to the accounts of public companies, and law no. 285 of the same date, which is applicable to the accounts of private companies.[56] Implementation took place in Belgium by means of two laws and two Royal Decrees [*arrêts royals*]. The two laws are the law of 1 July 1983[57] amending the law of 17 July 1975 governing the annual accounts of enterprises, and the lw of 5 December 1984[58] amending the co-ordinated laws on commercial companies of 30 November 1935. In addition to the two Royal Decrees, which were enacted in 1983 and 1986 respectively,[59] certain minor amendments[60] were made to other decrees for the purpose of helping to bring Belgian law into conformity with the Fourth Directive. Implementation took place in the Netherlands by means of the law of 7 December 1983,[61] as well as by means of two decrees, which were enacted on 22 December 1983[62] and 23 December 1983[63] respectively.

The French implementing legislation consisted of law no. 83–353 of 30 April 1983,[64] Decree no. 83–1020 of 29 November 1983 made in pursuance of law no. 83–353,[65] and the ministerial decree [*arrêt*] of 27 April 1982, approving the revised *plan comptable général* (national chart of accounts, already published in 1979).[66]

The Fourth Directive was implemented in Luxembourg by the law of 4 May 1984,[67] and in the Republic of Ireland by the Companies (Amendment) Act 1976. In the Federal Republic of Germany, the legislation required for the purpose of implementing the Fourth, Seventh and Eighth Directives is contained in the *Bilanzrichtliniengesetz* of 19 December 1985.[68] The necessary amendments to Greek law were made by two Presidential Decrees.[69] Implementation in Portugal took place through the medium of Decree Law 410/89 of 21 November 1989.[70] In Spain, the required implementing legislation is to be found in Law 19/1989 of 25 July 1989.[71]

THE SEVENTH DIRECTIVE

History and Scope

The Seventh Directive on consolidated accounts[72] was intended to implement the Fourth Directive on the annual accounts of companies. It appears from the preamble to the Seventh Directive that the philosophy underlying the requirement that Member States must make provision for the preparation of consolidated accounts is that all persons connected with an undertaking belonging to a group have an interest in being properly informed of the structure, assets, financial position and profits and losses of the group to which the undertaking belongs.

The Seventh Directive had a long gestation period. The first proposal for such a Directive was submitted by the Commission to the Council of Ministers on 4 April 1976.[73] This proposal was much influenced by German law, and encountered a considerable amount of criticism. The amended proposal of 1978 also encountered a number of criticisms, and the final version of the Directive departed from it in a number of ways. The Directive seems to be a compromise measure, which lacks certain harmonizing characteristics and incorporates certain features of the different national systems.

Consolidated accounts must cover all the subsidiaries of a parent undertaking, irrespective of where they are registered or what form they take. For the purpose of the preparation of consolidated accounts, a subsidiary of a subsidiary is treated under Article 3(2) as the subsidiary of the ultimate parent company. It follows from Article 3 that a subsidiary must be defined in implementing legislation so as to include all types of undertakings. Implementing legislation will also have to make it clear that all subsidiaries, wherever situated, must be included in the consolidation.[74] In addition, by Article 4(1) of the Directive, a parent undertaking is required to prepare consolidated accounts if that undertaking, or any of its subsidiaries, is established as a public or private limited company in one of the Member States. Thus, in contrast to the position which obtained before the implementation of the Seventh Directive in France,[75] the obligation to prepare consolidated accounts is imposed not only on parent undertakings which are listed companies, but also upon parent undertakings which are not listed companies or, indeed, companies of any kind.[76] German private limited companies, as well as public companies, which are parent undertakings have been required to draw up such accounts since the new form of Article 290 of the Commercial Code came into force on 1 January 1990.[77] Any Member State is permitted under Article 4(2) to exempt an undertaking from the obligation to prepare consolidated accounts if it is not established as a public or a private limited company under the law of that Member State. It should be clear from the new form of Article 290 of the Commercial Code that the exception will apply to German undertakings. France has not made any use of the exception. It follows from section 227(1) of the Companies Act 1985 – which was inserted therein by section 5 of the Companies Act 1989 – that the United Kingdom Parliament has taken advantage of this exception.[78]

Mandatory and Permissive Conditions for the Preparation of Consolidated Accounts

A parent undertaking is defined in the Seventh Directive as one which has a majority of the voting rights in and one which is a member of and has the right to appoint or remove the members of the administrative, management or supervisory body of the subsidiary undertaking.[79] Member States are required to adopt these two definitions. The requirement as to voting rights, which may be contrasted with that regarding equity share capital in the parallel provisions of the law, has necessitated the amendment of British law.

By Article 1(1)(c), consolidated accounts are also required to be prepared where a parent undertaking has the right, through the medium of an agreement with the subsidiary or under a provision of its memorandum or Articles which is valid under the law governing the subsidiary, to exercise a dominant influence over the sbubsidiary's undertaking. Article 1(1)(c), which is inspired by German law, does not contain any definition of what is meant by a dominant influence. Member States whose laws do not provide for such agreements or provisions are not required to apply the latter text. English law permits such contracts or provisions under certain circumstances and may therefore, perhaps, be said to provide for them.

Article 1(1)(d)(aa) and (bb) provide for the requirement to produce consolidated accounts in two more situations. These are where the parent undertaking is a shareholder or a member of an undertaking and:

1. a majority of the members of the administrative management or supervisory bodies of the subsidiary undertaking who have held office during the financial year, during the previous financial year and up to the time when the consolidated accounts are drawn up have been appointed solely as the result of the exercise of its voting rights; or
2. control alone, pursuant to an agreement with the other shareholders in or members of the subsidiary undertaking, a majority of shareholders' or members' rights in that undertaking.

Member States are permitted to introduce more detailed provisions concerning the form and content of such agreements. They are required to prescribe the arrangements referred to concerning voting agreements, but are not obliged to prescribe those relating to the designation of members of the board. Article 1(1)(d)(aa) is inapplicable if another company qualifies as the susidiary company under Article 1(1)(a), (b) or (c). Article 1(1)(d)(aa) is not clearly expressed, and fails to set out explicitly for how long the consolidation may take place, or to explain the meaning of the phrase 'solely as the result of the exercise of its voting rights'.

Article 2(1) sets out the rights which must be added to those of the putative parent undertaking for the purpose of determining whether a parent–subsidiary relationship exists for the purpose of Article 1(a), (b) and (d). These consist of the voting rights and rights of appointment belonging to any other subsidiary of the parent undertaking and the rights of any person acting in his own name, but on behalf of the parent undertaking. These rights, which must not be included in the calculation of the rights described in Article 2(1), are set out in Article 2(2), which contains some rather confusing provisions.[80]

In addition to the cases mentioned above, by Article 1(2) a Member State is permitted to treat an undertaking governed by the national law as a parent undertaking if it holds a participating influence (as defined in Article 17 of the Fourth Directive) in that undertaking and actually exercises a dominant influence over it, or is managed with that undertaking on a unified basis by the parent undertaking's management organ. A participating interest is a shareholding in the other undertaking which is intended to contribute to the parent undertaking's activities by creating a durable link with the other undertaking. A shareholding comprising 20 per cent of another undertaking's capital is presumed to be a participating influence. The purpose of this optional extension of the parent–subsidiary relationship was to accommodate German law. However, it has recently been adopted by the United Kingdom Parliament as the result of the incorporation of a new section 258 into the Companies Act 1985 by section 21 of the Companies Act 1989. It is noteworthy that the latter section not only incorporates the provisions of Articles 1(1)(a), (b), 1(1)(c) and (d), (bb), which are compulsory, but also those of 1(2), which are optional, into British law.[81]

The Department of Trade and Industry accepted the view that although the definition of a subsidiary in Article 1(1)(c) contains some elements of uncertainty, it was necessary that this provision should be implemented. Furthermore, it also took the view that although the implementation of Article 1(2) inevitably introduced an element of judgement into determining what is and is not a subsidiary, such implementation would go some way towards removing the problems which have arisen from off-balance-sheet accounting by which a company, which is effectively controlled by a parent, is used in such a way as to keep assets and liabilities off the consolidated balance sheet.[82]

The Department of Trade and Industry took the view that the two new definitions of a subsidiary which it proposed, based upon Article 1(2)(c) and 1(2), should be adopted merely for the purpose of consolidation. It also proposed that undertakings other than bodies corporate should not be regarded as subsidiaries otherwise than for the accounting purposes of the Companies Act. These two approaches are both adopted in the Companies Act 1989.[83] It should be noted that the approach which has been taken is similar to that which has been adopted in France, where there are a number of different definitions of a subsidiary for different purposes. It is also noteworthy that section 258 of the Companies Act 1985, which was incorporated therein by section 21 of the Companies Act 1989 and Schedule 9 of the same Act, contains a number of new provisions intended to implement the requirements of Article 2 of the Directive, which has been mentioned above. France has implemented the requirements of Article 1(1)(a), 1(d)(aa) and 1(1)(d)(bb) of the Seventh Directive.[84] Germany has implemented those of Article 1(1)(a)–(c), and 1(1)(d)(bb) and 1(2).[85]

Exemptions from the Requirement of Preparing Consolidated Accounts

(a) Exemptions for holding companies and small groups
It is not possible to give a detailed account of all exemptions. Article 5, which is mainly of significance for Luxembourg, provides that Member States may exempt parent undertakings which constitute financial holding companies from the obligation to prepare consolidated accounts. Article 6 provides Member States with the option of giving the parent undertaking of a 'small' group (as defined in Article 27 of the Fourth Directive, as amended)[86] an exemption from the need to consolidate. This exemption would be applicable except where one of the undertakings included in the consolidation was a company listed on a stock exchange in a Member State. The United Kingdom Parliament has exercised this option by enacting section 13(1) of the Companies Act 1989, which inserts a new section 248 making detailed provision for it in the Companies Act 1985; and legislative provisions taking advantage of it have been adopted both in France and Germany.

Exemptions for sub-groups
Each Member State is required to exempt from the obligation to produce consolidated accounts any parent undertaking governed by its law which is itself a subsidiary of another parent undertaking governed by the law of the same or another Member State.

However, this exemption is applicable only if the superior parent undertaking holds the whole or at least 90 per cent of the intermediate parent undertaking's share capital, and the remaining shareholders or members unanimously approve the application of the exemption.[87] The exemption was incorporated into the Seventh Directive at the request of the United Kingdom, and does not have to be given until the year 2000 if national laws require consolidated accounts. Furthermore, an intermediate parent undertaking will be exempted from preparing consolidated accounts only if consolidated accounts are prepared by the superior undertaking, or by the latter undertaking's superior undertaking governed by the law of a Member State, and the consolidated accounts cover the imtermediate parent company and its subsidiaries, and they and the consolidated annual report covering them are audited and published in accordance with the requirements of the Seventh Directive.[88] By Article 7(3), Member States are not required to apply Article 7 to companies the securities of which are admitted to listing on a stock exchange established in a Member State. The exemptions provided for by Article 7(1)(a) and (b) are mandatory, and their implementation by the United Kingdom Parliament will involve an extension of the exemptions already given by the old section 229(2) of the Companies Act 1985.

Article 8 empowers a Member State optionally to exempt intermediate parent undertakings governed by its law from the preparation of consolidated accounts where the superior parent undertaking holds less than 90 per cent of the share capital at the intermediate parent undertaking. This can be done only where the superior parent undertaking is governed by the law of a Member State, and the same conditions are complied with concerning the preparation, audit and publication of consolidated accounts by the superior parent undertaking, or its parent undertaking, as must be fulfilled under the mandatory exemption. Furthermore, no request for the preparation of consolidated accounts by the intermediate parent undertaking must be made at least six months before the end of its financial year by the holders of more than 10 per cent of its capital if it is a public company, or 20 per cent if it is not. Article 11 provides for a further permissive exemption from consolidation in the case of an intermediate parent undertaking whose superior parent undertaking is not governed by the law of a Member State. This exemption applies only where the intermediate parent company and its subsidiaries are included in consolidated accounts drawn up by the superior parent undertaking, or the latter company's own parent undertaking; and the consolidated accounts and the accompanying consolidated annual report are prepared and published in accordance with the requirements of the Directive, or in an equivalent manner, and are audited by an auditor authorized to audit accounts under the law of the State governing the superior parent undertaking, or its parent undertaking. The determination of what is meant by accounts equivalent to consolidated accounts drawn up in accordance with the Seventh Directive has given rise to difficulties, which have been discussed in the Contact Committee mentioned in Article 47 of the Directive.[89] The United Kingdom Parliament has not adopted the exception provided for in Article 11.

The permissive exemption contained in Article 11 is applicable only where no request is made by the holder of a fraction of the share capital of the intermediate parent company that it should prepare consolidated annual accounts. The rules contained in Article 8 governing the time within which the request must be made and the percentage of shareholders required to make it apply also to the extended exemption under Article 16. A Member State may apply for exemptions under that Article only if it provides for the same exemptions under Articles 7–10.

Article 9 provides for an additional Member State option in relation to Articles 7 and 8. The mandatory exemption under Article 7 may, at the Member State's option, be made conditional on the disclosure of certain additional information in the consolidated accounts of the ultimate parent undertaking, or in an appendix thereto, and/or the individual accounts of the intermediate parent undertaking.

Article 357–2 of the French law governing commercial companies of 1966, as amended, which is the only provision of that law specifically applicable to such group exemption, provides that parent companies other than those whose shares are listed on the stock exchange, and which comply with the requirements of paragraph 1^0 of that Article, as well as with those of Decree No. 86–221 of 17 February 1986,[90] will be exempted from the obligation to prepare and publish consolidated accounts. The requirements of paragraph 1^0 are that the parent company is itself under the control of another company which consolidates it into its accounts and that shareholders in or members of the exempted undertaking which hold at least 10 per cent of its share capital shall not have requested the preparation of consolidated accounts. The additional requirements contained in Articles 248–13 of the law governing commercial companies of 24 July 1966, as amended, like those requirements which have already been mentioned, would seem to be based upon Articles 8 and 11 of the Directive, rather than on Article 7 thereof. However, there may be little to object to in this, because the extended exemptions provided for by French law and by Articles 8 and 11 are more liberal than those provided for by Article 7, and are conditional on compliance with all or most of the provisions of Article 7(2).

It should be noted that the German sub-group exemption contained in the new form of Article 291 of the German Commercial Code, introduced by the law of 19 December 1985, also appears to be based upon Article 8 rather than Article 7.

(c) Omission of subsidiaries
Article 13 of the Seventh Directive contains five permissive exclusions from consolidation, and Article 14 provides for one mandatory one. The latter provision excludes from consolidation undertakings which are so dissimilar that their inclusion would derogate from a true and fair view. All the exclusions in question authorize the omission of one or more subsidiaries or sub-subsidiaries from consolidated accounts. The exclusions provided for in Article 13(3)(a)(aa) and (a)(bb) and in Article 13(3)(c) contained no direct parallel in the law of Great Britain, but the first and last of them have been implemented by section 229(3)(a) and (c) of the Companies Act 1985, incorporated therein by section 5(3) of the Companies Act 1989. Article 13(1), which corresponds to the old section 229(3)(a) of the Companies Act 1985, has been implemented by new section 229(2) of that Act. Article 13(3)(b) closely corresponds to both the old and new section 229(3)(b) of that Act. Article 14(1) resembles the old section 229(3)(d); Article 14(2), which limits the application of Article 14(1), is not very clearly drafted. Article 14 has been implemented in Great Britain by means of the new section 229(4) of the Companies Act 1985. French law provides for all the exemptions contained in Article 13;[91] German law also specifically provides for all the exemptions contained in Articles 13 and 14.[92]

Preparation of Consolidated Accounts

Basic requirements, accounting formats and valuation methods
The accounts in consolidated accounts comprise the consolidated balance sheet, the consolidated profit and loss account, and the notes to the accounts.[93] They must give a true and fair view of the assets, liabilities, financial position and profits and losses of the undertakings included therein taken as a whole.[94] As in the case of the Fourth Directive, the requirements of a true and fair view are paramount; they entail the provision of additional information when necessary[95] and also departures in exceptional circumstances from the provisions of the Directive relating to the preparation of consolidated accounts, as long as particulars of any departure, the reasons for it, and a statement of its effects appear in the notes to the accounts.[96] It should be noted that, as in the case of section 230(2) of the Companies Act 1985, the true and fair view does not relate to the definition of the group itself. However, when the accounts would not otherwise give a true and fair view, it may be necessary for additional information to be given about a non-subsidiary, or for the detailed accounting rules to be overridden in accordance with Article 16(5) of the Directives so that the amount of assets and liabilities and profits and losses of a body which is not a subsidiary is included in the consolidated accounts as though it were one.[97]

Consolidated accounts, including the annual report, must be prepared in accordance with the format and general rules as to the presentation of the annual accounts which are provided for in the Fourth Directive, subject to the essential adjustments necessary in respect of consolidation, and the requirements of the Seventh Directive.[98] As in the case of the formats to be employed when preparing consolidated accounts, the Seventh Directive makes reference to the relevant Articles of the Fourth Directive when determining the methods of valuation to be employed in consolidated accounts.[99] A number of options are thus available to Member States in relation to the enactment of valuation rules. Article 29(1) of the Seventh Directive provides that uniform methods must be applied in valuing all the assets and liabilities included in the consolidated accounts. To achieve this aim the valuation rules applied by the parent undertaking in drawing up its own annual accounts must be used by it in preparing consolidated accounts. However, an exception to this principle exists where the law of the Member State governing the parent undertaking requires or permits the use of other valuation rules contained in the Fourth Directive. The valuation rules must, in principle, be applied in a consistent manner to the assets and liabilities of all the undertakings in the group. It should be noted that there was formerly nothing in Schedule 4 to the Companies Act 1985 which required uniform accounting policies in the law of Great Britain, but this position has been changed by the incorporation of a new paragraph 11 into Sch. 4 of the Companies Act 1985 by Sch. 1, para. 5 to the Companies Act 1989.

Techniques of consolidation

The Directive makes provision for four techniques of consolidation which are in common use: these are acquisition accounting, merger accounting, the equity method of accounting for investments in associated undertakings, and the proportional consolidation of joint ventures. Article 25 provides that whatever methods are adopted for consolidation, they must be applied consistently from one financial year to another. Changes in the methods are permissible in exceptional circumstances if they are disclosed in the notes on the accounts, together with the reason for them and the effect which they will have on the figures shown in the accounts. This provision is necessary in order to achieve the fundamentally important objective that the accounts should show a true and fair view of the group as though it were a single entity.[100]

The assets and liabilities of all the undertakings included in a consolidation are required to be included in a consolidated balance sheet in full.[101] A similar rule applies to the income and expenditure of all the undertakings included in a consolidation.[102] The purpose of these provisions is to require line-by-line consolidation rather than pro rata consolidation.[103] The above method is normally employed in conjunction with acquisition accounting, which is in essence provided for by Article 19 of the Directive. However, Article 20 of the Directive permits merger accounting, an alternative which is employed in Anglo-American systems, under the circumstances mentioned below:

(a) Article 19 contains requirements governing the principal set-offs which achieve what is usually known as the acquisition method of accounting. The book values in the parent company's accounts of shares in the capital of subsidiary undertaking must be set off against the proportion they represent of the capital and reserves of the relevant subsidiary undertaking. The basic rule contained in Article 19(1)(a) is that the set-off should be calculated on the basis of book values as at the date when the undertakings are included in the consolidation for the first time. However, Article 19(1)(b) grants Member States the option of requiring or permitting set-offs on the basis of the value of identifiable assets and liabilities at the date of the acquisition of the shares or in the event of acquisition in two or more stages, at the date when the undertaking became a subsidiary. This has been exercised and made compulsory in Great Britain by para. 9 of Sch. 4A of the Companies Act 1985, which was incorporated therein by Sch. 2 of the Companies Act 1989. Article 19(1)(c) contains certain provisions governing the disclosure of differences arising from the set-off, which had to be implemented in legislation in the Member States.[104] It is noteworthy that the requirements of Article 19 have been implemented in Germany by the very detailed provisions of Article 301 of the Commercial Code, as amended. Thus, in essence, now that this provision has come into force, German law will be changed so as to require goodwill to be calculated on a fair-value basis on the acquisition of a subsidiary.[105]

(b) *Merger accounting*: Article 20 was inserted into the Seventh Directive at the request of the UK. This provision gives Member States the option, in rather limited circumstances,[106] to require or permit the use of merger accounting. They would thus be allowed by Article 20(1) to require or permit the book values of shares held in the capital of an undertaking included in the consolidation to be set off against the appropriate percentage of capital, provided that:

1. the shares held represented at least 90 per cent of the nominal value, or in the absence of a nominal value, of the accounting par value of the shares in that undertaking, other than shares carrying a limited right to participate in distribution;
2. the proportion referred to in (1) above has been obtained pursuant to an arrangement providing for the issue of shares by an undertaking included in the consolidation; and

3. the arrangement did not include a cash payment exceeding 10 per cent of the nominal value, or in the absence of a nominal value, the accounting par value of the shares issued.

Any difference arising under Article 20(1) must be added to or deducted from consolidated reserves as appropriate.[107] The application of the method known as merger accounting, the resultant movement in reserves, and the names and registered offices of the undertakings involved must be disclosed in the notes on the accounts.[108]

The implementation of Article 20, which is somewhat restrictive, has necessitated a number of minor changes in the law of Great Britain.[109] The abuse of this method of accounting has given rise to concern in the UK accountancy and legal professions in recent years. The provisions of the new form of Article 302 of the German Commercial Code, incorporated therein by the law of 19 December 1985, closely follow those of Article 20 of the Directive. French law does not contain any provision for merger accounting.

(c) *Equity accounting for associated companies*: Article 33, which covers a number of complex matters which cannot be fully considered in the present text,[110] is concerned with the situation where an undertaking included in a consolidation exercises a significant influence over the operating and financial policy of an associated undertaking which is not included in the consolidation, in which it holds a participating interest.[111] A participating influence is defined in Article 17 of the Fourth Directive. A group undertaking which holds a participating interest in another undertaking is presumed to exercise a significant influence over it, such as to make it an associated undertaking if the group undertaking and its subsidiaries and nominees for them together hold at least 20 per cent of the voting rights exercisable by shareholders of the associated undertaking. The internationally accepted manner of accounting for interests of the latter kind is the equity method, which is prescribed by Article 33(2) and adopted by paragraph 22 of Sch. 4A of the Companies Act 1985 (as amended). When an investment is first accounted for on an equity basis, the Directive requires it to be included in the consolidated accounts on one of two alternative bases. The associate may be valued at cost, and the difference between that value and the group's share of the net assets must then be disclosed separately in the consolidated balance sheet or the notes on the accounts.[112] The net amount represents the goodwill in the associate. The associate may be valued instead at the group's share of its capital and reserves. The purpose of the special rules governing interests in associates is to facilitate the partial consolidation of associated undertakings without requiring that they shall be fully consolidated with group undertakings.[113] Articles 311 and 312 of the Commercial Code, which were incorporated therein by the Law of 19 December 1985 and appear to be in general conformity with Article 33 of the Directive, provide for the introduction of both forms of equity accounting in Germany.

(d) *Proportional consolidation for joint ventures*: An investment in an associated company must be distinguished from a joint venture. By Article 32, Member States may require or permit undertakings which are managed by a member of the group jointly with one or more undertakings which are not part of the group to be proportionately consolidated. The proportional method, which involves a line-by-line approach, is an approach to consolidation under which a proportion of the assets, liabilities and profits of the undertaking invested in (which may, for example, been a partnership) is incorporated in the accounts of the investing group, so that any minority interest is eliminated. An investment which is proportionately consolidated is not accounted for on an equity basis.[114]

British law used not to make any provision for dealing with joint interests, but somewhat limited provision for proportional consolidation is now made by para. 19 of Sch. 4A to the Companies Act 1985. Article 310 of the German Commercial Code, which was incorporated therein by the law of 19 December 1985, also provides for proportional consolidation. The same is true of Article 357–3 of the French law governing commercial companies of 1966, as amended.

Notes on the Accounts
The provisions of Article 34, which require consolidated accounts to be accompanied by extensive notes, reflect those of Article 43 of the Fourth Directive.[115] Many of the requirements of Article 34 were incorporated into the law of Great Britain and made

applicable to consolidated accounts by virtue of paragraph 62 of Schedule 4 to the Companies Act 1985. However, the implementation of Article 34 has necessitated some minor changes in our law. Reference should be made to section 6 and Schedule 3 of the Companies Act 1989; the latter Schedule inserts a new Schedule 5 into the Companies Act 1985.

Some Other Important Features of the Seventh Directive

The remaining provisions of the Seventh Directive which appear to require discussion here are those relating to the directors' report and the audit and publication of consolidated accounts. Article 36 of the Seventh Directive corresponds to Article 46 of the Fourth Directive and deals with certain matters to be included in the consolidated annual report to accompany the consolidated accounts. This report is required to contain at least a fair review of the development of the business and position of the group as a whole, together with certain other prescribed particulars. In Great Britain, section 234 of and Schedule 7 to the Companies Act 1985, as amended, provide for the contents of the directors' report to accompany company accounts. Paragraph 2 of Schedule 7 takes account of the effect of the necessary inclusion of undertakings which are not companies in the definition of subsidiaries.[116]

The Seventh Directive also governs the audit and publication of consolidated accounts. The audit must be carried out by one or more persons authorized to audit the accounts of the parent undertaking which prepares the consolidated accounts.[117] The continued imposition of this requirement by sections 235(1) and 235(2) of the Companies Act 1985, as amended by Section 9 of the Companies Act 1989, has not necessitated any changes in English law. A copy of the consolidated accounts and the accompanying consolidated annual report and the auditors' report must be published in the national gazette appointed by the Member State.[118] The requirements of Article 38(1) concerning publication are now complied with under British law[119] as a result of the enactment of the new form of section 242 of the Companies Act 1985 incorporated in section 11 of the Companies Act 1989, which must be read together with section 711(1)(k) of the Companies Act 1985 (as amended by para. 14 of Schedule 10 to the Companies Act 1989).[120]

Implementation

At the time of writing, the Seventh Directive has been implemented by only eight Member States: the United Kingdom, France, Germany, Greece, Luxembourg, the Netherlands, Belgium and Spain. Implementation by the United Kingdom has so far taken the form of the relevant provisions of the Companies Act 1989, which made a number of amendments to the Companies Act 1985.[121] As already pointed out, implementation took place in France by means of law no. 85–11 of 3 January 1985,[122] relating to the consolidated accounts of certain commercial companies and public enterprises; and through the medium of Decree 86–221 of 17 February 1986.[123] In Germany, the Fourth, Seventh and Eighth Directives were all implemented by the *Bilanzrichtliniengesetz* of 19 December 1985.[124] In Greece, implementation took place through the medium of the two Presidential Decrees [125] which have already been mentioned in connection with the Fourth Directive. In Luxembourg, implementation took place through the law of 11 July 1988,[126] and in the Netherlands through that of 10 November 1988.[127] In Belgium, implementation took place through Royal Decree 90/763 of 27 March 1990,[128] whilst in Spain it took place through Law 19/1989 of 25 July 1989, and Decree Law 1564/89.[129]

AMENDMENT OF FOURTH AND SEVENTH DIRECTIVES

A draft Directive intended to amend the Fourth and Seventh Directives has been published;[130] it is designed to have two effects. As far as the Fourth Directive is concerned, a partnership, limited partnership or unlimited company would become subject to the requirements of the Directive if all its members with limited liability were public or private limited companies. Furthermore, as regards the Seventh Directive, a 'holding' company taking the form of a partnership, limited partnership or unlimited company would become subject to the requirements of that Directive if all the members with unlimited liability were public or private limited companies. The original version of the proposal had some drafting defects,[131] and encountered opposition on the ground that its adoption might place undue burdens on partnerships and limited partnerships.[132] Until recently the German government expressed continuous opposition to this proposal, which would have an important impact on the type of business organization encountered in Germany known as a GmbH & Co. KG. This consists of a limited partnership between a private company (which is the general partner) and its members (which are the limited partners). This type of business organization is used in Germany not only by small businesses but by large business organizations [*Publikumsgesell-schaften*]. It is understood that a common position was reached in the council on an amended version of the proposal on 29 June 1990.

However, as already indicated, a more recent proposal exists for the amendment of the Fourth and Seventh Directives.[133] If this proposal is adopted, its main impact would be on the Fourth Directive. It would extend the derogations now made available to small and medium-sized companies under that instrument and make them mandatory within Member States with a view to achieving greater harmonization of the treatment of such companies within the Community. In addition, it would give all companies the option to draw up and consolidate accounts in ECU, if they so wished. The draft Directive (the preamble to which makes reference to Article 54, EEC as the principal enabling provision), which enjoys the enthusiastic support of Germany, owes its origin to an idea included in the Commission's 1986 programme for small and medium-sized firms, and to discussions in the Accounting Directives Contact Committee. Article 1 thereof would exclude certain closely held companies from the ambit of the Fourth Directive. The criteria for these companies would be drafted in such a way as to ensure that there were no minority shareholders. Member States would be enabled to provide their own regime in respect of such companies, provided that it did not go beyond the requirements of the Fourth Directive. Such States would also be required to provide for penalties in the event of failure to keep proper accounts.

As already indicated, the existing exemptions for small companies would be made mandatory. Furthermore, such companies would be exempted by Article 8 from including certain further items of information in the notes on the accounts. By Article 10, small companies would be exempted from the requirement of preparing a directors' report, provided that information on important events and purchase of the company's own shares was disclosed in a note on the accounts. Article 4 would introduce an element of flexibility into the two financial thresholds relevant to the definition of small and medium-sized companies. These might be increased or decreased by up to 25 per cent. As far as the definition of such companies was concerned, Member States would be permitted to descend below the number of 50 employees to a minimum of 25. In order to simplify the administrative procedure for small and medium-sized companies, such companies would be allowed, in accordance with the conditions set out in Article 11, to keep the accounting documents available to the public at the registered office of the company instead of having to file these documents in a register in accordance with the provisions of the first company law Directive. Articles 13 and 14 of the draft Directive would provide that companies might draw up their individual accounts and consolidated accounts in ECU if they so wished.

The proposed relaxation of the rules governing small and medium-sized companies was avowedly intended by the Commission to make life easier for such companies. However, the United Kingdom government has expressed its opposition to the proposed Directive in a Consultative Document published by the Department of Trade and Industry. It is understood that a common position on the above proposal, which has undergone very considerable amendment during the process of negotiation, was reached by the Council on 12 June 1990. This revised version of the proposal, which would seem to delete certain of the controversial features mentioned above, may well be created by the Council in the fairly near future.

The Accounts of Credit Institutions and Insurance Undertakings
These matters will be considered in outline only. As already pointed out, a Council Directive on the annual accounts of banks and other financial institutions was adopted on 8 December 1986.[134] According to Article 27(1) thereof, Member States are required to bring into force the laws, regulation and administrative provisions necessary in order to comply with the Directive by 31 December 1990. However, by Article 27(2) these laws may stipulate that the provisions in the Directive need be first applied only to annual accounts for the financial year beginning in the calendar year 1993.

The Directive makes provision for minimum financial reporting standards for credit institutions and other financial institutions, which are known collectively as credit institutions for the purposes of the Directive. Because of their specific character, such institutions were excluded from the scope of the Fourth and Seventh Company Law Directives. However, the present Directive has the effect of extending the harmonization achieved by these Directives to credit institutions. The Directive is applicable to all deposit-taking companies and firms which are formed under civil or commercial law, and all financial institutions taking the form of limited liability companies which are not subject to the Fourth Directive.[135] The phrase 'financial institutions' has not been clearly defined in the Directive, because of the diverse nature of such institutions in the different Member States.

A further Directive on the accounting requirements of branches of overseas credit institutions and financial institutions was enacted on 13 February 1989.[136] This Directive must be implemented not later than 1 January 1991.[137] Nevertheless, a Member State may provide that the implementing provisions shall apply for the first time to annual accounts for the financial year beginning on 1 January 1993, or during the calendar year 1993.[138]

Credit and financial institutions are defined in the same way as in the above-mentioned Directive. The Directive stipulates, for the branches of such institutions established in a Member State and having their head offices outside that State, the documents, including accounting documents, which they must file at the relevant local registry.[139] The branches of such institutions whose head office is established in another Member State are required by the Directive to file accounts drawn up in accordance with Council Directive 86/635/EEC. Furthermore, Member States are given the option of requiring additional information concerning the branch itself to be filed. Branches of credit institutions whose head office is outside the Community are required to file accounts which are equivalent to accounts prepared in accordance with Council Directive 86/635/EEC.[140] Where equivalent accounts are unavailable, Member States may require the branches to publish annual accounts relating to their own activities.

A draft proposal for a Directive on the Anual Accounts of Insurance Undertakings was submitted by the Commission to the Council in January 1987. A revised proposal was published in

October 1989,[141] consequent upon the European Parliament's Opinion on the original proposal, which was given in March 1989. It is envisaged that the Directive would apply to all insurance undertakings falling within the scope of the Council Directive 73/239/EEC on the co-ordination of laws on direct insurance.[142] and Council Directive 79/267/EEC on direct life assurance.[143] The Directive would establish a framework for a common standard of accounting disclosure for insurance undertakings. Certain adaptations would be made for Lloyd's insurance undertakings. Credit and insurance institutions were excluded from the ambit of the Fourth and Seventh Directives.[144] It is envisaged in the Commission's latest proposal that certain provisions of these Directives will be made applicable to insurance companies, but that some account will be taken of the different character of insurance business. It is envisaged that insurance company accounts will have to give a true and fair view and that the definition, layout and valuation of items included therein will be standardized.

5

The Eighth Directive on the Approval of Auditors

History and Scope

Like the Fourth and Seventh Directives, the Eighth Directive had a long gestation period. The original proposal was made in 1978,[1] and amended in 1979.[2] The Directive was finally adopted on 10 April 1984.[3] It is principally concerned with the harmonization of the qualifications of auditors responsible for carrying out the statutory audits of the annual accounts of companies and firms, in so far as such audits are required by Community law; and of the qualifications of auditors responsible for carrying out the statutory audits of the consolidated accounts of bodies and undertakings, in so far as such auditors are required by Community law.[4] It will be remembered that the audit of individual accounts is required by Community law only when the firm in question is a public or private limited company, or a partnership limited by shares. Furthermore, it follows from Articles 4 and 37 of the Seventh Directive that the preparation of consolidated accounts – and hence their audit – is required by Community law only where either the parent undertaking or one or more of the subsidiary undertakings is one of the three types of entity already mentioned. In addition, it should be remembered that a Member State is permitted by Article 4(2) of the Seventh Directive to grant an exemption from consolidation when the parent undertaking does not fall within one of the three above-mentioned categories. The United Kingdom has taken advantage of this exemption. Hence, in this country and in certain other Member States, including Germany the only impact of the Directive will be on the qualifications of auditors of public and private limited companies, and (where applicable) of partnerships limited by shares.

The Eighth Directive is designed to supplement the Fourth and Seventh Directives. It should be evident that if the qualifications of auditors were not harmonized by regulating their professional competence and by stipulating for their integrity and independence, the two accounting Directives mentioned in the last chapter would not have a uniform effect throughout the Common Market.[5] The Directive provides that the auditors may, depending on the legislation of each Member State, be natural or legal persons, or other types of company, firm or partnership (firms of auditors as defined in the Directive). It was required to be implemented by Member States before 1 January 1988;[6] the implementation date is the same as that for the Seventh Directive.

No great difficulties may be anticipated with regard to the implementation of the Directive in Great Britain, where the matter has already been considered by the Department of Trade and Industry[7] and is dealt with in Part II of the Companies Act 1989. By section 215(2) of the latter Act, most of the relevant provisions thereof concerning auditors will come into force on such day as the Secretary of State may appoint by order made by Statutory Instrument. However, the new provisions of sections 119–24 of the latter Act, which inserted a number of new provisions in the Companies Act 1985 concerning the appointment, rights, remuneration and resignation of auditors, came into force on the Royal Assent.

It should be noted that a Directive on a General System for the Recognition of Higher Education Diplomas has recently been enacted.[8] This instrument differs in certain respects from the Eighth Directive, and will require implementation (almost certainly after an extensive process of consultation) by January 1991. Thus, certain further amendments to the laws of the Member States will have to be made in so far as auditors qualified in other Member States are concerned. In addition, the draft Fifth Directive contains a number of provisions on the auditing of accounts whose adoption would make certain further changes in the law relating to such matters as disqualifications from acting as an auditor and the dismissal and liability of auditors which are of a somewhat controversial character and whose enactment would require certain further changes in the laws of the Member States.

Rules on Approval
By Article 2(1), statutory audits may be carried out only by persons approved by authorities of the Member States. It follows from Article 2(2) that a professional organization may be authorized

by national law to grant approval.[9] Where the approved persons are natural persons, they must satisfy the complex conditions outlined in Articles 3–19, which are considered in outline only below. Where they consist of firms of auditors as defined in the Directive (which include legal persons), they must comply with the conditions stipulated in Article 2(1)(b). The most important of these are that the natural persons carrying out the audit on behalf of the firm satisfy, at least, the conditions imposed in Articles 3 to 19;[10] that a majority of the voting rights must be held by natural persons or firms of auditors who satisfy, at least, the conditions imposed in Articles 3 to 19 with the exception of Article 11(1)(b);[11] and that a majority of the members of the administrative or management body of a firm of auditors must be natural persons or firms of auditors who satisfy, at least, the conditions imposed by Articles 3 to 19.[12] The statutory prohibition which formerly existed on corporate auditors will be removed by section 25(2) of the British Companies Act 1989: paragraphs 4(1)(b) and 5 of Schedule 11 to that Act comply with the restrictions contained in Article 2 of the Eighth Directive.[13]

As already indicated, Articles 3–19 prescribe what may be called qualifying requirements. In principle, these may be classified under two headings: the normal and the exceptional requirements. In addition, Article 11 contains rules applicable to the approval of persons who have obtained all or part of their qualifications in another Member State. Article 3, which applies to both the normal and the exceptional requirements, provides that an auditor must be of good repute and not carry on any incompatible activity. It is understood that the provision on incompatible activities is designed to cater for the position in certain Member States, where statutory auditors are prohibited from holding positions as employees.[14] The Council Minute to the Directive, inserted at the instigation of the United Kingdom, makes it clear that Member States need not provide for any activity to be designated as incompatible with the audit function.

The normal requirements are set out in Article 4, which provides that a natural person may be approved to carry out statutory audits only after attaining university entrance level, then completing a course of theoretical instruction, undergoing practical training and passing an examination of professional competence of university final level. At least part of the examination of professional competence must be written.[15] The subjects which must be included in the syllabus of theoretical instruction are prescribed in very considerable detail in Article 6. For the most part, the subjects specified in Article 6 are already covered in British professional examinations: they all are, as far as the Institute of Chartered Accountants in England and Wales are concerned. A person who has passed a university or equivalent examination in any one of the subjects mentioned in Article 6 may be exempted from the test of theoretical knowledge in that subject.[16] The practical training must continue for a minimum period of three years.[17]

Article 9 allows persons who do not fulfil the conditions of Article 4 to be approved as statutory auditors if either they have acquired practical experience over a period of fifteen years and have passed the examination of professional competence, or they have worked in finance, law or accounting for seven years, completed the practical training required under Article 8, and passed the professional examinations. In addition, Article 10 would allow periods of theoretical instruction to be deducted from the years of professional activity specified in Article 9. The United Kingdom has made use both of the second option contained in Article 9, and of that embodied in Article 10.[18]

By Article 11, a Member State may admit a person of good repute if he has equivalent qualifications in another Member State and has furnished proof of a sufficient legal knowledge required in the Member State in which he is to carry out the audit. The authorities of that Member State need not, however, require such proof where they consider legal knowledge obtained in another Member State sufficient. Thus at present there is no obligation to accept qualifications obtained in another Member State.[19]

A number of transitional provisions are contained in Articles 12–22. It does not seem appropriate to give a detailed account of these provisions, the most important of which seem to be Articles 12, 18 and 19. Article 12(1) allows existing practising rights to be retained by individually qualified auditors who would not otherwise qualify; Article 12(2) permits existing practising rights to be retained by members of recognized professional bodies who would not otherwise qualify under the Directive.[20] By Article 18, existing students who would not satisfy the requirements at the time of the implementation of the Directive may nevertheless be approved for up to six years after implementation. The provisions of Article 19 will ensure that only those whom the competent authorities consider fit to carry out statutory audits qualify for approval under the latter derogation. In the Great Britain derogation under Articles 17–19 would seem to be possible under the provisions of section 31(4) and (5) of the Companies Act 1989.

Professional Integrity and Independence
Member States are required by Article 23 to prescribe that statutory auditors shall carry out such audits with professional integrity. Furthermore, Article 24 requires Member States to prescribe that auditors shall be independent in accordance with their national laws. Articles 23 and 24 are made applicable by Article 25 to natural persons who carry out statutory audits on behalf of a firm of auditors. Article 26 requires Member States to ensure that approved persons are liable to appropriate sanctions when they do not carry out audits in accordance with the provisions relating to integrity and independence. By Article 27, Member States are required to ensure that members of approved firms of auditors who do not personally satisfy the requirements of the Directive do not intervene in audits in any way which jeopardizes the independence of those conducting them.

Although – as should be apparent from what has been discussed above – the Directive places emphasis on the requirements of professional integrity and independence, it places the burden of enacting of detailed rules defining – and designed to safeguard – these requirements on the individual Member States. The implementing legislation enacted in Great Britain requires the supervisory bodies to have rules and practices which are adequate to secure that company audit work is conducted properly and with integrity. The implementation of the requirements of Article 27 is also left to the rules and practices of the supervisory bodies.[21] In the event that an auditor's professional integrity was called in question, the provisions of the ethical guidance and the evidence of the best current practice would doubtless be of assistance to the courts in determining the issue.[22] The British Companies Act 1985, as amended, contains a number of provisions which are designed to safeguard that the auditor shall be independent of the directors.[23] These statutory rules result, to a considerable extent, from the provisions of the Companies Act 1989.[24] The latter Act also places emphasis on strengthening professional guidance and ensuring that it is properly applied after implementation. Section 28 thereof provides for the imposition of sanctions on persons who act as auditors although ineligible for office, and would seem to be in accordance with Article 26 of the Directive.

Publicity

Member States are required by Article 28(1) to ensure that the names and addresses of all natural persons and firms of auditors approved by them to carry out statutory audits are made available to the public. The publicity requirements imposed by Article 28(2) in respect of firms of auditors appear somewhat extensive. As far as these are concerned, the names and addresses of the natural persons who carry out statutory audits on their behalf must be made available to the public. The same is also true of the names and addresses of the members or shareholders of the firms, and the names and addresses of the members of the administrative or management body thereof.[25]

Final Provisions

Article 29 provides that the Contact Committee set up under the Fourth Directive on Company Accounts will also deal with practical problems arising from, and advise the Commission on amendments to, the Eighth Directive. Article 30 requires the laws necessary to comply with the Directive to be brought into force before 1 January 1988, with the option not to apply them until 1 January 1990.[26]

Implementation

The Eighth Directive was implemented in Luxembourg by the law of 28 June 1984 concerning the organization of the auditing profession [*réviseurs d'entreprises*],[27] and by the Grand Ducal Regulation of 16 August 1984. In Belgium, implementation took place by means of the law governing the reform of the auditing profession of 21 February 1985,[28] whilst in Germany it occurred through the medium of the *Bilanzrichtliniengesetz*, as already mentioned.[29] Implementation took place in Spain by means of Law 19/1988 of 12 July 1988.[30] It took place in Greece through the medium of Presidential Decree no. 15/89 of 3 January 1989.[31] In France, two implementing decrees were enacted in January 1988, which modified earlier relevant legislation.[32] In Portugal, the relevant legislation consisted of a decree enacted on 2 September 1986, which made certain amendments to the Commercial Code.[33] Implementation has taken place by the United Kingdom through the medium of Part II of the Companies Act 1989 which, as already pointed out, has effect in Great Britain only. A number of additional regulations are being made by Statutory Instrument.[33A] The approach adopted in Part II is that the auditing profession should be supervised by the Secretary of State for Trade and Industry, who will approve certain monitoring bodies which comply with certain stated criteria. These bodies are likely to be the four accounting bodies mentioned in the old section 389(3) of the Companies Act 1985.[34] By section 47 of the Companies Act 1989, the Secretary of State will be empowered to transfer his functions of approving supervisory bodies and, with certain minor exceptions, all his other functions under Part II of the former Act, to a body corporate set up under an order made by a Statutory Instrument. Implementation in Northern Ireland took place through the Companies (Northern Ireland) Order 1990.[35]

Implementation in Denmark took place through the medium of three enactments; these are government notice [*bekendtgoreise*] no. 229 of 5 May 1986; law no. 815 of 21 December 1988; and government notice [*bekendtgoreise*] no. 56 of 19 January 1989.

6

The Draft Fifth and Vredeling Directives

INTRODUCTORY REMARKS

The draft Fifth Directive[1] contains somewhat controversial proposals for the involvement of employees in the management of public limited companies, and thus overlaps to some extent with the draft 'Vredeling' Directive,[2] which also contains proposals for procedures for informing and consulting employees. It should be noted that the first of these instruments is by far the more important and thus merits more detailed discussion than the Vredeling proposal. Neither of these instruments seems likely to be adopted in the near future,[3] and it appears possible that the Vredeling proposal may be abandoned. The need for the development of the right to information consultation and participation of workers received recent emphasis in the Commission's preliminary draft of a Community Charter of Fundamental Social Rights.[4] It is conceivable that these matters will be dealt with separately from the draft Fifth Directive, which may possibly be ultimately confined to matters of company structure. It is understood that the present discussions on the third reading of the draft Directive in the Council are so limited.

THE DRAFT FIFTH DIRECTIVE

History and Scope

A proposal for a Fifth Directive on the structure of public limited companies based on Article 54(3)(g) EEC was first presented to the Council of Ministers in 1972.[5] Because widely divergent views were taken of certain of the more radical proposals of the 1972 draft concerning the board structure of public limited companies and worker participation therein, the Commission published a

Green Paper in 1975 dealing with these issues.[6] The original proposal and the Green Paper have received exhaustive consideration from the Economic and Social Committee[7] and the European Parliament.[8] Following this consideration, the Commission issued a revised text of the Directive in August 1983.[9] A further revised text, which is unpublished, dates from 1988 and is available in a Consultative Document on the draft Directive published by the Department of Trade and Industry in January 1990. This is the text which is referred to below.

The draft Fifth Directive would apply to public limited companies only and contains a number of significant proposals on the structure and duties of the boards of such companies and the conduct of their general meetings and, as already indicated, controversial proposals for employee participation. There now appears to be some possibility that these proposals will be deleted from the draft Directive, but this is by no means certain. Member States would be permitted not to apply the Directive to public companies which were co-operatives.[10] Although it does not seem that a very detailed account of the Fifth Directive is appropriate, this instrument has given rise to a greater measure of controversy than any other Community instrument concerned with the harmonization of company law.

Although it purports to be based particularly on Article 54(3)(g), some have doubted whether in fact it can be properly based thereon, contending that employee participation lies outside the scope of Article 54(3)(g). However, it does not seem to do so if this provision is regarded as a means of excluding, as far as possible, the influence of individual Member States on the determining factors for the exercise of the freedom of establishment; these factors may well include the presence or absence of employee participation.[11] It would also seem that an employee is capable of being a party whose interests are worthy of protection for the purposes of Article 54(3)(g). It has been contended that the introduction of new legal institutions in Member States in which they do not exist cannot be called co-ordination; on the other hand, it has been argued that if a significant Community contribution is to be made to a particular economic area, it must be possible to achieve a certain degree of harmonization even in cases where not all Member States have special legislation.[12] Lutter[13] has questioned whether the large number of employee participation options which would be available to Member States under the revised draft Directive can be properly regarded as consonant with harmonization. However, as should already be apparent, other Directives contain precedents for this approach. Finally, others have questioned the necessity for a Directive involving matters of employee participation.[14] It is apparent, however, that the Community institutions have a considerable measure of discretion in determining whether a particular action is necessary.

It would thus seem that the employee participation provisions of the draft Fifth Directive may be regarded as having a proper constitutional basis. However, it is noteworthy that the United Kingdom government has consistently expressed its opposition to the present instrument in recent years. It has taken the somewhat doctrinaire standpoint that the introduction of Community-wide legislation in the area of employee participation would increase employers' costs and damage the competitive position of industry in the Community.[15] Furthermore, it has also emphasized the inappropriateness of such legislation to the general structure of industrial relations in this country. There has been comparatively little progress towards the adoption of the revised draft Directive in recent years: as the Department of Trade and Industry Consultative Document of January 1990 on the revised proposal points out, this instrument has recently completed its second reading in the Council of Ministers.

Single- or Two-Tier Boards
The revised proposal, which seems to have been influenced in this respect by French law, permits Member States to enact legislation providing for the continuance of the single-tier board system as a lasting alternative to the double-tier board system involving a supervisory and a management board. The revised proposal also provides that Member States may make provision for one of these systems only and not – as under the text of the revised Directive of August 1983 – simply a choice between the latter system and the two-tier board system. If a company given the choice under national legislation conforming with Article 2(1) adopted the former system, it would be required to have non-executive directors. A controversial attempt was made in the 1983 proposal to assimilate the position of these directors to that of the supervisory board under the two-tier system. It has been contended that

this suggested assimilation was misconceived, and should be resisted. Where the single-tier system was used, the administrative board would comprise a minimum of three members and the number of executive directors would be smaller than that of the non-executive directors.[16] The executive members would be designated by the administrative organ from among its members. However, where a company did not have employee participation under Article 21d or 21d(a), the laws of the Member States would be permitted to provide that the general meeting might not only appoint the members of the administrative organs but also designate the executive members.[17]

The supervisory board would be empowered to appoint, dismiss and supervise members of the management board.[18] The laws of the Member States or the memorandum or Articles of association or instrument of incorporation would be able to require that the execution of certain types of transaction by the management organ be subject to the authorization of the supervisory organ.[19] The laws of the Member States could provide that where the supervisory organ had refused to authorize a transaction in accordance with Article 12(1), the general meeting would be entitled to take a final decision on the request of the management organ. This rule would not be applicable to companies having employee participation in the members of the supervisory organ.[20] Where there was a unitary board, the laws of the Member States or the memorandum or Articles of association or the instrument of incorporation might provide that the execution of certain types of transaction might not be delegated to the executive members of the administrative organ.[21]

Members of the management board might be natural or legal persons.[22] The former provision that one member on the management board would have special responsibility for labour relations has been deleted.[23] By Article 11 the management board would be required to report to the supervisory board at least once every three months. The supervisory board would have the power to call for a report from the management board at any time, and extensive power to require information and undertake investigations. The latest version of the draft Fifth Directive does not contain any provisions governing the submission of the accounts by the management board to the supervisory board.[24] The normal rule under Article 48 would be that the accounts might be adopted by the general meeting. Member States would be permitted, however, to provide that the accounts should be adopted by the two boards, unless the latter decided otherwise or failed to agree on the adoption of the accounts. They might also stipulate that the single-tier board should approve the accounts if such an option were provided for in the instrument of incorporation or the Articles of association.

Employee Participation

The Commission's revised text would require employee participation in public companies which were not co-operatives, and which either alone or together with subsidiary undertakings[25] employed more than an average of 1,000 workers. Employee participation would not be required in subsidiary undertakings if the employees of such undertakings were included in the participation or representation system applicable to the parent company.[26] Participation would not be required where it was opposed by the majority of the company's employees.

If a Member State (such as Germany, the Netherlands or Denmark) decided to make provision for the two-tier board system only, it might adopt any one of four types of employee participation:

(i) participation in the supervisory board with the employees electing between one-third and one-half of the members thereof;[27]

(ii) participation through a system of co-optation to the supervisory board similar to that which exists in the Netherlands;[28]

(iii) participation through an employee representative council at company level (consultative council);[29] or

(iv) participation through a system agreed by collective bargaining, corresponding to the principles of one of the foregoing models.[30]

If no such collective agreement were reached within a fixed time limit, one of the other options would automatically apply.[31] If a Member State permitted its companies to choose between the two-tier board system and the single-tier board system or accepted the single-tier system only, it would be able to choose the same models for employee participation as in the case of the two-tier system, subject to certain modifications.[32] Thus, if it adopted the first model, participation would be within the group of non-executive directors, between one-third and one-half of whom would be elected by the employees.[33]

In all cases the choice of employees' representatives would be required to comply with democratic principles: the right of all workers to vote; freedom of expression of opinion; proportional representation and a secret ballot.[34] However, it is noteworthy that the revised draft Directive does not specifically require direct elections, or make it clear whether the right to participate includes the right to nominate candidates, and the right to stand as a candidate.[35] Although there is considerable reason to doubt whether this object is attained, the alternative systems of participation are intended to be equivalent in effect. This matter receives further consideration later in the present chapter.

Worker directors would have the same information as supplied to the other members of the supervisory board (or other non-executive members of the one-tier board, as the case may be). The representatives of employees under other systems of representation would also be granted certain rights to information. These would include the right to receive a report on the company's affairs every three months. Furthermore, under the consultative council option employees' representatives would have the right, in relation to the supervisory organ, to be informed and consulted before each meeting of the latter.

Criticisms of the Division between Managing and Supervisory Directors

Although there have been complaints of the occasional lack of activity and complaisance of the supervisory board, the two-tier board system, with the attendant division between management and supervisory functions, has worked fairly well in Germany. It has been argued that its introduction in the United Kingdom might encourage the management board to pursue progressive social policies and might also help to protect small investors. Although the Labour Party Green Paper of 1974 supported the two-tier board structure, the consensus of opinion has long been that it should not be introduced, or at least made compulsory, in the United Kingdom.[36] As has already been indicated, United Kingdom companies would not be required to comply with the two-tier model under the revised draft Directive. For this reason, detailed consideration of it may be inappropriate.

It would seem that the single-tier model was inspired by the situation in the United Kingdom, Ireland and France. However, as already indicated, the board is endowed with certain characteristics which are expressly intended to harmonize its functioning with the two-tier board. It has been severely criticized on this ground in para. 22 of the CBI paper, which contains a number of cogent objections to this model.[37] Although certain of these objections appear somewhat exaggerated and recent changes to the proposed structure of the single-tier board bring it much closer to the United Kingdom model, it seems very doubtful whether a unitary board modelled too closely on the two-tier system would prove acceptable to the United Kingdom. It may be thought that, although the employees might be given the power to elect a certain proportion of the directors belonging to a unitary board, all such directors should (as is posited in Article 21q(1)) have the same rights and duties and, perhaps, that all of them should be dismissable by the passing of an ordinary resolution in general meeting. The rather complex provisions of Article 21t do not adopt the latter perhaps too simplistic approach. It should also be noted that the amended proposal does not make provision for special notice of the resolution to dismiss an executive director, nor is such a director given the right to make representations prior to the decision concerning his dismissal. Despite the provisions of Article 21a(1)(b), it would seem that the draft Directive would permit a proposal to be carried against the wishes of the majority of the non-executive directors on the administrative board.[38]

Criticisms of Employee Participation Options
The employee participation options contained in the draft Fifth Directive are largely derived from German, French, Dutch and Italian models, and are obviously designed to ensure that an acceptable (but unfortunately not necessarily equivalent) model becomes available for each Member State. One can usefully compare the similar approach taken to the definition of a subsidiary undertaking under Article 1 of the Seventh Directive on Group Accounts. It would seem advantageous if the draft Fifth Directive were amended to permit individual companies rather than Member States to adopt one or more of the options. The provisions

governing employee participation were severely criticized by the Employment Secretary at the time, the Right Honourable Mr Tom King, in a press notice released by the Department of Employment and the Department of Trade and Industry on 9 November 1983. A critical approach to these provisions is also taken in the CBI paper on the draft Fifth and Vredeling Directives, and in the Consultative Document on these instruments issued jointly by the Department of Employment and the Department of Trade and Industry in November 1983.

The CBI paper makes a number of cogent, if somewhat exaggerated, general criticisms of the employment participation provisions of the revised draft Directive. It argues that certain assertions made by the Commission in the preamble to the 1983 instrument are questionable. It further contends that the employee participation provisions would undermine the competitiveness of industry in the United Kingdom by introducing delays in decision-making and increased cost burdens; that they would not provide for employee involvement and would have an adverse effect on voluntary arangements with the United Kingdom; and that their implementation would be detrimental to industrial relations and would lead to frequent disputes between employees and trade unions.

The objection that the introduction of employee participation would undermine the competitiveness of industry in the United Kingdom has not been borne out by experience in the Federal Republic of Germany and elsewhere. The second major objection may have a greater element of truth on it, but it is doubtful whether the postulated consequences would always arise, or whether voluntary arrangements might always prove a satisfactory alternative. The existence of a more fragmented trade-union structure in the United Kingdom than in certain other countries, especially the Federal Republic of Germany, may lend some force to the third objection. However, it appears that it would often be possible to reach compromises between different unions concerning the selection of candidates for the supervisory board, or for co-option to that board. Nevertheless, it seems possible that the introduction of the consultative council option might interfere with existing negotiating procedures, and lead to disputes with unions. Furthermore, such disputes might arise in consequence of the introduction of the collective bargaining option, which might interfere with existing methods of communication between employers and workers.

The provisions of the draft Fifth Directive also give rise to some problems in relation to the rights of employees to reject employee participation. It is not clear which employees would be taken into account in order to determine whether a majority of the employees were opposed to the introduction of employee participation. Thus, for instance, it is doubtful whether a company in one Member State would be obliged to introduce employee participation where its own employees were outvoted by the employees of its subsidiaries in another Member State. Additional problems arise in relation to groups of companies.[39] Thus, for example, the involvement of representatives of companies in decisions made by a group board concerning subsidiaries whose employees did not have their own representatives but were included in the system of participation or representation applicable to the group undertaking in accordance with Article 63b(2) might well damage relations within a group.

Lack of Equivalence between the Different Options

Although the preamble to the revised draft Directive states that the provisions for employee participation enable Member States to choose between a number of equivalent arrangements there is, as already pointed out, some reason to doubt the equivalence of the available models. It is thus questionable whether the co-option model is equivalent to the other models provided. It hardly appears correct to say that a limited right to veto a candidate for the supervisory board is equivalent to the right to elect up to half the members of that board. Furthermore, where employee participation took place through the supervisory board, the latter would be able to appoint and dismiss the members of the management organ.[40] However, where the single-tier system is used, it is no longer proposed that the executive members of the administrative board shall be dismissable by the non-executive members thereof. In addition, where participation took place through the consultative council, the latter would have no powers of dismissal. Moreover, considerable differences arise in relation to the powers of the supervisory board, the non-executive directors and the consultative council in certain defined categories of transaction.[41] Thus it should be abundantly clear that the different options are not really equivalent.

Provisions Dealing with Purely Company Law Matters

The fact that the revised draft Directive contains a number of other Articles dealing with purely company law matters which are considered in some detail in the Department of Trade and Industry's Consultative Document of 1990 on the amended proposal is sometimes overlooked. These comprise directors' duties and their enforcement, the conduct and powers of the general meeting and the functions and liability of auditors. The often lengthy and detailed provisions concerning these matters are frequently modelled on French, German and Italian law, and many have proved controversial, although a more positive attitude to certain of them is displayed in the Consultative Document of 1990. Those relating to directors' civil liability;[42] the minority shareholders' right to sue the directors for damages on behalf of the company;[43] shareholders' rights to obtain information;[44] the general prohibition of non-voting shares;[45] and the nullity or voidability of certain company resolutions[46] appear especially controversial, and certain of the proposed rules enshrined therein may require some rethinking. The same remarks are applicable to certain of those relating to auditors.

The revised draft Directive also contains provisions relating to groups of companies, certain of which have given rise to controversy. The most important relaxation of the provisions of the draft Directive on behalf of groups of companies consists of the ability that would be granted to Member States by Article 63b(2) to derogate from Article 14 of the Directive governing the liability of board members for wrongful acts in the case of a subsidiary, to the extent necessary to allow subsidiaries to be run in accordance with group strategy, provided that the parent company assumed responsibility for all the debts and obligations of the subsidiary and the members of its boards, and provided that the subsidiary's employees were included in the same system of participation as that applicable to the employees of the parent company. It may be difficult for groups which operate in a number of Member States to take advantage of this and other group derogations, because such a group may be faced with many different systems of participation, in addition to which not all such Member States may have opted for the group derogation.[47]

Reasons for Failure to Adopt the Revised Draft Fifth Directive

The failure to adopt the above instrument so far may be explained by the opposition which it has encountered from certain governments and from employers' organizations such as the Institute of Directors and the Confederation of British Industry. Although certain of the purely company law provisions of the instrument are highly controversial, it seems that, had the draft Fifth Directive always been confined to these or analogous provisions, it would have been enacted by the Council with certain modifications some years ago. In view of the lack of substantial equivalence of the different proposed systems of participation, and given that such an approach might well be acceptable to employers' organizations such as the CBI, there seems to be some force in Professor Schmitthoff's suggestion[48] that the draft Fifth Directive should admit a fifth alternative method of employee involvement, namely voluntary consultation schemes complying with certain minimal requirements. However, such an approach would be highly unlikely to prove acceptable to the Commission, or to trade-union organizations within the Member States. There seems little reason to anticipate the early enactment of the Fifth Directive in its comprehensive form. It may, however, be possible to enact this instrument by confining it to purely company law matters, which might well, in view of certain recent Commission proposals, include certain new provisions governing the elimination of barriers to takeovers. The question of employee participation may well be left to later Directives enacted for the purpose of supplementing the Social Charter.

THE DRAFT VREDELING DIRECTIVE

Because of the unlikelihood of this draft instrument being enacted in its present form, only a brief account is thought appropriate of the Draft Vredeling Directive for informing and consulting the employees of undertakings with complex structures.[49] Although the amended proposal has some drafting defects and displays certain inconsistencies with other Community instruments on employment matters (such as the revised draft Fifth Directive), much of the opposition to it may be explained on political grounds. It is noteworthy that employees' organizations, unlike employers' organizations, have adopted a sympathetic approach to the Vredeling proposals.[50]

Article 2(1) of the amended proposal defines the employees for whose benefit the obligation to inform and consult would be imposed. The amended proposal would apply if the total number of persons employed in the Community by a parent undertaking and its subsidiaries, or by an undertaking and its establishments, was at least 1,000, irrespective of the number employed by an individual subsidiary or establishment.[51] Article 2 would attempt to deal with the situation where the management on which obligations were imposed was not within the Community, and not within the jurisdiction of any Member State. It follows from Article 2(2) that if such a management was not represented in the community by an agent authorized to fulfil the requirements regarding information and consultation laid down by the Directive, the management of each subsidiary to which the parent had failed to give information would be obliged to communicate to itself, and to the management of any fellow subsidiary which has not been so informed, the information which it had not received from its parent.[52]

Whether an undertaking was treated as a parent undertaking in accordance with Article 1 would depend not only on the provisions of Article 1 of the Seventh Directive but also (in the case of an undertaking within the Community) upon the legislation applicable to the parent or (in the case of an undertaking outside the Community) upon the legislation applicable to the subsidiary. The application of the definition of parent and subsidiary in the Seventh Directive for the purposes of the Vredeling Directive would give rise to many uncertainties.[53]

The management of a parent undertaking would be required to provide information giving a clear picture of the activities of that undertaking and its subsidiaries as a whole to the management of each of its subsidiaries in the Community at least once a year. This information would have to include in particular the five matters specified in Article 3(2).[54]

Article 4 of the amended proposals, which contains provisions concerning consultation of a rather detailed character, has been subjected to a good deal of criticism.[55] According to this draft provision, where the management of an undertaking proposed to take a decision liable to have serious consequences for employees interests, it would be required to communicate information to the management of each subsidiary, giving details of the grounds for the decision, its legal, economic and social consequences, and the measures planned for the employees.[56] The management of each subsidiary concerned would be required to communicate this information without delay to employers' representatives and to consult them with a view to reaching agreement on the measures planned for the employees' representatives. The proposed decision would not be implemented until the latter had given their opinion, or until thirty days had elapsed from the time when the information had been communicated. When information was defined as secret under Article 7(1), the management of the subsidiary would still be required to consult employees' representatives on the measures planned before the decision was implemented. However, it is apparent that it might prove difficult to discuss the implementation of a decision without its basis being disclosed.[57] Article 4 has a number of other defects. There appear to be some flaws in the consultation provisions. Furthermore, the procedure enshrined in Article 4 might also lead to damaging delays. In addition, disputes might well arise as to whether a particular decision fell within Article 4 and whether information had been rightly withheld on the ground that it was secret. Finally, the provisions of Article 4 differ in some respects from the corresponding ones of the draft Fifth Directive.

It does not seem appropriate to discuss the remaining provisions of the amended proposal in detail in the present text. All of them appear to have some defects: this seems especially true of those of Article 7 concerning secrecy and confidence.[58]

7

Miscellaneous Draft Directives

INTRODUCTORY REMARKS

The Directives which have already been enacted by the Council of Ministers in the field of company law have been discussed above, as also have certain draft instruments. No discussion has taken place of Council Directive 88/627/EEC of 12 December 1988 on the information to be published when a major holding in a listed company is acquired or disposed of.[1] This is because this instrument appears to be more concerned with securities law than with company law.[2] It requires a natural person or a legal entity under public or private law who acquires or disposes of a holding in a listed company so that, following that acquisition or disposal, the proportion of voting rights held by that person or legal entity reaches, exceeds or falls below the thresholds of 10 per cent, 20 per cent, one-third, 50 per cent and two-thirds to notify the company and the competent authority or authorities within seven calendar days of the proportion of the voting rights he or it holds following that acquisition or disposal.[3] Member States are permitted to impose stricter requirements or requirements additional to those of the Directive,[4] but the Contact Committee has as one of its tasks the facilitation of consultations so as to bring the requirements imposed in all the Member States into line.[5] Member States are not required to implement the Directive until 1 January 1991,[6] and in view of its modest requirements it is clear that such implementation will not prove burdensome for the United Kingdom.[7]

The instruments which will receive most detailed consideration in this chapter consist of the Eleventh Directive on disclosure requirements in respect of branches[8] and the Twelfth Directive on single-member private limited companies.[9] Some brief mention will first of all be made on the draft proposal for a Ninth Directive on the Conduct of Groups of Companies.[10] Although the draft Ninth Directive deals with the important subject of group liability, it is not thought appropriate to discuss this proposal at length because there is at present no indication that any further steps will be taken by the Community in this area in the immediate future.[11] The preliminary draft Directive is very much modelled on German *Konzernrecht*, and proposals for its amendment, and would seem to pay insufficient attention to the evolution of the law dealing with groups of companies in other countries; thus, for example, it contains no provisions relating to the sale of controlling blocks of shares. It would be applicable to groups of companies containing a public limited company as a subsidiary and would also affect public limited companies controlled by another undertaking, whether or not that undertaking was a company.[12] The exclusion of private limited liability companies and partnerships from the ambit of the draft Directive has been much criticized.

The Directive would provide harmonized legal structures for the unified management of a group consisting of a public limited company and any other undertaking which had a controlling interest in it, irrespective of whether that undertaking was itself a company. There would be two methods of constituting a group, either through the medium of a control contract or through that of a unilateral declaration of control.[13] Both these methods would provide for unified management and consequential compensation to the shareholders in the dependent companies. The Directive would also contain rules governing the conduct of *de facto* groups which were not managed on a unified basis. It is noteworthy that these rules would apply only to the relations between the parent undertaking and those members of the group which were public companies. Unless an undertaking which exercised a dominant influence over a public limited company had formalized its relationship by one of the methods prescribed for constituting a group, it would be liable for any losses suffered by such a dependent company which resulted from that influence and were attributable to a fault in management, or to action which was not in the dependent company's interests.[14] Many of the provisions of the proposed Directive appear to require some revision, and it is unlikely to be adopted in its present form. A definitive proposal was promised in 1988, but this has not materialized.

THE ELEVENTH DIRECTIVE

History and Scope

The Eleventh Directive is concerned with disclosure requirements in respect of branches established by a foreign company in a Member State.[15] Such a company may be governed by the law of a Member State, or that of a third country. An early version of the draft Directive was submitted by the Commission to the Council of Ministers on 29 July 1986.[16] An amended proposal was submitted by the Commission to the Council on 5 April 1988,[17] and this proposal was adopted, with certain amendments, on 21 December 1989.

The Directive requires a company which is subject to the law of a Member State, other than that in which it sets up a branch, to deliver certain documents to the companies registry of the Member State where the branch is situated. The purpose of this proposal is to protect persons dealing with foreign companies that carry on business within a State belonging to the European Economic Community. As is correctly pointed out in the preamble to the Directive, there is at present a disparity between the protection afforded to those dealing with subsidiary companies and those dealing with branches of companies. A subsidiary is required to comply with the various company law Directives, which have been discussed above, in so far as they have been implemented in the different Member States. However, the branch of a foreign company is not subject to the disclosure requirements contained in the company law Directives, and in particular to those provided for in the First, Fourth, Seventh and Eighth Directives. The Directive is designed to eliminate this disparity in order to provide an equivalent level of protection for those concerned. It is applicable to all foreign companies, but certain exceptions apply to credit institutions and other financial institutions covered by Directive 89/117/EEC, and to insurance companies.[18] One major difficulty with the present Directive is that it contains no definition of what is meant by a branch.[19]

Principal Characteristics

Part I of the Directive contains provisions which are applicable to branches of companies from other Member States, whilst Part II contains provisions which are applicable to branches of companies from third countries. The requirements of Part I would seem to be maximum requirements, whilst those of Part II are minimum ones. Part I consists of six Articles, 1–6. Article 1 imposes a general duty of disclosure and applies the proposed Directive, in so far as any particular Member State was concerned, to all companies set up in another Member State.[20] Where disclosure requirements in respect of a branch differed from those in respect of a company, the branch's disclosure requirements would take precedence with respect to transactions carried out with the branch. The particulars which have to be disclosed are stated in Articles 2(1) and 3. Those required under Article 2(1) include: (a) the address and activities of the branch; (b) particulars of the register in which the company's file is kept, and its registration number in that register; (c) the name and legal form of the company and the name of the branch, if different from the name of the company; (d) details of directors and other permanent representatives of the company; (e) the winding up of the company and the appointment of liquidators, and particulars concerning them; (f) the accounting documents required by Article 3; (g) the closure of the branch. Article 2(2) stipulates that the Member State in which the branch was situated may provide for the disclosure of certain further matters including the instruments of constitution of the company and particulars as to securities on the company's property in that State.

As already indicated, Article 2 and 3 appear to require maximum disclosure. In that case, minor amendments will have to be made to sections 691–703 of the Companies Act 1989 so as to delete certain additional obligations to which overseas companies are subject.[21] Certain of the requirements of the Directive will be additional to those of English law: one may instance the need to give particulars of the address and activities of the branch and particulars of the company registration.

Article 3 is concerned with accounting requirements and makes provision for a maximum disclosure rule. The branch is required to file copies of accounts drawn up and audited in accordance with the law of the Member State by which the company was governed. These accounts must be drawn up in accordance with the Fourth, Seventh and Eighth Directives[22] and be accompanied by an annual report. The implementation of Article 3 will require only fairly minor changes in British law. Thus, when this provision is implemented, foreign companies carrying on business in Great Britain would no longer be required to file annual accounts and consolidated accounts on the same basis as companies incorporated in Great Britain, as they are at present under new Section 700(1) of the Companies Act 1985. The Secretary of State is empowered to make an order exempting an overseas company from such a requirement under new section 700(2) of the Companies Act 1985 (both subsections were incorporated therein by Schedule 10, Part I, Chapter II to the Companies Act 1989). It is noteworthy that the new section 700(1) of the Companies Act 1985 changes British law so as to require an overseas company to file an annual report and cause to be prepared such an auditor's report as would be required if the company was formed and registered under the Act. The Secretary is empowered to modify these requirements by section 700(2).

As already indicated, the provisions of Part II of the draft Directive, which are contained in Articles 7–10 thereof, are of a minimal character and might therefore be supplemented by domestic legislation, which might require matters additional to those prescribed in Article 5 to be disclosed. The matters which have to be disclosed under Article 8 include certain particulars not at present required under British law, such as the address of the branch and its activities. Difficulties might arise in respect of a jurisdiction in which a company was not required to have objects. The accounts requirements are contained in Article 9, which requires the accounting documents of the company to be drawn up, audited and disclosed pursuant to the law of the State which governs the company. If such documents are not drawn up in accordance with or in a manner equivalent to the Fourth and Seventh Directives, Member States may require that the accounting document relating to the activities of the branch be drawn up and disclosed. Member States would be able to prescribe penalties for non-compliance with Articles 1, 2, 3, 7, 8 and 9.

Evaluation

The enactment of the draft Directive is unlikely to cause serious problems for the United Kingdom. Where implementation is necessary, this will probably take place through the medium of subordinate legislation. The requirements of an annual report and audit will be more onerous than those imposed on foreign companies under British law prior to the enactment of new section 700 of the Companies Act 1985 by Part I, Chapter 2 of Schedule 10 to the Companies Act 1989. Furthermore, the need to comply with the requirements of the Fourth Directive imposed by new section 700 will place a greater burden upon such companies than did Schedule 9 to the Companies Act 1985 in its old form, which used to be applicable to their accounts. As the majority of the information which would have to be disclosed, including the accounts, would relate to the company rather than to the branch, the new provisions might well benefit British companies carrying on business in other States in the Community. At present, some Member States require companies to file branch accounts rather than company accounts.[23]

THE TWELFTH DIRECTIVE

History and Scope
Single-member private limited companies may be formed in a number of States belonging to the European Communities including Germany,[24] Denmark,[25] France,[26] Belgium,[27] and the Netherlands.[28] Member States which do not permit the formation of single-member companies either require the winding up of the company or the personal liability of the single member where all the shares come to be held by a single shareholder.[29]

In November 1986, the Council of Ministers approved an Action Programme which placed a good deal of emphasis on the need to encourage the development of small and medium-sized enterprises. In the same year, it also emphasized the need to encourage one-man businesses. A recent Commission document[30] contained a draft Directive which was intended to harmonize the law governing one-man private companies throughout the Community. The Commission's explanatory memorandum emphasized the absence of such a business form in certain Member States, and the disparities which existed in the laws of those Member States which permit one-man private companies. As is also the case with a number of other harmonizing directives, including the one discussed immediately above, the draft (and finalized) Directive are said to be based, in particular, on Article 54 EEC, which has often been widely interpreted as giving an extensive mandate for the harmonization of European company law. The draft proposal contained a number of fairly stringent provisions which were criticized by UNICE, *inter alia*, and do not appear in the Directive, which was enacted by the Council, which accepted certain amendments proposed by the European Parliament, in December 1989.[31]

Principal Characteristics

Article 1 of the Directive provides that the instrument is applicable only to private limited liability companies. However, it is noteworthy that Article 6 provides that where a Member State (such as the Netherlands) permitted the formation of a single-member public company, the provisions of the Directive are applicable. By Article 2(1) a company might have a single member either when it was formed, or when all the shares came to be held by one person. Thus, the reduction of the membership of a private company below two persons would no longer be a permissible cause of nullity, as it is under Article 11(2)(f) of the First Directive. It appears to follow from the absence of any provision to the contrary in the Directive that the shares in a single-member company may be in a nominative (registered) or bearer form. Article 2(2), which replaces certain more stringent provisions which existed in the draft Directive and were subjected to a good deal of criticism, provides that Member States may, pending the co-ordination of national provisions relating to groups, lay down special provisions for cases in which a natural person is the sole member of several companies or a single-member company, or any other legal person is the sole member of a company. It follows from the sixth recital to the preamble that the sole aim of the latter provision is to take account of the differences which exist with respect to this matter in national laws, and that for this purpose Member States may in specific cases lay down restrictions on the use of single-member companies or remove the limits on the liability of single members.

By Article 3, publicity has to be given to the fact that a company has become a single-member company. Article 4(1) provides that the sole member shall exercise the powers of the general meeting and may not delegate them. Article 4(2) would stipulate that decisions taken by the sole member when exercising the powers of the general meeting should be recorded in minutes or drawn up in writing.[32] Agreements between the sole member and the company as represented by him would be required by Article 5(1) to be drawn up in writing. However, Article 5(2) provides that Member States are not required to apply the former provision to current operations under normal conditions.

Certain Member States are reluctant to accept the notion of single-member companies for theoretical reasons. Such reasons are not operative in the United Kingdom, where the corporation sole has been recognized since the Middle Ages. Countries like Portugal, in which they appear to be relevant, may still provide for limited liability for sole traders. Member States choosing such an arrangement would be required by Article 7 to provide safeguards covering such traders which would be equivalent to those imposed by the Directive or by any other Community provision applicable to the companies mentioned in Article 1 thereof. Such provisions would obviously include the Directives applicable to the annual accounts and consolidated accounts of such a company. Article 8 would require Member States to implement the Directive by 1 January 1992; however, they would be permitted to prescribe that, in the case of companies already in existence on that date, the Directive would not apply until 1 January 1993.

Evaluation

Although there may be no urgent necessity for the introduction of one-man companies throughout the Community because sole entrepreneurs can always make use of nominees, the principle contained in the draft Twelfth Directive would seem to be generally worthy of support. It is noteworthy that this instrument concerns itself only with certain questions relating to the introduction of the single-member company, and leaves such matters as the taxation and liquidation of such companies, opening the veil of incorporation and the qualification of persons to be directors thereof to the different systems of law of the Member States. Thus, for example, its implementation would do nothing to resolve the problems which have been discussed by German textwriters concerning the capacity of a single-member company in the process of formation to enter into legal transactions with the founder.

It is evident that the enactment of this instrument and its implementation by the United Kingdom will necessitate a number of minor amendments to the Companies Act 1985, the Insolvency Act 1986, and a number of related Statutory Instruments in order to introduce a concept of the one-man company. It will also be necessary to make certain additional changes to British law to accommodate other features of the proposals. No Consultative Document is expected to be published. It is not clear what effect such changes would have in inducing individual businessmen to form themselves into companies. The reaction of such persons to the adoption of the Directive may be awaited with some interest.

8

Supranational Instruments

INTRODUCTION

Substantive Community law with a direct effect in the Member States may be enacted by means of a Community regulation. Many such regulations have been based upon Article 235 of the EEC Treaty, which requires the fulfilment of three conditions in order to be invoked. The first of these is that action by the Community must be necessary in order to achieve one of the objectives of the Common Market. The second is that the powers provided for in the Treaty must be insufficient. The third is that it must be enacted by the Council unanimously.[1] Article 235 has been called one of the most controversial provisions of the EEC Treaty, and so far only two instruments have been based on it in the field of company law.[2] These are the draft Regulation for the European Company Statute put forward in 1970 and revised in 1975, and the Regulation on the creation of a European Economic Grouping, which was enacted in July 1985. The Commission took the view that an optional European Companies Act and a new European legal framework for co-operation were necessary, but that the powers provided for in the EEC Treaty seemed inadequate for these ends. Thus, these two measures had to be based on Article 235. The question of the necessity of both these measures, however, remains problematic. It has been argued that this was particularly true of the European Company Statute.[3] Because the draft Regulation for the European Company Statute has not yet entered into force (and despite the new Treaty basis of Article 100A EEC which was given in 1989, there remains some measure of doubt whether it will do so), it has been thought appropriate to consider the European Economic Interest Grouping first of all. It should be noted that it is clear from the governing regulation that the legal regime applicable to this entity will not be entirely based upon the mandatory provisions of this Regulation which prevail over contrary provisions of national law.[4] The governing regime is complex, and sometimes it will be necessary instead for reference to be made to national legal systems, the provisions of the contract for the formation of the grouping, and the internal law of the Member State where the grouping has its official address, for the purposes of determining the relevant rule of law.

THE EUROPEAN ECONOMIC INTEREST GROUPING

History and Scope

The *groupement d'intérêt économique*, a new legal form with legal personality intermediate between the *société* and the *association*, was introduced in France in 1967.[5] It was intended as a method of co-operation between enterprises wishing to maintain their independence. By setting up a GIE undertakings can, for example, pool or co-operate in their sales, export, import or research activities. A GIE is fiscally transparent – i.e. only its members are taxed. The GIE proved very successful in France, and certain such entities have taken on an international aspect. This success led to the suggestion that a similar legal form should be introduced for the Community as a whole. On 21 December 1973 the Commission submitted to the Council a proposal for a Regulation on the European Co-operation Grouping EEIG(G).[6] In April 1978[7] the Commission submitted to the Council an amended proposal which took account of the opinions of the European Parliament[8] and the Economic and Social Committee[9] in accordance with the provisions of Article 149(2) EEC. Detailed discussion of this proposal took place in a number of Council Working Parties, and the Regulation was adopted on 25 July 1985.[10] The Regulation provides a somewhat original framework for natural persons, companies and firms within the meaning of Article 58(2) EEC, and other entities governed by public or private law,[11] to enable them to co-operate effectively when carrying on business activities across national frontiers. As already indicated, EEIGs will not be governed only by supranational provisions of this Regulation. It is also noteworthy that it follows from the fifteenth recital that, except where the Regulation expressly provides that the law of the Member State in which the official address of the grouping is situated applies, the economic activities of the grouping are subject to the rules generally applicable to persons carrying on economic activities. Furthermore, it follows from the sixteenth recital that in matters not covered by the Regulation, the laws of the Member States[12] and Community law are applicable, for example, in relation to social and labour law, competition law[13] and intellectual property law. Finally, the seventeenth recital provides that the Member States are free to apply or adapt any law, regulation or administrative measures which do not conflict with the scope or objectives of the Regulation. It is noteworthy that many of the provisions of the Companies Act 1985 concerning the investigation of companies and their affairs, books and papers have been made applicable to EEIGs with an official address in Great Britain.[14]

The grouping has some of the features of a contractual arrangement, and some of those of a business association. It follows from Article 43 of the Regulation that the necessary implementing legislation must be passed by 1 July 1989. The Regulation was implemented in Germany in 1988,[15] and has been implemented by the United Kingdom through the medium of a Statutory Instrument containing regulations called the European Economic Interest Grouping Regulations, which extend only to Great Britain, and through the medium of the Statutory Rules for Northern Ireland 1989 (S.I. 1989, No. 216). These two instruments are in almost identical terms: only the Regulations will be considered in this chapter. Perhaps unfortunately, these Regulations tend to assimilate the grouping to an unregistered company rather than to a partnership. An extensive literature exists on the grouping.[16]

Objects of the Grouping

Article 3(1) of the Regulation provides that the purpose of a grouping shall be to facilitate or develop the economic activities of its members, and to improve or increase the results of those activities. This provision (which is much influenced by French law) also states that a grouping's purpose is not to make profits for itself and that its activities shall be related to the economic activities of its members and must be no more than ancillary to those activities. It follows from the fifth recital to the preamble to the Regulation that a grouping must not replace its activities of its members. Furthermore, Article 3(2) contains provisions which are not paralleled by those of French law, which set out certain specific restrictions to the objects or purposes of an EEIG. These prohibitions are considered below. Although one cannot be quite certain of this, groupings may prove a useful vehicle for collaboration between small and medium-sized firms. They might well be used for such purposes as research and development, buying and selling, the packaging of finished products, the processing of goods, and the provision of services for their members.

It seems implicit from Article 3(1) that a grouping may make profits for its members. This is confirmed by Articles 21 and 40. The former provision states that the profits of a grouping shall be deemed to be the profits of its members, and shall be apportioned among them in the proportion laid down in the contract for the formation of the grouping or, in the absence of any such provision, in equal shares. Like its French counterpart, the EEIG is fiscally transparent. Thus Article 40 provides that the profits or losses resulting from the activities of the grouping shall be taxable only in the hands of members. It follows from the fourteenth recital that legislation will have to be passed by the Member States stating what profits made by EEIGs shall be subject to taxation, and to stipulate the basis on which they shall be apportioned between members for the purposes of Article 40. It is uncertain, however, in what country the profits should be taxed in the hands of the members. This would seem to be the permanent or usual residence of the members, but in some circumstances at least such profits may be taxable in the country of registration of the EEIG.[17]

Specific Prohibitions

The object of the prohibitions contained in Article 3(2) are disparate. The rationale of those contained in Article 3(2)(a) and (b) is to prevent the creation of an integrated enterprise to the detriment of the autonomy of the participating ones. Article 3(2)(a) provides that a grouping may not exercise, directly or indirectly, a power of management or supervision over its members' own activities, or over the activities of another undertaking, in particular in the fields of personnel, finance and investment. Article 3(2)(b) provides that a grouping may not directly or

105

indirectly, on any basis whatsoever, hold shares of any kind in a member undertaking. It adds that the holding of such shares shall be possible only in so far as it is necessary for the achievement of the grouping's objects, and if it is done on its members' behalf.[18]

According to Article 3(2)(c) the EEIG may not employ more than 500 persons. The aim of this limit is to prevent the application to such groupings of the German legislation concerning employee participation in management. Article 3(2)(d) contains certain complex prohibitions on the uses of an EEIG by a company to make loans to its directors, or for the transfer of property between a company and a director in circumvention of national rules of company law.[19] The more general problem of the abuse or circumvention of the laws of a Member State is dealt with in the sixteenth recital in the preamble to the Regulation. Finally, Article 3(2)(d) provides that an EEIG may not be a member of another EEIG. The purpose of this is to prevent the creation of a chain of liabilities, which might diminish the liability of individual members in a context already rendered difficult by reason of its international dimension.

Criteria for Membership
Each of the members of an EEIG must have pursued an economic activity of some kind (the latter phrase is widely interpreted) prior to the formation of the EEIG.[20] Natural persons who are members of the professions may participate in a grouping, but it is clear from the fifth recital that such a grouping may not itself practise a profession with regard to third parties. The scope of Article 4(1)(d), which enumerates the different types of companies, firms or legal entities which may participate in the formation of a grouping, is also wide. An EEIG must have at least two members, who belong to different Member States. In order that a company or firm may belong to a grouping, it must have its registered office and/or central administration within the Community. Natural persons are required to demonstrate their link with the Community by carrying out any industrial, commercial, craft or agricultural activity or by providing professional or other services in the Community.[21] The term 'professional services' has, of course to be interpreted in accordance with Community law.

There is no limit to the number of members of an EEIG. However, Article 4(3) provides that a Member State may provide that groupings registered in its registries in accordance with Article 6 may have no more than twenty members. Furthermore, the Member State may provide that for this purpose in accordance with its laws, each member of a legal body formed under its laws, other than a registered company, shall be treated as a separate member of a grouping. Further, Article 4(4) provides that any Member State may, on the grounds of public interest, prohibit or restrict participation in groupings by certain classes of natural persons, companies, firms or other legal bodies. Member States are required by Article 41(2) to inform the Commission of any such prohibition or restriction. It is understood that the inclusion of this provision in the Regulation resulted in part from concern felt about the possibility that British savings banks might become members of an EEIG, and that in consequence losses might be sustained by their investors.

The Formation of an EEIG
The formation of an EEIG requires the conclusion of a contract and registration in a registry designated by the Member State in which the official address is situated.[22] A contract for the formation of a grouping is required to be in writing and its minimum contents are set out in Article 5.[23] An EEIG may not be registered in Great Britain by a name which included any of the following words or expressions, or abbreviations thereof, i.e. 'limited', 'unlimited', or 'public limited company' or their Welsh equivalents.[24] Furthermore, a grouping may not be registered if the name of the grouping is the same as a name appearing in the registrar's index of company names.[25] In determining whether one name is the same as another, the words 'European Economic Interest Grouping' or the initials 'EEIG' may be disregarded. In addition to the prohibition already mentioned, other prohibitions or restrictions on the registration of a grouping on the ground that the name of the grouping is objectionable are provided for by Schedule 4 to the European Economic Interest Grouping Regulations.[26] These Regulations also provide that an EEIG which is registered in a name which, in the opinion of the Secretary of State, is too similar to a name appearing at the time of registration in the registrar's index of company names, may be required to change its name.[27] The present rules would seem to be justified by the seventeenth recital to the Regulation, which provides that Member States are free to

apply or adopt any laws, regulations or administrative measures which do not conflict with the scope or objectives of the Regulation.

It is provided by Article 1(2) of the Regulation that a grouping shall, from the date of its registration, have the capacity, in its own name, to have rights and obligations of all kinds, to make contracts or accomplish other legal acts, and to sue and be sued.[28] Further-more, Article 1(3) permits member States to determine whether groupings registered at their registries pursuant to Article 6 have legal personality. It was found impossible to confer legal personality on the EEIG because of the fact that different tax repercussions attach in different Member States to 'legal capacity' and 'legal personality'. The provisions of Article 1(3) permit an EEIG to benefit from fiscal transparency. EEIGs will have legal personality in most of the Member States.[29]

The formation of a grouping is made subject to certain rules on the filing and publication of documents and particulars thought to be necessary for the purpose of informing third parties who enter into business transactions with the EEIG.[30] By Article 11, the formation and liquidation of a grouping must be published in the *Official Journal of the European Communities*, but it would seem arguable from the different wording of Article 9, concerning the effect of publications in the official gazette, that such publications cannot be relied upon against third parties.

The Official Address

By Article 17, the official address of a grouping must be situated in the Community. It must be fixed either where the grouping has its central administration or where one of the members of the grouping has its central administration or, in the case of a natural person, his principal activity, provided that the grouping carries on an activity there. Thus, one of the activities of the grouping must be carried on at the place where it has its official address, although this need not be the principal activity. The official address of an EEIG may be transferred within the Community. Such a transfer includes transfers within a Member State, such as the United Kingdom, in which more than one legal system exists.[31] Such transfers have no effect upon the legal capacity of an EEIG. Publicity must be given to a proposed transfer such that third parties may take appropriate precautions before the transfer takes place, although they are not allowed to oppose it.[32] However,

Article 14(4) was inserted in the Regulation in order to allay the fears of the United Kingdom, which may be the only country in which it is implemented.[33] This provision states that the laws of a Member State may provide that, as regards a grouping registered under Article 6 in that Member State, the transfer of the official address which would result in a change of the law applicable shall not take effect if, within the two-month period after the publication of the proposal, a competent authority in that Member State opposes it.[34] Such opposition may be based only on grounds of public interest. Review by a judicial authority must be possible.

Structure and Functioning of the Grouping

(i) Organs

Although the Regulation makes provision for certain binding rules and rules which apply in the absence of an express agreement to the contrary, the grouping is intended to be a flexible instrument which may, in principle, be adapted to the needs of the participants therein. A grouping is required by Article 16 to have at least two organs, which are the members acting collectively and the manager or managers. However, the contract may make provisions for other organs – for example, for a supervisory body comparable to the German *Aufsichtsrat*. The members acting collectively constitute the decision-making body of the EEIG, and Article 16(2) provides that they may take any decision for achieving the objects of the grouping. The Regulation does not contain detailed rules concerning the functioning of this body, and covers only essential matters. Thus Article 17(1) provides that each member shall have one vote, but that the contract may give more than one vote to certain members, provided that no member shall have a majority of the votes. A unanimous decision is always required for the matters enumerated in Article 17(2)(a)–(e). It is also necessary for the matters mentioned in Article 17(2)(f) and (g), except where the contract otherwise provides. It follows from Article 17(3) that in all other cases, the contract may prescribe the conditions for a quorum and the majority by which decisions, or certain of them, shall be taken; if it fails to do so, unaminity is necessary. Article 18 provides that each member shall be entitled to obtain information from the manager or managers concerning the grouping business, and to inspect its books and business records. The members of a grouping do not appear to be bound to one another by a partnership like duty of good faith.

A grouping must be managed by one or more natural persons appointed in the contract or by decision of the members. Persons who are disqualified from managing a company or other undertaking may not manage a grouping.[35] A Member State may provide that legal persons may be managers of groupings registered at its registries under the conditions provided for in Article 19(2).[36] The powers of the managers must be set out in the contract, or determined by a unanimous decision of the members.[37] A manager who exceeded his powers would incur liability to the grouping. Each of the managers binds the grouping as regards third parties when he acts on its behalf, even where his acts do not fall within the objects of the grouping, unless the grouping proves that the third party knew, or could not have been unaware, that the act fell outside its objects. The mere publication of these objects does not constitute proof of this matter.[38] It should be noted, however, that the contract may validly provide that the grouping shall be validly bound only by two or more managers acting jointly.[39]

(ii) Contributions

The contract, or a decision of the members, may provide for contributions to be made to the grouping in cash, or in kind, or by way of services. Article 21(2), which deals with the situation when no such provision is made for contributions, provides that the expenditure of the grouping shall be met in accordance with the contract and, in the absence of any such contractual provision, in equal shares.

(iii) Assignment or charging of a participation

These matters are dealt with in Article 22, which seems to indicate that a grouping has some of the characteristics of a personalistic association. Article 22(1) provides that any member of a grouping may assign his participation in the grouping, or a proportion thereof, either to another member or to a third party, and that the assignment shall not take effect without the unanimous authorization of the other members. It is noteworthy that this text does not provide how an assignment is to take place, nor does the Regulation state how a member's rights in a grouping are to be represented. It may follow from Article 22(1) that the validity and effect of an assignment against the grouping is determined by the law of the Member State where the grouping has its official address. This matter depends on whether the matter can be regarded as one relating to the internal organization of the grouping. Article 22(2) provides that a member of a grouping may use his participation as security only after the other members have given their unanimous authorization, unless otherwise laid down in the contract for the formation of the grouping. The holder of the security may not at any time become a member of the grouping by virtue of that security. This would seem to indicate that a security which has a comparable effect to a charge by way of legal mortgage may not be created in respect of a member's participation.[40]

(iv) Rules governing liability
The rules governing liability in a grouping resemble those which are applicable to a partnership. By Article 24(1), the members of a grouping shall have unlimited joint and several liability for its debts and liabilities of whatever nature. The tenth recital makes it clear that these include arrears of taxes and social security contributions, and that the liability of one or more members in respect of a particular debt may be restricted by contract. The consequences of joint and several liability are determined by national law. The European Economic Interest Grouping Regulations do not contain any provision governing this matter, but it may be anticipated that the British courts would apply partnership-like rules to determine these consequences.[41]

The liability of a new member of a grouping is provided for in Article 26. This provision permits such a new member to be exempted from the payment of debts and other liabilities arising out of the group's activities before he became a member, provided that such exemption is provided for in the contract for the formation of the grouping, or the instrument of admission thereto,[42] and provided also that the relevant provision has been published in accordance with Article 8. The rules contained in Articles 34 and 37(1), which govern members who cease to belong to a grouping, are more severe. It follows from these provisions that any member who ceases to belong to a grouping remains liable for a period of five years from the publication of notice of the cessation of his membership for debts and other liabilities arising out of the grouping's activities before he ceased to be a member.

(v) Cessation of membership

The personalistic character of a grouping is also reflected in the rules governing resignation therefrom. Article 27(1) provides that a member of a grouping may withdraw in accordance with the conditions laid down in the contract and, in the absence of such conditions, with the unanimous agreement of the other members. A member of a grouping may in addition withdraw on just and proper grounds. Furthermore, any member of a grouping may be expelled in accordance with the provisions of Article 27(2), which is modelled upon the provisions of German law relating to the civil and commercial law partnership. Article 28(1) provides that a member of a grouping shall cease to belong to it on death, or when he no longer complies with the requirements of Article 4(1). The former provision also permits a Member State to provide – for the purposes of its liquidation, winding up, insolvency or cessation of payments laws – that a member shall cease to be a member of any grouping at the moment determined by those laws.[43] The legal consequences of a person ceasing to be a member of a grouping are regulated by Articles 29, 30, 33 and 37 of the Regulation.

(vi) Winding up

Articles 31, 32 and 35 govern the winding up of groupings on grounds other than that of insolvency or cessation of payments. Article 31 provides for the voluntary winding up of a grouping in certain circumstances. By Article 31(1), a grouping may be wound up by a decision of its members which will be unanimous unless the contract otherwise provides. A grouping may be wound up by a decision of its members in the circumstances mentioned in Article 31(2) and (3). Article 32 provides for the winding up of the company by the court in certain circumstances. Thus, Article 32(1) states that on application by any person concerned or by a competent authority, in the event of the infringement of Article 3 (purpose of the grouping), 12 (situation of the official address) or 31(3) (winding up by decisions of members when requirements of Article 4(2) as to membership are no longer fulfilled), the court must order a grouping to be wound up. It need not, however, do so if the affairs of the grouping can be put in order before the court has delivered a substantive ruling. Article 32(2) provides that the court may order a grouping to be wound up on just and proper grounds on the application of a member. Finally, Article 32(3) provides that a Member State may provide that the court may, on application by a competent authority, order the winding up of a grouping which has its official address in the State to which that authority belongs, wherever the grouping acts in contravention of that State's public interest, if the law of that State provides for such a possibility in respect of registered companies or other legal bodies subject to it. It may be noted that section 440 of the Companies Act 1985 (as amended) contains such a provision. Article 32(3) may be contrasted with Article 38, which does not contain the limitation as to official address. By Article 38, where a grouping carries on any activity in a Member State in contravention of that state's public interest, a competent authority of that Member State may prohibit that activity. Review of the competent authorities decision by a judicial authority must be possible.[44]

By Article 35(1) the winding up of the company and its dissolution are governed by national law. This rule is applicable even though the ground for winding up is prescribed by Community law – i.e. the rules contained in Articles 31 and 32. Groupings are made subject by Article 36, sentence one, to national laws governing insolvency and the cessation of payments. This solution, which is in some ways unsatisfactory, was rendered necessary by the failure of the Member States to agree on the draft Convention on bankruptcy, winding-up arrangements, compositions and similar proceedings.[45] However, it follows from Article 36, sentence two, that insolvency proceedings against an EEIG do not have the same effect as they do against a French GIE. This provision stipulates that the commencement of proceedings against a grouping on the ground of its insolvency or cessation of payments shall not of itself cause the commencement of such proceedings against its members. If the law were otherwise, the creditors in the State in which insolvency proceedings were commenced might well derive an unfair advantage.[46]

Regulation 8 of the European Economic Interest Grouping Regulations provides that EEIGs will be wound up as unregistered companies under Part V of the Insolvency Act 1986 in Great Britain. It appears to follow from section 221(4) of the Insolvency Act 1986 that no such company may be wound up voluntarily under it. However, it may well be that despite the latter provision, a grouping can be wound up voluntarily by a decision of its members under Article 31. Furthermore, under Part V of the

Insolvency Act 1986, if a grouping was unable to pay its debts, it would be liable to winding up. It is arguable that this may not be an appropriate solution for a grouping in view of the right of action of any unsatisfied creditor against a member of that grouping. In appropriate circumstances managers of groupings might become liable for fraudulent or wrongful trading under s.213 and s.214 of the Insolvency Act 1986. Furthermore (although this would often be inappropriate), it follows from Regulation 19 of the Statutory Instrument that it would be possible for an administrative receiver to be appointed by a debenture holder where a grouping had been financed by means of a debenture. No provision is made for the appointment of an administrator of a grouping.

The Legal Regime Applicable to the Grouping
This matter has already been mentioned above, but it is thought appropriate to discuss it in more detail at this stage.[47] The Regulation contains provisions governing the structure and functioning of EEIGs from formation to winding up in the areas normally covered by company law. The governing hierarchy of rules applicable to groupings in these matters is as follows: (i) the mandatory provisions of the regulation itself; (ii) the contract for the formation of the grouping in many situations where the Regulation is silent as well as where the Regulation makes specific reference thereto; (iii) the provisions of the Regulation where it follows from the Regulation that the contract shall or may provide certain rules and it fails to do so; and (iv) the internal law of the Member State where the grouping has its official address.[48]

The structure and functioning of the grouping are to a very considerable extent governed by the mandatory provisions of the Regulation. This is true to a perhaps greater extent as far as the principal protection of members and third parties at different stages in the existence of the grouping is concerned.[49] These mandatory rules of law, and the words and phrases used in them, have, of course, to be interpreted in accordance with Community law. Sometimes, instead of attempting to provide for a particular matter itself, the Regulation grants options to Member States to enact legislation governing this matter. Furthermore, as has already been pointed out, national law governs the liquidation of a grouping and the whole winding-up process (including the making of the winding-up order) in the event of insolvency or cessation of payments.

As should be apparent from what has been discussed above, the Regulation sometimes fails to contain mandatory provisions, and instead leaves specific matters to be settled by the contract or a decision of the members. In such an event, the Regulation will contain provisions which will be applicable in default of the contract containing any appropriate provision, or of a decision of the members.[50]

In so far as problems concerning the contract for the formation of the group and its internal organization cannot be resolved by the application of the above-mentioned rules, they must be resolved by applying the internal law of the Member State where the grouping has its official address.[51] An exception to this rule is made as regards the status and capacity of persons, which is governed by the law applicable to their personal status.[52] It would appear that the actual scope of Article 2 is somewhat limited.[53]

It has already been pointed out that national laws may be applicable to groupings in circumstances additional to those mentioned above. As is apparent from consideration of the eleventh, fourteenth, fifteenth, sixteenth and seventeenth recitals,[54] the final text of the Regulation (the adoption of which required careful negotiation) represents a delicate balance between the desire – which may have been felt especially by the Commission – to introduce an entity having a number of significant supranational features, and the more conservative need felt to submit it to national law in certain areas, especially in some of those which would not be covered by the Regulation.

The complex legal regime governing the grouping will probably result in the fact that few businesses will be willing to use this entity without taking legal advice. It may not be possible to understand the impact of this regime fully before the European Court of Justice has given some preliminary rulings on the meaning of certain of the provisions of the Regulation (for example, Article 2 thereof)[55] in preliminary rulings under Article 177 EEC. Although it is difficult to predict how popular the grouping will become, the partnership-like system of unlimited liability, and perhaps the detailed publicity requirements,[56] may also act as a disincentive to its use. Business undertakings wishing to engage in cross-frontier co-operation involving the creation of some common body may still prefer to form a joint subsidiary, or to enter into some kind of contractual arrangement. However, it

115

might prove that the fiscal transparency of the EEIG will encourage its use. It is certainly the case that the English firm of solicitors Pannone Blackburn has established connection with lawyers in Belgium, France, Italy and Spain by means of an EEIG in order to form a unified European law firm. A number of other instances where the formation of an EEIG has taken place or is contemplated have been reported. It is thought that groupings might prove particularly useful in the form of multidisciplinary consortia to tender for large public contracts.

Implementation in the Member States

Although the Regulation came into force on 3 August 1985, Member States were given until 1 July 1989 to enact the implementing legislation; this was necessary because the Regulation leaves a number of matters to national law. No groupings can be set up before that date. The extended time interval may be explained by a number of factors. Thus Member States were required to enact legislation providing for the registration of groupings and the publication of their principal acts.[57] It was necessary for such states to enact legislation governing and supervising the activities of groupings, providing for their taxation and extending their laws governing winding up and the conclusion of liquidation, insolvency and the cessation of payments to them.

The European Economic Interest Grouping Regulations of 1989 take the form of a Statutory Instrument made by the Secretary of State for Trade and Industry under section 2(2) of the European Communities Act 1972, which is thus subject to negative parliamentary resolutions. As already pointed out, like virtually all the implementing legislative provisions enacted by the United Kingdom Parliament considered in any detail in this book, they extend to Great Britain only. However, a parallel instrument has been made in respect of Northern Ireland. It is interesting to contrast the relative complexity of the European Economic Interest Grouping Regulations (S.I. 1989, No. 638) with the simpler statute enacted in Germany in 1988. The latter statute was supplemented by a regulation made on 19 June 1989.[58] In Denmark, implementation has taken place through the medium of Law No. 217 of 5 April 1989,[59] and by means of the administrative regulations of 7 August 1989.[60] Implementation took place in France as a result of Law No. 89–377 of 13 June 1989,[61] and the Decree of 20 June 1989,[62] concerning the registration of the grouping. Only one law has been passed for the purpose of implementing the Regulation on the EEIG in the Netherlands.[63] The position is different in Belgium, where two implementing laws and one implementing decree have been enacted.[64] The European Economic Interest Grouping Regulations enacted in Northern Ireland took the form of a Statutory Instrument.[65] Implementing legislation is under active consideration in the five other Member States.

Companies and other undertakings will not be required to wait until all Member States have enacted the necessary implementing legislation before they can form EEIGs. They will be able to form such groupings in Member States which permit them to be registered.[66] Furthermore, Member States which have not yet enacted the required legislation will not be able to prevent EEIGs which have been lawfully registered in another Member State from pursuing activities on their territory. It remains to be seen whether frequent use will be made of this entity, which is, as already indicated, governed by a rather complex Regulation.

THE DRAFT REGULATION FOR THE EUROPEAN COMPANY STATUTE

History and Scope
Proposals to adopt a comprehensive company law by means of an international Convention were first put forward by French legal practitioners in 1959. The concept of a European Company (sometimes called Societas Europea or SE) was first dealt with in some detail by Professor Sanders in an inaugural address delivered at the Rotterdam School of Economics in the same year. Because of the clear potential which such a company – which many contended should be governed by the same, or substantially the same, legal regime in all Member States – might have for stimulating industrial co-operation, the Commission showed itself sympathetic to the idea and set up a working group of experts, chaired by Professor Sanders, to investigate the possibilities. This group quickly prepared the basis for a possible Commission proposal in 1967. The Commission's initial proposal, made in 1970, was largely based on the 1967 draft. The amended proposal, adopted by the Commission in 1975,[67] was much influenced by the

117

suggestions made by the European Parliament in connection with the earlier proposal.[68]

Like the 1970 proposal, the 1975 proposal was expressly based upon Article 235 EEC, and thus took the form of a directly applicable Regulation which would have direct effect in the Member States. In the first two recitals to the 1975 proposal, the Commission contended that one of the objectives of the Community is the realization of economic union, and that a condition for its realization was the reorganization of enterprises at Community level. It adds that this condition might be fulfilled only by the creation of European Companies. Many would doubt whether this is in fact the case. The 1975 proposal was very complex and contained 284 separate Articles and a further 170 paragraphs and 4 Annexes. After six years of fairly frequent discussion in a Council working group which discontinued work in 1982, a first reading had been given to less than one-third of the document.[69] This was achieved only by leaving contentious matters such as board structure and worker participation on one side, and concentrating on the less contentious Articles. As already pointed out, the Commission circulated a Memorandum on 15 July 1988 to the European Parliament, the Council of Ministers, and to employers' and employees' organizations, requiring comments on a proposal to revive earlier plans to create an optional legal framework for the formation and operation of European Companies.[70] The Memorandum contained alternative mandatory schemes for worker participation, and gave some information on the taxation aspect, but otherwise gave practically no information on the detailed content of a statute for the European Company. It did, however, indicate that its earlier proposal of 1975 could be simplified to some extent, particularly by leaving some matters to be dealt with by earlier directives or national laws.

NEW PROPOSALS

Basis and Nature
Definitive new proposals for a Council Regulation and a Directive complementing the Statute for a European Company contained in the former Regulation were presented by the Commission to the Council, the European Parliament and the Economic and Social

Committee in August 1989.[71] These proposals are contained in the same text, the first part of which brings together in a draft Regulation based upon Article 100a EEC[72] all the rules supposedly required for the creation and operation of the European Company, apart from those dealing with the involvement of the employees in such a company. These rules rather controversially form the subject of a complementary draft Directive, based upon Article 54 EEC, purportedly in view of the fact that the great diversity of the rules and practices of the Member States governing employee participation makes it difficult to lay down uniform rules on the involvement of employees in the SE. The two instruments are treated as a composite whole, and it is intended that they should be applied together. When considered together, they contain significantly fewer Articles than did the 1975 proposals. Because both instruments may well undergo a considerable degree of amendment before their eventual adoption, it is not intended to consider their provisions in very great detail in the present text. It is noteworthy that a critical attitude was taken to them in the Department of Trade and Industry's Consultative Document on the proposal for a European Company Statute of December 1989.

There are a number of reasons for the comparative brevity of the combined instruments. Although the new draft Regulation is based to a considerable extent on the 1975 proposal, certain topics such as groups of companies, which were dealt with in some detail in the latter proposal, are no longer subject to detailed regulation in the 1989 proposal. Furthermore, it has been found possible in the latter instrument to make reference to the provisions of the Fourth, Seventh and Eighth Directives (and to options granted in the former two instruments) for the purpose of regulating matters related to accounts and auditing. finally, the 1989 proposal makes reference to the law of the Member State where the SE has its registered office for the purpose of regulating a number of other matters.

Like an EEIG, an SE would be subject to a rather complex legal regime. The draft Regulation of 1989 contains provisions which are in principle directly applicable and are generally of a mandatory character, for the purpose of regulating matters covered by it. However, in drafting the proposed Regulation the Commission has placed a very considerable degree of reliance on previous Directives or proposed Directives. Thus Title III is closely based on the Second Company Law Directive, and Title IV on the proposed Fifth Directive. Furthermore, much of Title V consists of the application of the Fourth and Seventh Directives to SEs. In addition, much of Title II is derived from the draft Tenth Directive and thus depends on extensive reference to national implementation of the Third Directive. In addition to making reference to specific national laws implementing Directives, as already indicated, there are a number of other references to the national law of the Member State where the SE is registered. It follows from Article 3 of the draft Regulation that if a question of law arose on a matter covered by the draft Regulation but not expressly mentioned therein, it would be governed by the general principles on which the draft Regulation was based and, if these did not provide a solution, by the law applying to public limited companies in the State of registration. The meaning of the latter provision is far from clear. It is certain, however, that SEs formed in different Member States would not be subject to the same legal regime. Matters not covered by the draft Regulation (such as competition law, employment law and intellectual property law) would be governed by the laws of the Member States and Community law. The draft Regulation provides no criteria by which the relevant Member States can be identified. Furthermore, it is by no means clear from the foregoing provisions whether the relevant provisions of United Kingdom law relating to such matters as the registration of charges, the appointment of receivers and the protection of minorities from unfair prejudice would apply to an SE registered in the United Kingdom.[73] None of these matters is dealt with in the draft Regulation.

An SE would have legal personality, a capital divided in shares and denominated in ECU, and would also have limited liability.[74] In each Member State it would be subject to the express provisions of the draft Regulation, and have the same rights, powers, and obligations as a public company incorporated under national law.[75] Furthermore, it would also enjoy a simplified tax position.[76]

Methods of Forming an SE

Article 2 of the draft Regulation would provide for three methods of forming an SE. By Article 2(1), public limited companies formed under the law of a Member State and having their registered office and central administration within the Community might form an SE by merging or by forming a holding company, provided that at least two of them had their central administration in different Member States. Furthermore, by Article 2(2), companies or firms within the meaning of Article 58(2) EEC, and other legal bodies governed by public or private law which had been formed in accordance with the law of a Member State and had their registered office and central administration within the Community, might set up an SE by forming a joint subsidiary, provided that at least two of them had their central administration in different States. According to Article 3, an existing SE might be party to the formation of another by merger, or by the formation of a holding company or joint subsidiary. Although an SE would also be permitted to set up one or more subsidiaries, an SE which was itself a subsidiary of another SE could not create further subsidiary SEs. Some have argued that the restrictions on the methods of formation are unjustified. It is clear that they could be circumvented in practice.

The minimum capital for an SE would be 100,000 ECUs in all cases, except where the SE carried on the business of a credit institution or insurance undertaking.[77] By Articles 13–15 the forms of the instrument of incorporation and the statutes (if these were in a separate instrument), the examination of non-cash consideration, and the supervision of the formation procedure would be governed by the law applicable to public limited companies of the State in which the SE was to have its registered office. It is not clear from the proposal whether an SE may change the location of its registered office from one Member State to another. It is understood, however, that the Commission has indicated that this somewhat controversial facility will exist. The latter office would be specified in the statutes and would be the same as the place where the company had its central administration.[78] An SE would have legal personality as from the date set by the law of the State in which it was to have its registered office.[79]

The procedure for formation by merger[80] would be based largely on the Third Company Law Directive, supplemented to take account of the cross-border aspects of the proposal for a Tenth Directive. No provision is made in the draft Regulation for the formation of an SE by a take-over. The wording of Article 17, which would describe the type of merger envisaged, is based on the two instruments mentioned above. The rights of the employees of the merging companies would be protected in each Member State in accordance with Directive 77/589/EEC.[81] The draft terms of merger, which would be common to all the founding companies, would be required to contain certain prescribed details, and to be published.[82] The board of each of the merging companies would be bound to draw up a detailed report to shareholders justifying the merger. This report would be examined by experts, who would be responsible in particular for checking, on behalf of shareholders, whether the share exchange ratio was fair and reasonable.[83] The merger would have to be approved by a general meeting of each of the founder companies. The resolution approving the merger would be subject to the same conditions as are applicable to domestic mergers.[84] Creditors whose claims originated before the publication of the draft terms of merger and had not reached maturity at the time of such publication would be governed by those provisions of the national law governing the founder companies which related to the arrangements for the protection of the interests of creditors.[85] The provisions of Articles 24 and 25, which relate to the supervision and control of compliance with merger requirements, would prescribe certain rules for synchronizing supervisory procedures. The date on which the merger took effect would thus follow the completion of all the checks carried out by the founder companies, and would be determined by the law of the Member State in which the SE was to have its registered office.[86] The merger would be required to be made public before it could become effective against third parties. It would entail the transfer of all the assets of the founder companies to the SE.[87] The complexity of the procedure envisaged leaves room for doubt whether much use would be made of it.

The formation of an SE holding company, which would take place by means of an exchange of shares by which the holding company became the sole holder of all the shares in the founder companies, would be subject to the requirements of Articles 31–3.[88] The formation of a joint subsidiary where one of the parent companies is an SE would be governed by Articles 34 and 35. Articles 36 and 37 govern the formation of a subsidiary by an SE. An SE, acting alone, would be permitted to set up a subsidiary having the same legal form as the parent company.

Capital, Shares and Debentures

Capital, shares and debentures would be dealt with by Title III of the draft Regulation. The capital of an SE would be divided into shares denominated in ECU. Shares issued for a cash consideration at the time of the registration of the company would have to be paid up to the extent of at least 25 per cent.[89] Where shares were issued for a non-cash consideration at the time of such registration, that consideration would have to be transferred to the company in full within five years of the date on which the company was incorporated or acquired legal personality.[90] Furthermore, when such an issue took place, the provisions of national law concerning the examination of such consideration, adopted in the State in which the SE was to have its registered office pursuant to Article 10 of the Second Company Law Directive, would be applicable.[91]

The capital might be increased by an alteration of the statutes, which would require a resolution of the general meeting passed by a two-thirds majority.[92] Such an increase might take place by means of the issue of new shares paid up in full, or by the capitalization of reserves.[93] Where new shares were issued for a non-cash consideration, a report prepared by one or more independent experts would have to be submitted to the general meeting.[94] If shares were issued on a capitalization of reserves, they would be distributed among the shareholders in proportion to their existing holdings.[95] It would be possible to increase capital through the creation of approved capital, which might be issued by the administrative or management board during the following five years. Such approved capital might not exceed one-half of the issued capital.[96]

If the capital were increased by issuing shares for cash, the existing shareholders would be entitled to subscribe for new shares in proportion to their existing holdings, but the general meeting which resolved on the increase might waive this right on the written recommendation of the management board.[97] The statutes, the instrument of incorporation, or the general meeting might give the power to restrict or withdraw the right of pre-emption to the administrative or management board which was empowered to decide on an increase of subscribed capital within the limits of the authorized capital.[98]

The reduction of capital, except on the order of the court, would require at least a two-thirds majority of the votes attaching to the securities represented or to the subscribed capital represented.[99] Where there were several classes of shares, the decision of the general meeting concerning a reduction of the subscribed capital would be subject to a separate vote, at least for each class of shareholders whose rights were affected by the transaction.[100] Unless the reduction was because of losses, creditors would be entitled at least to obtain security for their claims, and the reduction would be void or no repayment might be made for the benefit of the shareholders until the creditors had obtained satisfaction, or the court within whose jurisdiction the registered office of the company was situated had decided not to accede to their claims.[101] The capital of an SE might not be reduced below 100,000 ECU.[102]

An SE and companies controlled by it within the meaning of Article 6, or in which it held a majority of the shares, would not subscribe for or acquire shares in the SE.[103] However, a number of exceptions to the general principle would be provided for in the case of the acquisition by an SE of shares in itself.[104]

It would be possible to issue classes of shares with different rights attached, but non-voting shares might be issued only to the extent of one-half of the SE's capital, and the shares carrying multiple voting rights might not be issued.[105] If the holders of a class of shares were adversely affected by a resolution passed at a general meeting, it would be valid only if approved by a class meeting by a majority of not less than two-thirds of the votes attached to the subscribed capital represented at the meeting.[106] Shares might be in registered or bearer form, and the statutes might permit conversion.[107] The issue, replacement and cancellation of share certificates and the transfer of shares would be governed by the laws of the state where the SE had its registered office.[108]

An SE would be permitted to issue debentures.[109] The laws of the State in which the SE had its registered office would apply to the body of debenture holders.[110] Where convertible bonds were issued, approved capital must be created to cover their eventual conversion and the pre-emptive rights of existing shareholders might be excluded as far as the shares used on conversion were concerned.[111] An SE would also be able to issue debentures carrying the right to a share of the profits.[112]

Principal Organs

As far as the principal organs of the SE were concerned, the proposed regime would be based upon national company law and on the amended proposal for a Fifth Company Law Directive. Provision would be made for a separation of powers between the general meeting of shareholders, which would decide certain matters of business, and the bodies which would manage and represent the SE.[113] The latter task would be the function either of a management board with a supervisory board monitoring its activities (the two-tier board system) or of an administrative board (the single-tier board system). The SE's founder companies would be authorized to choose between the two systems. Detailed rules for each system would be provided for in Articles 62–5 and 66 and 67 respectively. Articles 68–80, which are not considered in detail below, provide for rules common to both systems. Finally, Articles 81–100, which will also not be subjected to detailed consideration, would contain rules governing the general meeting.

Where the two-tier system was used, the members of the management board would be appointed by the supervisory board, which would be empowered to remove them at any time.[114] No person would be able to serve on both boards at the same time.[115] The members of the supervisory board would be appointed by the general meeting and, where the SE used a model of employee participation which so required, by the employees as well.[116] The supervisory board would be required to receive a report at least every three months from the management board on the management and progress of the company's affairs, including the companies controlled by it, and on the company's situation and prospects.[117] The supervisory board would also be empowered, at any time, to require the management board to provide information or a special report on any matter concerning the company or other undertakings controlled by it.[118]

The fundamental characteristics of the single-tier structure would be defined in Article 66, which would require the administrative board to have at least three members appointed by the general meeting and, where the model of participation in used required it, by the employees. All the members would be required to designate one or more executive members from among their own members and to delegate the management and representation of the company to them. The main function of the other members would be to supervise the executive members. In order that the position of the non-executive members might be strengthened, they would be more numerous than the executive members.[119] All members of the administrative board would have the same rights and duties apart from the actual management of the company.[120]

The rules outlined in the present paragraph would be applicable both to the single- and two-tier board systems. Members of the governing bodies might be appointed for a period not exceeding six years, but their reappointment would be possible.[121] The rules governing the representation of the company in dealings with third parties would be closely modelled on those contained in the First Company Law Directive.[122] Certain operations might be effected by the management board only following prior authorization by the supervisory board or by the administrative board as a whole.[123] Conflicts of interest would be governed by Article 73. Each member of a board would, in principle, have the same rights and duties. One of the main obligations of board members would be to protect confidential information. Members of the governing bodies would be required to act in the interests of the company, the shareholders and employees.[124] When the board was composed of more than one member, all the members would be jointly and severally liable without limit in respect of wrongful acts committed by members of the board in carrying out their duties.[125] However, a member might be relieved of liability if he could prove that no fault was attributable to him personally.[126]

A resolution of the general meeting would be required before certain actions could be taken by the company.[127] No distinction would be made between ordinary and extraordinary general meetings, but a qualified majority vote rather than a single majority vote would be required for resolutions amending the statutes or the instrument of incorporation, which would have to be passed by a two-thirds majority of the votes attached to the subscribed capital represented at the meeting.[128] A shareholder or his or her representative would not be able to exercise votes attached to her or her shares or to a third person where the subject matter of the resolution related to the assertion of claims against the shareholder, or the commencement of legal proceedings to establish his or her liability to the company, or to the waiver of the right to bring such proceedings.[129]

A general meeting would have to be held at least once a year.

Other general meetings could be called by the board of management or the administrative board at any time.[130] In addition, one or more shareholders together holding 10 per cent of the capital of the SE might request the SE to call a general meeting and to settle the agenda therefore. General meetings would be called by at least thirty days' notice in the national gazette specified in the legislation of the State of the registered office, or in one or more large-circulation newspapers.[131] Every shareholder would be entitled to appoint a proxy to represent him or her at the general meeting. Restrictions on the categories of persons who might be appointed as proxies might be laid down in the laws of the Member State where the company had its registered office, or in its statutes.[132] Further rules contained in Article 88 would be applicable where the proxies appointed were persons acting in a professional capacity.[133] The invitation to make such an appointment would have to be extended to all shareholders, and would have to set out the agenda of the meeting, require instructions as to voting, and state how the proxy would vote in the absence of such instructions.

If a general meeting was called to approve the annual accounts and to decide on the appropriation of the profits, certain documents – in particular the annual accounts and an auditors' report – would have to be made available to every shareholder, at the latest by the date of despatch or publication of the notice convening the meeting.[134] At a general meeting, a shareholder might require information on the affairs of the company relevant to the agenda, and this could be refused only where giving it was likely to prove seriously prejudicial to the company or to a controlled company, or if its disclosure would be incompatible with a legal obligation of confidentiality.[135]

A shareholder's voting rights would normally be proportional to the fraction of the subscribed capital which he or she had, but the statutes might authorize certain restrictions upon voting rights.[136] Where there were several classes of shares, any resolution of the general meeting would require a separate vote at least for every class of shareholders whose rights were affected by that resolution.[137] Resolutions of general meetings might be declared invalid on application to the court within whose jurisdiction the registered office of the SE was situated witin three months of the closure of the meeting on the ground that they violated the Regulation governing SEs, or the statutes of the SE.[138]

Annual Accounts and Consolidated Accounts
As far as the preparation, publication and auditing of annual accounts is concerned, the draft Regulation refers to the three accounting Directives – the Fourth, Seventh and Eighth Company Law Directives – and to Directive 86/635/EEC, which governs the drawing up, auditing and publication of annual accounts and consolidated accounts of credit and financial institutions; and to the forthcoming Directive which will govern the same matters in relation to insurance companies.[139] An SE would be entitled to make use of the options which the Fourth and the Seventh Directives grant Member States. A detailed treatment of the relevant accountancy provisions does not seem appropriate in the present work.[140]

Groups of Companies
Controlled undertakings and controlling undertakings are defined in Article 6 of the draft Regulation. The proposed definition is based on Article 8 of Directive 88/627/EEC,[141] and may be comparatively easy to apply.[142] Although the draft Regulation does not contain any provisions which would be applicable to the management of a group whose parent company was an SE, these rules are necessary in order to determine the law which would be applicable under Articles 114(1) and (2). The former provision would stipulate that where an undertaking controlled an SE, that undertaking's consequent rights and obligations relating to the protection of minority shareholders and third parties would be those defined by the law governing public limited companies in the State where the SE had its registered office. The latter provision would stipulate that this would not affect the obligations imposed on the controlling undertaking by the legal system which governed it.

Winding up, Liquidation, Insolvency and Suspension of Payments
Winding up and liquidation are matters which have not yet been harmonized within the Community. It is likely that an English insolvency practitioner will find the provisions of Articles 115–28, which would govern these matters, somewhat fragmentary. A detailed account of them will not be attempted. The proposed Regulation would restrict the grounds on which an SE could be automatically wound up, and would also seek to facilitate

the taking of a decision to wind up the company by the shareholders.[143] In addition to the latter kind of winding up, winding-up proceedings might also be brought by any interested party in the court of the place where the SE had its registered office.[144] It is not clear whether, as in the case under section 116 of the Insolvency Act 1986, a winding up by the members could be converted into a winding up by the court. The draft Regulation contains no provision corresponding to section 89 of the Insolvency Act 1986, which permits the directors of a solvent company which is to be wound up voluntarily to make a declaration of solvency.[145]

By Article 119, an SE which was to be wound up as the result of a resolution to that effect by the general meeting might continue in existence so long as there had been no distribution, provided that the general meeting so resolved.[146] The winding up of an SE would entail the liquidation of its assets, which would be carried out by one or more liquidators, who would be appointed in one of three ways indicated in Article 120(2). The liquidator would be empowered to take all appropriate steps to liquidate the SE and, in particular, to terminate pending transactions, collect debts, convert remaining assets into cash when this was necessary for their realization, and pay the sums owing to creditors.[147]

The liability of liquidators, accounting documents, and information to be supplied to creditors would be dealt with respectively by Articles 123, 124 and 125. No distribution might be made to the beneficiaries designated in the statutes or in the instrument of incorporation or, failing such designation, to the shareholders, until all creditors had been paid in full.[148] The liquidator or liquidators would be required to draw up a plan for the distribution of the net assets of the company. This might be challenged by any shareholder or beneficiary in the court of the place where the SE had its registered office within three months of the date when it was brought to the attention of the general meeting or that beneficiary.[149] The termination of the liquidation would be governed by Article 128.

By Article 129, as far as insolvency and suspension of payments proceedings are concerned, the SE would (somewhat controversially) be subject to the law of the place where it had its registered office. Under English law, such insolvency proceedings would appear to include insolvent voluntary winding-up proceedings, the compulsory winding up of a company on the ground of its inability to pay its debts, most types of administrative receivership and also administration proceedings.[150] Publicity in respect of insolvency or suspension of payments proceedings would be governed by Article 130.

Mergers

Under Article 131, an SE would be permitted to merge with other SEs and with public limited companies incorporated under national law, either by taking them over or by forming a new SE jointly with them. The reverse procedure would also be authorized: an SE might be taken over by a national public limited company and might set up a new national public limited company together with another such company, or with another SE or SEs.

Taxation

The only provisions contained in the draft Regulation concerning the taxation of SEs are those embodied in Article 133 thereof. The desirability of the inclusion of these provisions in the draft Regulation has been questioned by the United Kingdom government, and it is uncertain whether they will be included in the final version thereof. The draft Regulation does not contain any provisions which would permit an SE to deduct losses of subsidiary companies, or govern the imposition of taxation where an SE transferred its registered office from one Member State to another. Where an SE conducted taxable business through permanent establishments abroad, losses suffered by those establishments would, generally speaking, not be taken into account for tax purposes in its country of residence if profits from foreign business were exempt from tax in that country under national tax law or bilateral treaties. This rule might result in an SE being more heavily taxed. In order to prevent this situation, Article 133(1) would provide that such losses might be deducted from an SE's profits. To safeguard the interests of the Member State of the SE, Article 133(2) would provide that subsequent profits made by such permanent establishments were to be added to the SE's profits up to the amount of the losses previously deducted. Article 133(4) would take into account the fact that in Member States applying the imputation system a tax treatment identical to that already mentioned is actually applied.

The above provisions appear rather fragmentary, and it appears necessary for them to be coupled with certain other measures – some of which will be applicable to companies in general – which would also facilitate the formation and operation of SEs. These include provisions governing the taxation of mergers and of profits received by parent companies from subsidiaries in Member States, which have only recently been adopted by the Council.[151] Furthermore, the operation of SEs will be assisted by the adoption of the 1976 proposal for a Directive providing for an arbitration procedure which would eliminate double taxation arising from transactions between associated companies.[152] In addition, it may well be that SEs, as well as other companies, will be assisted by the enactment of measures governing corporate tax also.

Final Provisions
Article 136 would provide that an SE might be formed in any Member State which had implemented in its national law the provisions of the complementary Directive dealing with the involvement of employees in the SE. This provision would thus prohibit the creation of an SE in a State which had not implemented the latter Directive. By Article 137, the draft Regulation would not enter into force until 1 January 1992. In view of the length of the process of negotiation, a later date now appears virtually certain.

Employee Participation
The suggested constitutional basis of the complementary Directive is now said to be, in particular, Article 54 EEC. As already indicated in an earlier chapter, some have argued that this provision does not permit legislation on questions of employee participation: the matter remains in dispute. Article 2 of the proposed Directive would provide that employees of an SE would participate in its supervision and strategic development. The mechanism for choosing between the different models of participation would be governed by Article 3, which would allow a Member State to restrict the choice to one or more models. If only one model was permitted the SE would have to adopt it. Where the choice was between the three models proposed, the management of each of the founder companies would be required to choose a model, if possible with the agreement of the representatives of the

131

employees of the companies. Where no agreement could be reached, the management would chose the model. An SE could never be set up until one of the available models of participation had been chosen.

Two types of employee participation on the supervisory board (the two-tier system) from the administrative board (the one-tier system) would be provided for by Article 4. If the first model was chosen, all the employees of the SE and its various establishments would be entitled to elect representatives to the supervisory board or administrative board of the SE itself. These board members (at least one-third and not more than one-half) would sit alongside the shareholders' representatives (at least one-half and not more than two-thirds). According to the second type, the employees' representatives might instead be co-opted to the board in accordance with rules similar to those applicable under Dutch law.

Article 5 would make provision for a model of employee participation through a body which represented the employees at company level, but was separate from the company supervisory or management structure. If this model were chosen, all employees of the company and its various establishments, in whatever Member State they might be employed, would elect representatives to sit on this body. The mechanism for setting up this body envisaged in Article 5(1) might give rise to practical difficulties. the body representing the employees would have the rights to be informed and consulted as stipulated in Article 5(2). These rights would not be so great as where employee participation existed in the supervisory or administrative board. Thus, for example, the prior authorization of the supervisory or administrative board would be necessary before certain operations listed in Article 72 were implemented; the separate body envisaged by Article 5 would be required only to be informed and consulted about such operations.

Under Article 6, other models of participation might be established in the SE by means of a collective agreement to be negotiated between the managements of the founder companies and the representatives of those companies' employees. The agreement would have to contain the minimal provisions stipulated in Article 6(2). Where it provided for a collegiate body representing the employees, that body would be able to require the management board or the administrative board to supply the information necessary for the performance of its duties.[153] Article 6(4) would impose obligations as to discretion in relation to any confidential information they hold on the SE similar to those that would be imposed on members of the boards by Article 74(3), and on members of the separate body by Article 5(3). The provision contained in Article 6(5), which would permit the withholding of such information in certain circumstances, would only apply the Article 6 models of participation. A Member State which so desired would be permitted by Article 6(8) to make use of a type of model, called a standard model, in accordance with the most advanced practice in the country. The standard model would apply in the SE where the two parties had so decided, or where no agreement had been reached. The SE's representatives would have to be granted at least the minimal rights to quarterly information on the progress of the company's business and to information and consultation mentioned in Article 6(2). Where the employees were represented by a collegiate body, that body would have the right to require the information necessary for the performance of its duties under Article 6(3).

The election of the representatives of the SE's employees would be governed by Articles 7–10. Article 11 would make provision for agreements providing for employee participation in the SE's profits or losses. Member States would be required by Article 12 to implement the Directive by 1 January 1992.

Evaluation

As has already been pointed out, the constitutional basis of both the draft Statute and the draft Directive give rise to a measure of doubt, and if they remain unaltered there may be some possibility of these instruments being challenged by Member States before the European Court under Article 173 EEC. Although the new draft Statute represents a considerable degree of simplification when compared with the 1975 model, it still has a number of defects.[154] As already indicated, some would argue that the restrictions on the methods of formation may be unjustified. The proposed new legal regime remains complex and, as already indicated, it is unclear in certain ways. Furthermore, the draft Statute fails to provide, or to provide adequately, for a number of matters which company lawyers in the United Kingdom would generally consider to be of cardinal importance, such as powers of investigation and the enforcement of fair dealing by directors.

The proposed new legal regime might well prove too complex for small and medium-sized companies to use. Furthermore, such companies might not be subject to employee participation in their own countries and might find its compulsory use in the Regulation rather unwelcome. Companies might also be dissuaded from using the SE by reason of the fact that, apart from the provisions of Article 133, an SE would not be granted any special tax advantages.

It is rather surprising that the draft Directive says nothing about employee participation in groups of companies. The different models of employee participation proposed in the draft Directive would not, as has already been indicated, give the employees or their representatives equivalent rights. It is thought that the third model, in its two different guises, may be sufficiently undemanding eventually to meet British objections to compulsory employee participation, which seem to be of a rather doctrinaire character.[155] It is likely that the Commission will publish a significantly modified version of the draft Directive and the draft Regulation in 1991, after the European Parliament has given its opinion on these instruments.

9

Mutual Recognition

Introductory Remarks

Article 220 EEC requires Member States, as far as is necessary, to enter into negotiations with each other with a view to securing for the benefit of their nationals the mutual recognition of companies and firms within the meaning of Article 58(1). When one speaks of the recognition of a company, one is really talking about more than one question. The fundamental question is whether the company exists as a legal entity. However, if that question has been answered in the affirmative, one has to ask what laws the forum should apply to the company's internal and external affairs. As has frequently been pointed out, it is difficult to separate these two questions. However, it is certain that an unrecognized company would be denied the right to hold property, conclude contracts, sue or be sued.

The six original Member States concluded a Convention on the Mutual Recognition of Companies and Firms, which they signed on 29 February 1968. It appears highly unlikely that this Convention will come into force in the near future. Indeed, because of the prolonged failure of the Netherlands to ratify the Convention and the Additional Protocol of 1971 conferring jurisdiction on the European Court of Justice, and of the doubts entertained by the new Member States which undertook to accede to the Convention by Article 3 of the respective Acts of Accession and to negotiate modifications necessary for this purposes, it appears quite likely that the Convention will never come into force. In recent years some have expressed the doubt whether it still meets the necessity criterion embodied in Article 220 EEC.[1] It is understood that a working party which was considering what changes might be needed in the Convention is no longer functioning. The need for the Convention may perhaps have been lessened by the continuing harmonization of company law by means of Directives under

Article 54(3)(g), which have reduced disparities between national systems of laws. Although no attempt will be made to give a very detailed account of the provisions of the Convention, a succinct account has seemed justified by reason of the fact that the Convention continues to be discussed in all the available texts. Furthermore, recent experience with the draft Statute for European Companies leads to the conclusion that a Community text may sometimes remain dormant (or nearly so) for many years and then become reactivated as the result of some new initiative.

The Originally Perceived Need for a Convention

The chapter in the EEC Treaty on establishment does not say anything about recognition. However, the view has generally been taken that the Treaty intended recognition to companies to go hand in hand with the progressive realization of the freedom of establishment.[2] It is also clear that it was very desirable that the provisions of the Convention on Mutual Recognition should be compatible with those of the Treaty. Articles 52 and 58 EEC provide for Community-wide freedom of establishment and supply of services for companies which are formed in accordance with the law of a Member State and have their registered office, central administration (real seat) or principal place of business within the Community. These provisions have been said effectively to espouse the incorporation rule, which is explained below. Article 58 clearly does not require that the real seat must be in the State where the company is formed or, indeed, within the Community. However, it appears to follow from Article 52(1) that a company which simply has a registered office within the Community cannot benefit from the provisions on freedom of establishment and supply of services.[3]

To a large extent, the mutual recognition of companies has already been achieved among the Member States by a number of bilateral treaties, legislation and case-law.[4] However, there are certain disparities and inadequacies in the protection afforded in this way. Because of this, and because it is possible for the question of recognition to arise where there is no question of freedom of establishment or supply of services, the Member States undertook in Article 220, so far as necessary, to enter into negotiations with each other for a new and improved recognition.[5] One might also add that specific rules on recognition are required to remove all doubts on the interpretation of Articles 52 and 58 of the EEC Treaty.

The perceived need for the conclusion of a Convention was felt by reason also of factors additional to those mentioned above. Thus, of the six original Member States, the Netherlands adopts the rule that the law applicable to the recognition of companies (and of their powers and capacities) is that of their State of incorporation; whilst the other five adopt the rule that the law of the place of the company's real seat (central administration) governs this matter.[6] The protagonists of the incorporation rule point to its certainty; its opponents argue that it may facilitate certain abuses which do not arise under the real-seat rule. It was contended by a number of textwriters that whilst recognition was governed by such fundamentally different national rules, freedom of establishment within the Community could not be safeguarded. Thus it is noteworthy that the application of the real-seat rule might result in the refusal of recognition when the real seat of the foreign company was in the State where recognition was requested. This approach has been adopted in certain German decisions.[7] The application of the real-seat rule might instead lead to the application of the law of the forum to the foreign company.[8] In addition to the difficulty already outlined, the further difficulty arises that existing bilateral agreements do not cover all the types of company and legal person included under Article 58 EEC. Finally, the traditional exception of public policy was thought to be too wide for Community purposes.[9]

Beneficiaries of, and Conditions for, Recognition

The preamble to the Convention stipulates that the recognition of companies and firms within Article 58(2) should be as liberal as possible. The adoption of incorporation theory in Articles 1 and 2 would seem to have been influenced by this approach but, as will be shown later, Articles 3 and 4 provide for significant limitations and exceptions to this rule of recognition which may be invoked by Member States which adhere to the real-seat theory. Article 1 provides that recognition as a matter of right shall be accorded to all companies formed under civil or commercial law, including co-operative societies, which are established in accordance with the law of a contracting State which grants them the capacity to have rights and obligations and have their registered office in the territories to which the Convention applies. Article 8 makes it clear that any such company may not be denied recognition, even if it does not have the legal status of a body corporate under the law by which it was formed. Thus such legal entities as the English partnership,[10] the German commercial partnership [*offene Handelsgesellschaft*] and the French economic interest grouping [Groupement d'Intérêt Economique] may claim recognition under Article 1. It should also be noted that [despite the wording of Article 58(2) EEC] non-profit-making companies are not excluded from the ambit of Article 1, which enshrines a very liberal rule of recognition which is influenced by Article 58(2) EEC but departs from it in some respects.

This liberal approach to recognition is also adopted by Article 2 of the Convention. This provision stipulates that recognition shall also be granted as of right to legal persons under public and private law, other than the companies referred to in Article 1, if their principal or subsidiary purpose is to engage in an economic activity which is normally carried on for remuneration, or if they in fact continuously engage in such activity, without thereby violating the law under which they were formed. The concept enshrined in Article 2 of an economic activity normally performed for remuneration is somewhat vague, and deliberately differs from the gainful purpose criterion contained in Article 1.

As already indicated, the concessions made to the advocates of the incorporation theory in Article 1 and 2 are in part revoked by Articles 3 and 4. Thus, a Member State is permitted by Article 3 to declare that it will not apply the Convention to any company or firm whose real seat is outside the territories to which the Convention applies if the company or firm has no real connection with the economy of one of those territories.[11] The real seat of a company or firm is defined in Article 5 as the place where its central administration is located. this may be very difficult to determine in some cases, especially in that of a partnership. The somewhat vague limitation contained in Article 3 is modelled upon the General Programmes, and although it departs from their wording it is equally objectionable on the ground of its uncertainty.

Article 4 is intended to deal with the position of a company which claims recognition in a Member State, party to the Convention, in which its real seat is situated, but was formed in another Member State where it has its registered office. It permits a State to declare that it will apply the mandatory provisions of its own law to a foreign company whose real seat is in its territory. Such a State is permitted to apply non-mandatory (optional or suppletive) provisions to the company only if the company's charter fails to contain a reference to the law under which it was formed, or if the company is unable to prove that it has actually conducted its activity during a reasonable time in the state of its formation. The provisions of Article 4 have been said to lead to considerable uncertainties[12] and possibly to conflict with the requirements of Articles 52 and 58 EEC.[13] It may not always be clear which provisions of a given system of law are mandatory. In addition, the real-seat doctrine may be very hard to apply in marginal cases. Despite the defect of Article 4, five out of the six original Member States made a declaration under it.

The Effects of Recognition
The provisions of Article 6, which reflect the traditional solution under private international law,[14] stipulate that without prejudice to the application of Article 4, all companies or legal persons recognized by virtue of the Convention shall have the capacity accorded to them by the law under which they are formed. Uncertainties arise as to what is meant by 'capacity' and as to what rules of law govern those questions relating to a company and its activities which do not come within the ambit of this concept.

It will be noted that Article 6 gives the forum State freedom to apply the rules of its own law to the capacity of the company in the circumstances mentioned in Article 4. Furthermore, by Article 7, the State in which recognition is sought may deny the foreign company specific rights which under its own law are not accorded to companies of a corresponding type, but such restrictions may not have the effect of depriving the company of its basic capacity to have rights and obligations, to enter into contracts and undertake other legal acts, and to sue and be sued. The foreign company is not, however, permitted to invoke the limitations permitted by Article 7.[15] It is noteworthy that the Convention does not attempt to regulate the converse situation to that provided for in Article 7: where the law of the State in which recognition is claimed gives the company a more extensive capacity than the law of the Member State in which the company is incorporated.

Public Policy

When the exception of public policy is invoked by a forum State, this is in order to permit that State to deny the application of foreign law which would otherwise be applicable under its own choice of law rules. The application of this exception is limited by Article 9 of the Convention to situations where the company claiming recognition violates – through its charter purpose, through the objective it seeks to achieve, or through the activities in which it is in fact engaged – principles which the forum State considers to be a matter of public policy within the meaning of private international law.

Although Article 9 is given a deliberately narrow ambit, its application is somewhat uncertain and some have contended that there was no need for this provision to be inserted in the Convention.[16] Article 9 also provides for one situation in which the exception of public policy may not be invoked. It stipulates that if a so-called 'one-man' company may lawfully exist in its own State, it cannot be denied recognition in the other Member State on grounds of public policy. As was pointed out in an earlier chapter, the one-man company is now recognized in a number of Member States, and a Directive has recently been adopted in relation to such companies. It thus appears that the aforementioned provisions will have little or no effect if the Convention ever comes into force.

Final Provisions and Interpretation

The relationship between the Convention and other conventions to which the contracting parties are or will become parties is determined by Article 11 of the Convention. The territorial ambit of the Convention is stated by Article 12 thereof to consist of the European territories of the contracting states, the French overseas departments and the French overseas territories. The provisions of Article 14 are of special interest, because their wording has prevented the Convention from coming into force. This Article stipulates that the Convention shall enter into force on the first day of the third month following the deposit of the last instrument of ratification. The revision of the Convention is provided for by Article 18.

Common Declaration No. 3 of the Convention expresses the readiness of the parties thereto to examine the possibility of conferring jurisdiction to interpret the Convention on the European Court of Justice. The Additional Protocol of 1971, which is worded very similarly to Article 177 EEC, provides for the conferment of such jurisdiction on the Court. The Netherlands has not ratified this Protocol and thus, like the Convention, it is not yet in force.

Evaluation

As already indicated, the failure of the Convention to enter into force is explained by the doubts entertained by the Netherlands and certain of the other Member States about some of its provisions. As already indicated, it is unfortunate that the Convention contains so many vague provisions and gives rise to many uncertainties. The view has indeed been taken that the adoption of the Convention would lead to a more unsatisfactory position in relation to the recognition of companies within the EEC than is the case at present. Although the revival of interest in the Convention cannot be excluded, its adoption in its present form seems highly unlikely. It is noteworthy that no Convention has yet been adopted under Article 220 in the field of company law: preliminary discussion took place in 1960 concerning the transfer of seat of companies, but nothing came of them. It seems unlikely that the somewhat unsatisfactory decision of the Court of Justice in the *Daily Mail* case will act as a spur towards further work in this area.

10
Conclusion

Some Final Observations on the Work so far Accomplished by the Community Institutions

In view of the very considerable differences between the company laws of the Member States, attempts at harmonization might seem both difficult to accomplish and, indeed, unrealistic and unpractical. It is perhaps surprising that, although until recently there was a considerable slackening in the place of enactment of Directives harmonizing company law,[1] a number of harmonizing Directives in this area, covering many very important topics which together constitute a large part of company law, have been adopted. It has also been possible to enact the Regulation of 25 July 1985,[2] on the European Economic Interest Grouping. In addition, substantial progress has been made with the enactment of harmonizing Directives in the fields of the free movement of capital,[3] securities law[4] and banking law,[5] which are obviously related to company law. It is difficult to determine to what extent, if at all, such harmonization has, or will, really promote European integration. It would appear that the decisions of the competent European institutions to harmonize European company and securities law in specific areas have had at least as much to do with more immediate political and social considerations as with the examination of the question of whether such harmonization will promote the objectives of the EEC Treaty. Although a number of economic theories have a significant impact on the question of what role harmonization has to play in a common market, there seems to be little evidence that the Community institutions have been influenced by these theories. These institutions, and in particular the Commission, have proceeded on an *ad hoc* basis and have not engaged in the difficult task of making a consistent effort clearly to identify areas of company law and securities law in special need of harmonization.

It is noteworthy that the competence of the relevant Community institutions to engage in company law harmonization in a particular field has sometimes been based upon a somewhat bold interpretation of the EEC Treaty; in certain cases, the precise basis of this competence has (often deliberately) not been very clearly defined. Such harmonization should be facilitated by Article 100A EEC, which provides for majority voting and possibly has a less limiting effect than Article 100, which requires the legal provisions to be approximated to affect directly the establishment and functioning of the common market. On the other hand, Article 100A requires such provisions to have as their object the establishment and functioning of the internal market. It is perhaps only of minor significance that the declaration made pursuant to Article 100A gives precedence to Directives as instruments of harmonization. It appears unlikely that the national safeguards admitted by Article 100A(4) will give rise to difficulties in the present context.

Certain real or apparent defects in the process of harmonization as it is at present carried out have already been discussed in some detail in the introductory chapter, where something was also said about the blocking or congealing effect of Directives. However, a little more will be said about some of the relevant issues in this conclusion. It has already been pointed out that certain Directives, which include the Second Company Law Directive, contain very specific provisions. This is also true of the draft Fifth and Ninth Company Law Directives. Some have argued that this approach is wrong, and that Member States should be given some measure of freedom to enact the detailed provisions of their legislative enactments implementing Directives.[6] However, the relevant cases support the view that Directives can enter into any necessary degree of particularity.[7] It has been contended that the Council's power to specify detail in Directives, especially those governing legal harmonization, has become a matter of European customary law.[8] Some doubts still exist, however, as to whether this is really so.

The opposite problem is encountered in relation to the Fourth and Seventh Directives, which leave a number of options open to the Member States. Although the grant of certain of these options may well have unsatisfactory results, most of them would seem to have been politically necessary. As is pointed out correctly by Buxbaum and Hopt,[9] the European accounting professions have had no single uniform basis and have not accepted any common accounting principles comparable to those which are accepted in the United States; considerable divergences of accounting practice still occur in the different Member States. It may thus be the case that the perhaps rather limited degree of harmonization which it was possible to obtain through the enactment of the Fourth – and to an even greater extent the Seventh – Company Law Directives was not far from the maximum which could be hoped for in the relevant circumstances. The need for the inclusion of a number of options in a particular instrument often results from the need to compromise, and it may thus be reduced by the more frequent employment of majority voting. In many situations, harmonization through the extensive use of options would seem undesirable. However, the use of options may well have a significant role to play in the field of securities law.

It has already been pointed out that many of the Company Law Directives have had a prolonged gestation period and many Member States have failed to implement them on time. It is doubtful whether a greater use of the Treaty mechanisms governing majority voting will necessarily do much to remedy the former situation. In addition, recent experience seems to suggest that the piecemeal or 'salami' tactics of harmonization already referred to in the introductory chapter will continue to be employed in the fields of company and securities law. The complexity and technicality of many areas make it easier for them to be considered in isolation.

As has already been indicated, the requirements of certain provisions of the Company Law Directives have been implemented in rather different ways in various Member States. Thus, for example, it would seem that Articles 98 and 113 of the French law governing commercial companies of 24 July 1966, as amended, correspond more exactly with the requirements of Article 9(1) of the First Directive than did the old section 35 of the Companies Act 1985, or the rather complex new section 35A(1) of that Act, which has been incorporated by the Companies Act 1989. The French provisions do not use the concept of good faith but stipulate that a company is not bound in dealings with third parties by the acts of the administrative board, or the president thereof, which are not within the scope of the company's objects, if it can prove that the third party knew that the act was not within the company's objects, or that under the circumstances, it could not have been ignorant of this. Mere publication of the statutes is not treated as constituting proof. It is evident from the history of the relevant legislation that British draftsmen have experienced considerable difficulties in transforming the requirements of Article 9 of the First Directive into British law. Although it may be hard to envisage how this could be done, it is clear that a procedure should exist for determining whether Directives have been properly implemented, either at the level of the Commission or, more probably, through the medium of a national supervisory body.[10] A number of examples of defective implementation of Directives could be cited in addition to the British ones already mentioned.

A number of commentators[11] have placed emphasis on the blocking or congealing effect a Directive is said to have against later revision, which is thought to prevent enactments of implementing Directives from being amended or repealed.[12] There is some controversy about the exact scope of this blocking effect, and German writers have expressed certain constitutional objections to it. It may be, however, that at the present stage of development of national company laws, this blocking effect is more of theoretical than of practical interest. It would appear desirable, however, for Directives to contain some mechanism providing for their revision in accordance with changing social and economic needs. Some in fact do; one may instance Directive 85/374 on product liability.[13] The use of contact Committees, which is provided for in the accounting and certain of the securities Directives, appears to be a step in this direction. The difficulty of revising Directives may be exaggerated: certain Directives have been revised repeatedly.

Whatever their shortcomings, and whatever difficulties may have been experienced in their transformation by the Member States, the Company Law Directives in force cover a substantial part of the company laws of the Member States. However, it is noteworthy that such important draft instruments as the draft Fifth and Ninth Directives have not yet been enacted. In the case of the former instrument, this failure can be based upon the differing (and sometimes surprisingly emotive) attitudes to worker participation which continue to be manifested in the various Member States. These attitudes often appear to be based upon little or no empirical research or evidence. Nevertheless, it must be agreed that difficulties may well occur in transplanting a particular model which has proved successful in one Member State to other Member States which have different legal structures, patterns of labour relations, and trade-union attitudes. It seems unfortunate that no expert study of the effects of codetermination comparable to the German Biedenkopf Report of 1970 has been undertaken. At present, failure to enact the Fifth Directive appears to be due to the somewhat dogmatic opposition of one or more Member States. It will be remembered that certain of the provisions of this instrument are comparatively uncontroversial.

Like the Fifth Directive, the draft Ninth Directive has encountered opposition from representatives of industry. The various forms of this instrument would seem to be too complex, and too much based upon German *Konzernrecht* and proposals for its reform, to be generally acceptable in other Member States. In addition, the different preliminary drafts which have been made available do not consider a number of important questions relating to groups of companies – for example take-over bids. The failure hitherto to adopt the Commission's proposal for a Directive[14] extending the ambit of the Fourth and Seventh Directive to certain partnership like bodies such as the German GmbH & Co. KG[15] can be explained on the basis of widespread and persistent opposition to such extension in Germany. It is interesting to speculate whether the more frequent use of qualified majority voting consequent upon the Single European Act will result in the adoption of the draft Fifth Directive or the draft Statute for a European Company, in the near future.

Whatever the ultimate fate of the draft instruments mentioned in the above paragraph, the Council has recently adopted the Eleventh and Twelfth Directives, concerning branch accounts and single-member private companies. Other Community Directives may be expected in the field of company law, perhaps relating to such matters as liquidations and private companies.

An important and highly controversial new draft Directive on take-over bids has recently been published.[16] This instrument would seem to be more concerned with securities law than with company law. However, as most commentators are agreed, the exact boundaries of these two disciplines are somewhat hard to define. United Kingdom companies are becoming increasingly involved in cross-border take-overs. Take-over bids have been of great importance in the United Kingdom for a long time, and have almost entirely replaced assets mergers in this country. However, take-over bids are becoming increasingly important in other Member States, particularly in France. For these reasons, a brief account of the proposed Directive appears appropriate. Article 4 thereof would require a company which had acquired at least one-third of the securities conferring voting rights in another company to make a bid to acquire all the securities conferring voting rights in that company. by Article 10, the offeror company would be required to give a number of particulars in its offer document which would include details of its intentions regarding the continuation of the business of the offeree company, including the use of its assets, the composition of its board, and its employees. Particulars would also have to be given of any future indebtedness of the company to finance the bid. The latter requirement would be specially relevant to leveraged buy-outs, which rely on borrowing.

By virtue of the provisions of Article 8, the offeree company would be unable to engage in defensive tactics (including the issue of new securities carrying voting rights) without the consent of the general meeting between the time when the bid was made public and the time when the period for acceptance had expired. In the absence of such consent, the offeree company would be restricted to current operations under normal conditions during this offer period. Member States would be required by Article 6 to designate a supervisory authority or authorities to discharge certain functions specified in the draft Directive. The authorities thus designated would be able to delegate all or part of their powers to other authorities, or to associations or private bodies. It would thus seem that the United Kingdom Take-Over Panel could be given a continuing role in accordance with the provisions of the draft Directive, which seem to require certain amendments but do not appear more onerous than the United Kingdom Code on Take-Overs and Mergers.[17] However, it would seem that the rules governing take-overs would have to be placed on a statutory basis. It is understood that because of the latter contingency and because of uncertainties about the position of the Take-Over Panel, the United Kingdom government has expressed some preliminary reservations about the present proposal, which may well undergo some revision: it will be unable to veto the proposal, because it will be subject to qualified majority voting under Article 54(3)(g) EEC.

It should already be apparent that regulations have played a less important role in the field of European company law than have Directives. This will probably remain true in the future, despite the new power to enact Directives by a majority vote provided for by Article 100A EEC. As already indicated, despite the complexity of the legal regime which it establishes, it seems likely that the Regulation on the European Economic Interest Grouping will be of some use to firms wishing to engage in cross-frontier co-operation. The proposal for a Council Regulation on the Statute for a European Company is somewhat complex and its constitutional basis, together with that of the accompanying proposal for a complementary Directive with regard to employee participation, has given rise to controversy. The proposals contained in the former instrument concerning taxation and board structure, and those contained in the latter concerning employee participation, have been regarded as unsatisfactory by certain commentators.[18] Whilst Regulations may have a limited role to play in the future unification of European Company Law, it may be doubted whether Conventions under Article 220 EEC will have any great significance in the field of European company law in the near future. The Mutual Recognition Convention would seem dormant at present, and because of its many defects it appears likely to remain so. There is no indication, at present, of any plans to formulate and work on proposals governing the transfer of the seat of EEC companies.

Notes

Abbreviations

AllER	All England Law Reports
BGBl.	Bundesgesetzblatt
Bull. EC	Bulletin of the European Communities
Ch.	Chapter
CMLR	Common Market Law Reports
CML Rev.	Common Market Law Review
Co. Law	Company Lawyer
ECR	Reports of the European Court of Justice
ELR	European Law Review
ICLQ	International & Comparative Law Quarterly
JBL	Journal of Business Law
JO	Journal Officiel
JöR n.f.	Jahrbuch des Öffentlichen Rechts der Gegenwart, neue Folge
LIEI	Legal Issues of European Integration
LQR	Law Quarterly Review
MLR	Modern Law Review
OJ	Official Journal (of the EC unless otherwise stated)
RTDE	Revue trimestrielle de droit européen
SJ	Solicitors' Journal
ZGR	Zeitschrift für Unternehmens- und Gessellschaftsrecht
ZHR	Zeitschrift für das gesamte Handelsrecht und wirtschaftsrecht

CHAPTER 1: INTRODUCTION

1 OJ No. C23 of 25.1.1985, pp. 11–15.
2 Bulletin of the EC, Supp. 13/73, with a report by Prof. B. Goldman.
3 OJ No. L295 of 20.10.1978, pp. 36–43.
4 OJ No. L199 of 31.7.1985, pp. 1–9.
5 Bulletin of the EC, Supp. 4/75.

6 Thus a Directive has recently been adopted concerning insider dealings: see OJL1989, 334/30, 18 Nov. 1989. This instrument is based on Article 100A EEC.

7 The term 'British' is usually used in this work to mean belonging to Great Britain. The company law of Northern Ireland is in general similar to that of Great Britain, but there are a few minor differences. The comparatively small differences between the company law of England and Wales, and that of Scotland, are not of great significance for the present work. An examination of the company law of Northern Ireland also appears irrelevant for its purposes.

8 Note in this sense Schmitthoff in *Encyclopedia of European Community Law*, Sweet & Maxwell/W. Green & Son, Part B10–135.

9 Case 205/84 [1987] 2CMLR 69, 100.

10 See the discussion of this matter by Advocate General Darmon in Case 81/87, *R v. HM Treasury and others, ex parte Daily Mail and General Trust plc*, [1989] 1AllER 328.

11 See the critical notes on this case by Schmitthoff, 'The *Daily Mail* Case in the 'European Court' [1988] JBL 454 and Frommel, 'EEC Companies and migration – a setback for Europe' [1988] Intertax 409. Professor Schmitthoff specifically mentions English law. He says that the common law admits such a transfer, and cites old precedents to this effect. The Commission impliedly adopted the view in its observations that such a transfer was permitted not only by English law, but by United Kingdom company law as a whole: see [1989] 1AllER 341.

12 JO 1962, pp. 32–46.

13 Note in this sense Ficker, 'The EEC Directives on Company Law Harmonization', in *The Harmonization of European Company Law*, ed. Prof. C.M.S. Schmitthoff, UKNCCL 1973, pp. 66–82.

14 Ibid., pp. 68–9.

15 Ibid., p. 69.

16 See his article 'La régime juridique des sociétés dans la CEE', *Revue trimestrielle du droit européen* 1965, 11, 16. A more restrictive approach was adopted by R. Rodière in his article 'L'harmonisation des législations européennes dans le cadre de la CEE', *idem* 1965, 336, 345; he contends that the Commission is competent to act only where the legislation and practice of certain Member States constitute an impediment to the freedom of establishment of companies belonging to other Member States. See also Y. Scholten, 'Company Law in Europe', 4CML Rev. (1966–7) 377.

17 This is true, for example, of many of the provisions of the First, (OJ No. L69 of 14.3.1968, pp. 8–12), Fourth (OJ No. L222 of 14.8.1978, pp. 11–31) and Seventh (OJ No. L193 of 10.7.1983, pp. 1–17) Company Law Directives. It is probably too late to question the constitutional propriety of such provisions. The process of harmonization through the medium of

Directives may result in too much or too little detail. In the latter case, too much discretion may be left to Member States.

18 Note, for example, case 51/76, *Nederlandse Ondernemingen v. Inspecteur der Invoerrechten* [1977]ECR 113 and case 301/81, *Commission v. Belgium*, [1983] ECR 467.

19 Note in this sense case 32/74, *Friedrich Haaga GmbH* [1974]ECR 1201 and case 14/83, *Von Colson and Kamaan v. Land Nordrhein-Westfalen* [1984]ECR 1891. See also, in the same sense, *International Sales and Agencies Ltd v. Marcus* [1982] 3AllER 551, an instructive English case including the implementation of Article 9 of the First Company Law Directive by s.9(1) of European Communities Act 1972.

20 Note in this sense Ehlermann, 'The Internal Market following the Single European Act', 24CMLR 36, 387. The learned writer takes the view that the exclusion of the free movement of persons contained in Article 100A(2) applies only to natural persons. However, it follows from Article 100A(2) that Article 100A is inapplicable to the rights and interests of employed persons. It is not quite clear whether Article 100A continues to be applicable after 31 Dec. 1992, but the better view may be that it does; note in this sense Glaesner, 'Die Einheitliche Europäische Akte', 21 Europarecht 1986, 119, 133.

21 OJ No. L65 of 16.3.1968, pp. 8–12.

22 OJ No. L26 of 31.1.1977, pp. 1–13.

23 OJ No. L295 of 20.10.1978, pp. 36–43.

24 OJ No. L222 of 14.8.1978, pp. 11–31.

25 OJ No. L314 of 14.12.1984, p. 28.

26 OJ No. L378 of 31.12.1982, pp. 47–54.

27 OJ No. L193 of 18.7.1983, pp. 1–17.

28 OJ No. L126 of 12.5.1984, pp. 20–26.

29 OJ No. L372 of 31.12.1986, pp. 1–17.

30 Directive 89/117/EEC, OJL 44/40, 16 Feb. 1989.

31 OJ No. L395 of 30.12.1989, pp. 36–9.

32 OJ No. L395 of 30.12.1989, pp. 40–42.

33 OJ No. C240 of 9.9.1983, pp. 3–28. An amended version of this proposal has been published in a Consultative Document issued by the Department of Trade and Industry in January 1990.

34 OJ No. C217 of 12.8.1983, pp. 3–16. The original proposal may be found in OJ No. C297 of 15.11.1980, pp. 3–8.

35 OJ No. C23 of 25.1.1985, pp. 11–15.

36 OJ No. C144 of 11.6.1986, pp. 10–11. See also COM(88) 292-Final-SYN 158, Brussels, 14 October 1988, and OJN C318 of 20.12.1989, pp. 12–20.

37 OJ No. C131 of 18.5.1987, pp. 1–21.

38 Note in this sense White Paper from Commission to European Council, completing the Internal Market, COM(85) 310 Final, point 144.

Proposals on liquidations and take-over bids may also be anticipated: see p. 29 of the timetable for completing the internal market contained in the former document ('Cockfield Report').

39 Note, for example, P. Storm in *Business Law in Europe*, Kluwer Law and Taxation, Deventer 1982, 38–9.

40 See B. Goldman and A. Lyon-Caen, *Droit commercial européen*, 4th edn, Dalloz 1984, 138 and G. Beitzke, 'Anerkennung und Sitzverlegung von Gesellschaften and Juristischen Personen im EWG – Bereich', 127ZHR (1964)1, 24ff.

41 See the French law governing commercial companies of 24 July 1966, Articles 31, 60 and 154, and the Italian Civil Code, Article 2368.

42 Case 81/87, *The Queen v. HM Treasury and Commissioners of Customs and Excise, Ex parte Daily Mail and General Trust plc*, *The Times*, 29 Sept. 1988, [1988] STC 787; [1989] 1AllER328.

43 Italian law recognizes them provided that they are approved at the level of the Italian company: if this is a public limited company [*Società per Azioni*], such approval must be given by an extraordinary general meeting deciding on the basis of the quorum and the majority prescribed for changes to the statutes. It may be that shareholders who voted against the merger would be entitled to exercise the right of withdrawal provided for by Article 2437 of the Civil Code. This liberal feature of Italian law would facilitate mergers in which an Italian company was taken over by a Belgian, French or Luxembourg company.

44 OJ No. L199 of 31.7.1985, pp. 1–9.

45 See OJ 1989 No. C24/3 of 16 Oct. 1989 and COM (89) 268 Final.

46 See the Commission's paper for the European Company (Com(88)) 320 Final, p. 25; note, however, as to the doubts as to whether the harmonization of company law is a necessary condition for the achievement of the internal market on the same pages. Some would argue that the Commission's harmonization programme has not been very successful, and has not done very much to foster European integration.

47 See R. Buxbaum and K.J. Hopt, *Legal Harmonization and the British Enterprise*, de Gruyter 1988, p. 204, in a similar sense. It is sometimes contended that haronization is not a necessary condition for the functioning of the Common Market: for mention of this contention, see Internal Market and Industrial Co-operation, Doc COM(88) 320, p. 26.

48 It has been argued that the desired approximation of employee participation provisions goes beyond the creditor and shareholder protection provided for in Article 54(3)(g): see M. Lutter, 'Die Entwicklung des europäisches Gesellschaftsrechts in Europa' (1975) Europarecht 44, 48–51, and J. Pipkörn, 'Zur Entwicklung des Gesellschaftsrechts-und Unternehmensrechts', 136ZHR (1972) 499, 511.

The necessity for a Directive on the Conduct of Groups was disputed in the memorandum by the Law Society's Standing Committee on Company Law on the proposed Ninth Company Law Directive of July 1982.

49 Note in this sense Schmitthoff, 'The Future of the European Company Law Scene', in *The Harmonization of European Company Law*, UKNCCL 1973, pp. 6–7; also Ficker, op. cit., p. 66, in the same sense.

50 OJ 1970, C124.

51 For some useful criticisms of the Commission's methods of harmonizing company law by means of directives, see P. Storm, 'European Company Law', pp. 13–18 in *Business Law in Europe*, Kluwer Law and Taxation Publishers, December 1982.

52 BGBI.1.2355.

53 This occurred, for example, in relation to the Second Directive.

54 Note in this sense COM(88) 320 Final, pp. 2–3, 5–11.

55 Note in this sense COM(88) 320 Final, p. 10.

56 Note, for example, German *Aktiengesetz*, Articles 78 and 80(1).

57 Ibid., Article 4b.

58 Ibid., Article 21d.

59 Ibid., Articles 4c, 21d(e).

60 Ibid., Articles 4d, 21e.

61 Ibid., Articles 4e, 21f.

62 The GIE was introduced in France by Ordonnance 67–821, 23 September 1967, French Official Journal of 28 September 1967.

63 The so called structural provisions of this instrument are comparatively non-controversial and their enactment might well be possible in the near future if they were contained in a separate instrument, unconcerned with worker participation.

64 Article 302 of the new form of the German Commercial Code incorporated therein by the *Bilanzrichtliniengesetz* of December 1985 closely follows the provisions of Article 20 of the Seventh Directive; France has enacted no legislation on this subject.

CHAPTER 2: THE FIRST AND SECOND COUNCIL DIRECTIVES

1 There is considerable literature on the present Directive. It is dealt with very thoroughly in the excellent work by E. Stein, *Harmonization of European Company Law*, Bobbs-Merrill Company, Indianapolis 1970. See also Y. Scholten, op. cit., 4CMLRev. (1966–7), 377; N.J. Ault, 'Harmonization of Company Law in the European Economic Community', 20 Hastings Law Journal 1968, 77 and F. Wooldridge, 'The Harmonization of Company Law', Acta Juridica 1978, 327. For articles in French, see R. Houin, op. cit., RTDE 1965, 11 and R. Houin, Les pouvoirs des dirigeants dans la CEE, 2RTDE1966, 307; R. Rodière, op. cit. 1RTDE 1965, 336 and P. van Ommerschlage, 'La première directive du Conseil du 9 mars 1968 en matière des sociétés', CDE 1969, 495–563, 619–65. One of the best articles in German is that by M. Lutter, 'Die Erste Angleichungs-Richtlinie zu Art 54 Abs 3(g) ENGW und ihre Bedeutung für das geltende deutsche Unternehmensrecht', (1969) Europarecht 1.

2 JO 1964, 3295. For a discussion of this draft, see W. Fikentscher, and B. Grossfeld, 'The Proposed Directive on Company Law', 2CMLRev. (1964–5)259.

3 JO 1966, 1519.

4 Directive 68/151/EEC, OJ 1968; 41.

5 See Act of Accession of the United Kingdom, Denmark and Ireland of 22 January 1972, Article 29, Annex I, Part III, 4; Act of Accession of the Hellenic Republic of 19 November 1979, Article 21, Annex I, Part II(c), point 1; and Act of Accession of Kingdom of Spain and the Portuguese Republic of 12 June 1985, Annex I, part II(d), point 1.

6 See Article 1 of the Directive, as amended.

7 Ibid., Article 2(1)(a) and (b).

8 Ibid., Article 2(1)(c).

9 Ibid., Article 2(1)(d). The European Court held in case 32/74 *Friedrich Haaga GmbH* [1974] ECR 120 that this clause made it necessary for companies which entrusted the power to act on their behalf to a single person to state explicitly in the national register in which the company was registered that he was the sole representative empowered to act on behalf of the company. The Commission has taken the view that British law does not fully comply with Article 2(1)(d), because it does not provide for the disclosure of the arrangements concerning the powers of managing director; see OJC 289/1 16 March 1977.

10 Ibid., Article 2(1)(c).

11 Ibid., Article 2(1)(f), Act of Accession (1985), Article 26, Annex I, Part II(d), point 1. In the case of private companies (except United Kingdom private companies, which were treated as a kind of public company for this purpose), application of this provision was postponed

until EC Council Directive 78/660 (The Fourth Directive) on annual accounts was implemented: EC Council Directive 68/151, Article 2(1)(f). The Fourth Directive was adopted on 25 July 1978, and was implemented in Great Britain by the Companies Act 1981. The First Directive seems to have acted as a stimulus to the recognition of the difference between public and private companies in all Member States: note in this sense Schmitthoff, 'The Second EEC Directive on Company Law', 15CMLRev. (1978) 43, 46.

12 Ibid., Article 2(1)(g).

13 Ibid., Article 2(1)(h).

14 Ibid., Article 2(1)(1).

15 Ibid., Article 2(1)(j).

16 Ibid., Article 2(1)(j).

17 Note, for example, Companies Act 1985, s.10 (registration); s.242 (accounts); ss.524 and 573 (winding-up order); ss.534(1)(a) and 600 (appointment of liquidator); and ss.585.(3) and 595(3) (final meeting and dissolution). Account has been taken of the amendments made to the Companies Act 1985 by that of 1989 in the present chapter, and elsewhere. In principle, the provisions of these Acts extend to Great Britain only, and not to N. Ireland: note s.745 of the Companies Act 1985 (as amended) and ss.213 and 214 of the Companies Act 1989. The last-mentioned section governs the making of corresponding provision for Northern Ireland by Orders in Council. The implementation of the First Law Directive in Northern Ireland is at present governed by the Companies (Northern Ireland) Order 1986, S.I. 1986 No. 1032 (N.I. 16).

18 Ibid., ss.711(1), 718(1) and Sch.22.

19 Thus in France, the Federal Republic of Germany, Italy and Belgium, the register which companies are registered in is maintained by the local courts, whereas in the Netherlands, it is kept by local chambers of commerce. In Spain, registration takes place in the Mercantile Registry of the capital of the Spanish Province in which it is intended to establish the company. The Mercantile Registries are placed under the authority of the Ministry of Justice.

20 This provision is given effect in the United Kingdom through the procedure of official notification: see Companies Act 1985, s.711. For the defects of this procedure see L. Sealy, *Company Law and Commercial Reality*, Sweet & Maxwell 1984, p. 33.

21 Section 42(1) of the Companies Act 1985 (as amended) is intended to give effect to section 3(5) of the Directive in Great Britain, but it is not clearly worded and gives rise to considerable difficulties in interpretation: see Prentice, 'Section 9 of the European Communities Act', 89LQR (1973) 518, 537–40 in this sense. See also Sealy, op. cit., p. 8.

22 See Schmitthoff in *Encyclopedia of European Community Law*, Sweet & Maxwell/W. Green & Son, Part C3-006, where a wide

interpretation of this phrase is advocated. Section 351 of the Companies Act 1985 (as amended) gives effect to Article 4 in Great Britain.

23 See Article 41 of the German *Aktiengesetz* and Article 11(2) of the German *GmbH Gesetz* (as amended).

24 See Italian Civil Code, Articles 2331, 2475.

25 Problems have arisen concerning the meaning of the words 'subject to any agreement to the contrary' and 'he shall be personally liable on accordingly' in section 9(2) of the European Communities Act 1972 and section 36(4) of the Companies Act 1985: both these texts were intended to implement Article 7. See Prentice, 'Section 9(2) of the European Communities Act 1972', 89 LQR 518, 530–33, for an expression of the view that section 9 may not have altered previous rules of the common law concerning pre-incorporation contracts. However, the Court of Appeal took a different view of this question in *Phonogram Ltd v. Lane* [1982] 3AllER 182.

26 German law thus made a distinction between *Vertretungsmacht* (power to represent) and *Geschäftsführungsbefügnis* (the authority to represent actually granted by the represented person). Lack of such authority would have consequences only between the principal and the agent, but would have no influence on the validity or the contract with the third party. This approach is enshrined in Article 82(1) of the German *Aktiengesetz*.

27 A similar approach is taken under Danish and Dutch law. Belgian and Italian law are now also influenced by the organic theory.

28 See Law of 24 July 1966 (as amended), Articles 98, 113.

29 See Articles 124 and 126 of the French law of 1966 concerning commercial companies (as amended).

30 See R. Pennington, *Company Law*, 5th edn, Butterworths 1985, p. 114 in this sense.

31 See the old section 35 of the Companies Act 1985, which was in very similar terms to section 9(1) of the European Communities Act 1972, which it replaced.

32 Note in this sense Prentice, 'Section 9 of the European Communities Act 1972', 89LQR (1973) 518; Farrar and Powles, 'The Effect of section 9 of the European Communities Act 1972 on English Company Law', 36MLR (1973) 270. It is noteworthy that the French Ordonnance 69–1176 of 20 December 1969 avoids the concept of good faith, and is drafted in clearer terms than the English implementing legislation. However, it is noteworthy that the corresponding Italian legislation, Article 2305 *bis* of the Civil Code, also employs the concept of good faith [*buona fede*].

33 Lawson J. held in *International Sales and Agencies Ltd. v. Marcus* [1982] 2AllER 551 that good faith had to be interpreted in accordance with the First Directive. However, Nourse J. took a different view in *Barclays Bank Ltd v. TOSG Trust Fund Ltd* [1984] BCLC1, 17–18.

34 For an expression of the contrary view, see R. Pennington, *Company Law*, 5th edn, Butterworths 1985, pp. 104–5. Professor Pennington adopts the view that, to the extent that *International Sales and Agencies Ltd v. Marcus* determined otherwise, it was wrongly decided.

35 Note in this sense the speech of Lord Wedderburn in the House of Lords, Parliamentary Debates, Official Report, 8 November 1989, columns 676–7.

36 See ibid., column 682. It is noteworthy that in France (see law governing commercial companies of July 1967, Articles 49(5), 98 and 113) the Netherlands (see Civil Code, Book 2, Section 6), Ireland (Companies Act 1963, s.8) and Denmark (Law No. 370 of 1973, paras 60, 61; Law No. 371 of 1973, paras 41, 42) use has been made of the exception provided for in Article 9(1) of the Directive, whereby an act is not binding if the third party knew, or must in the circumstances have known, that the transaction was outside the objects of the company.

37 S.I. No. 163 of 1973. Paragraph 6(1) provides that the acts of the organs of the company shall bind the company to third parties acting in good faith. It defines the organs of the company as the board of directors and any other person registered under the regulations as authorized to bind the company.

38 See Wedderburn, op. cit., cols 685–7, in this sense.

39 (1856) 6E and B327.

40 Thus in France, the registration of the company used to be thought to have a declaratory effect only.

41 Article 360 of the French law concerning commercial companies of 24 July 1966 (as amended) limits the application of the general contractual rules governing nullity as far as public and private limited companies are concerned, but it has been criticized on the ground of its unclear drafting, and may provide for nullity on grounds additional to those stated in the First Directive: see Ripert, *Traité Elémentaire du Droit Commercial*, 12th edn, Roblot, Paris 1986, p. 672.

42 Ibid., Article 12(2) and (3).

43 For the implementation of the First Company Law Directive in Northern Ireland, see Companies (Northern Ireland) Order 1986, S.I. 1986 No. 1062 (N.I. 12); and also Articles 44–47 of Companies (No. 2) (Northern Ireland) Order 1990, S.I. 1990, No. 1054 (N.I. 10).

44 Journal officiel de la République Française no. 69–193 of 28 December 1969.

45 Staatsblad van het Koninkrijk der Nederlanden 285, 1971.

46 Moniteur Belge (Belgisch Staatsblad) of 23 June 1973, 7681.

47 November 1979. See M. Forde, *Company Law in Ireland*, The Mercier Press, Cork and Dublin, 1985, p. 418.

48 This matter is dealt with in Regulation 6, which implements Article 9(2) of the Directive.

49 Lex, January–June 1970, 321: Gazetta Ufficiale della Repubblica Italiana no. 35 of 10 February 1970, 782.

50 BGB. 1.1146 (1969).

51 Memorial A no. 72 of 13 December 1972, 1586–94.

52 Lovtidende (1973) 1025 (public companies); 1063 (private companies).

53 Greek Official Journal, FEK 191A of 28 November 1986.

54 Greek Official Journal, FEK 197A of 10 December 1986.

55 Boletín Oficial del Estado, 27 July 1989. See also Decree Law 1564/1989 of 22 December 1989, Boletín Oficial del Estado, 27 December 1989.

56 OJ No. C48 of 24.4.70, p. 8.

57 OJ No. L26 of 31.3.77, pp. 1–13.

58 Ibid., Article 1(1).

59 Ibid., Article 1(2).

60 Note in particular R. Keutgen, *La Deuxième Directive en Matière des Sociétés*, *Revue Pratique des Sociétés* (1971)1; J.T. Lang, 'The Second EEC Company Law Directive', Irish Jurist 1976, 37; G. Morse, 'The Second Directive: raising and maintenance of capital', (1977) European Law Review 126; C. Schmitthoff, 'The Second EEC Directive on Company Law', 15CMLRev. 43; and F. Wooldridge, op. cit., Acta Juridica 1978, 334–45. The book by Professor Stein already referred to contains a valuable account of the history of the Directive.

61 Note in particular Companies Act 1985 (as amended), ss.3(1)(a), 11, 25(1), 27(4), 101, 112 and 118. See also Palmer, *Company Law*, 24th edn (Schmitthoff and others), vol. 1, Stevens & Co. 1987, pp. 57–8.

62 A private company continues to be designated as limited (ltd); Companies Act 1985 (as amended), ss.25(1) and 27(4).

63 The term 'statutes' corresponds with the memorandum and articles in the United Kingdom.

64 The phrase 'instrument of incorporation' corresponds with the memorandum in the United Kingdom.

65 This requirement does not appear to be complied with under English law: section 117(3)(b) of the Companies Act 1985 (as amended), which contains a similar one, applies only to newly incorporated public companies and seems to be designed to implement Article 3(g) of the Directive: see also Companies Act 1985 (as amended), ss.711(1)(g) (official notice and registration).

66 This concept is found only in British, Dutch, Irish and French company law.

67 This provision has not given rise to any specific implementing legislation in Great Britain: see Wooldridge, op. cit., Acta Juridica 1978, 335–6 for a more detailed discussion.

68 Article 4 was implemented in Great Britain by section 117(8) of the Companies Act 1985.

69 The authorized minimum in Great Britain is £50,000, but it may be varied by Statutory Instrument: Companies Act 1985 (as amended), section 118. This amount is well in excess of that required by the Directive.

70 Ibid., Articles 7 and 8: see Companies Act 1985 (as amended), ss.99, 100.

71 Article 7: see Companies Act 1985 (as amended), s.99(2).

72 Ibid., Article 9(1). See Companies Act 1985 (as amended), s.101, which provides that a public company shall not allot a share except as paid up to one quarter of its nominal value and any premium on it. Article 36a of the German *Aktiengesetz*, which was incorporated therein by the law of 13 December 1978, is in similar terms. See also the French law of 24 July 1966 concerning commercial companies, Article 75.

73 French and Italian law do not contain such complex provisions concerning the valuation of contributions in kind: see French Law of 1966 concerning commercial companies as amended, article 80, and Italian Civil Code, article 2343.

74 Article 11 is implemented in Great Britain by the Companies Act 1985 (as amended), sections 104, 105, 109 and 110. For certain defects in sections 104 and 105, see Boyle and Birds, *Company Law*, 2nd edn, Jordans 1987, p. 258.

75 Ibid., Article 12.

76 Ibid., Article 13.

77 See Companies Act 1985 (as amended) section 80, which makes it clear that an issue out of the authorized capital (a concept known only in the United Kingdom, France, the Republic of Ireland and the Netherlands) will require a resolution of the general meeting, or the grant of specific authority to the directors by the articles or the general meeting; such authority may be renewed by the general meeting. The deregulation of private companies by section 113 of the Companies Act 1989 will entail that a resolution in writing signed by or on behalf of all the members of the company will have the same effect as a resolution in general meeting. See also the special rules applicable to such companies contained in section 80A of the Companies Act 1985, which has been incorporated therein by section 115 of the 1989 Act. Article 25(1) and (2) are implemented in France by Article 180 of the law governing commercial companies of 24 July 1966 (as amended); for the position in Germany, see Articles 182, 183, 192–4 and 202 AktG.

78 Section 101 of the Companies Act 1985 (as amended) deals with both matters. For the position in France, see law governing commercial companies of 24 July 1966 (as amended), Article 15; for that in Germany, see Article 36a AktG.

79 Ibid., Article 27(4).

80 For the present law in these countries, see Companies Act 1985, ss.89–96 and s.711; French law governing commercial companies of 24 July 1966 (as amended), Articles 183ff.; Articles 186–7, AktG; Italian Civil Code, Article 2441.

81 See Companies Act 1985 (as amended), s.89, which makes provision for the conferment of pre-emptive rights on existing equity shareholders when further shares are allotted, and is subject to a number of qualifications and exemptions; note section 95 in the latter connection. See also the adaptations made to s.95 by new Sch. 15A of the Companies Act 1985, which was incorporated therein by s.114 of the Companies Act 1985, and is applicable to private companies only.

82 See Companies Act 1985 (as amended), s.89(1) and (2), which are subject to the permissive exemptions contained in Article 29(2) of the Directive.

83 The relevant period is 21 days in Great Britain: see Companies Act 1985 (as amended), s.90(6). Note also Article 188 of the French law of 24 July 1966 concerning commercial companies as amended (twenty days) and Article 186(1) AktG (two weeks).

84 The provisions of Article 29(4) (other than those relating to publicity) are implemented in Great Britain by the Companies Act 1985 (as amended), s.95(2); in France by Article 186–3 of the law governing commercial companies of 1966, as amended; and in Germany by Article 182(3) and (4) AktG.

85 See Companies Act 1985, s.711.

86 See Companies Act 1985, s.95(1).

87 Note in this sense, P. Storm, op. cit., p. 22.

88 See Companies Act 1985 (as amended), s.264, which provides that a public company may distribute profits only if at the time the amount of its net assets – i.e. the excess over liabilities – is not less than the total of its called-up capital and undistributable reserves, and only to the extent that the distribution does not reduce the amount of the net assets to less than that total. Note also French law of 24 July 1966 governing commercial companies (as amended), Article 346(3) and Articles 57, 58 and 150 AktG.

89 The profits available for distribution are thus defined in accordance with the balance sheet surplus method, as they are under section 263(3) of the Companies Act 1985 (as amended). This provision applies to all companies (whether public or private) except investment companies as defined in section 266, which are governed by section 265. See also French law of 24 July 1966 governing commercial companies (as amended), Article 346(1).

90 See Companies Act 1985 (as amended) ss.263, 264 and 272 (applicable to public companies). Note also French law of 14 July 1966

governing commercial companies (as amended) and Article 347(2) and Article 59 AtkG.

91 See Companies Act 1985 (as amended), s.277; French law of 24 July 1966 governing commercial companies (as amended), Article 347(3).

92 The present provision under French law is contained in the law governing commercial companies of 24 July 1966 (as amended), Article 241.

93 Article 92 AktG.

94 This is because the company is not required to consider any specific measure when the meeting is invoked.

95 See Companies Act 1985 (as amended), section 143; French law governing commercial companies of 24 July 1966 (as amended), Article 217; Article 56 AktG.

96 See Companies Act 1985 (as amended), ss.164(4) (off-market purchase); s.166(4) (market purchase); French law governing commercial companies of 24 July 1966 (as amended), Article 217-2.

97 This requirement is somewhat surprisingly not adopted under British law, which contains complex provisions concerning the purchase by a company of its own shares, which otherwise conform with the requirements of the Directive in so far as they concern public companies. The relevant rules are contained in the Companies Act 1985 (as amended), sections 143(a) and 162–77, and differ in accordance with whether the purchase is a market or off-market purchase, as defined in section 163. Private companies may purchase their own shares out of capital subject to compliance with the complex rules contained in sections 171–7. Minor adaptations to ss.164, 165, 167, 173, and 174 applicable to written resolutions of private companies are contained in paras 5–6 of the new Sch. 15A to the Companies Act 1985. The 10 per cent requirement may be found in Article 217-3 of the French law of 24 July 1966, (as amended) and in Article 71(2) AktG.

98 See Companies Act 1985 (as amended), ss.160 and 162, French law governing commercial companies of 24 July 1966 (as amended), Article 217-3; Article 71(2) AktG.

99 Companies Act 1985 (as amended), ss.159, 162 and 171; French law governing commercial companies of 24 July 1966 (as amended), Article 217-3.

100 See Wooldridge, op. cit., Acta Juridica 1978, for a more detailed account of the German provision.

101 See also Article 39. Note also Companies Act 1985 (as amended), ss.143(3) 159–61 and section 171 (power of private companies to redeem or purchase their own shares out of capital.)

102 See Companies Act 1985 (as amended), s.143(3)(c); note also Article 71(1) No. 3 AktG.

103 See Companies Act 1985 (as amended), s.143(3)(d).

104 See Companies Act 1985 (as amended), s.143(3)(b).

105 See Companies Act 1985 (as amended), s.146. The exclusion contained in section 146(1)(b) appears very wide. Note also French law of 24 July 1966 concerning commercial companies (as amended), Articles 217–6 and 217–7; and Article 71c AktG.

106 Second Directive, Article 21.

107 See Companies Act 1985 (as amended), s.146(4); French law of 24 July 1966 concerning commercial companies (as amended), Article 164; Article 71b AktG.

108 Second Directive, Article 23. See Companies Act 1985 (as amended), ss.151–4, 155–8 (special rules applicable to private companies); French law of 24 July 1966 concerning commercial companies (as amended), Article 217–9; Article 71d AktG.

109 Article 23, ibid. See Companies Act 1985 (as amended), s.150; French law of 26 July 1966 concerning commercial companies (as amended), Article 217–9; Article 71d AktG.

110 Companies Act 1985 (as amended), section 136(2); French law of 24 July 1966 concerning commercial companies (as amended), Article 216; Article 229 AktG [*vereinfachte Kapitalherabsetzung*], governing a simplified reduction, in the event of which creditors are not entitled to security under Article 225, but other provisions exist for their protection).

111 See Companies Act 1985 (as amended), s.125(2)(a) and (b) and (3); it appears likely that the existence of Article 31 will not prevent British courts from continuing to take a narrow view of class rights. Separate class meetings are held in practice in France, but there does not seem to be any statutory rule requiring such meetings, as there is in Germany: see Articles 222(2), 229(1) and 237 AktG.

112 See Article 229(1) of the German *Aktiengesetz*.

113 Articles 237ff. AktG.

114 *Hopkinson v. Mortimer, Harley & Co.* [1917] 1Ch. 646.

115 Now see ss.159–61 of the Companies Act 1985 (as amended); note also the complex rules contained in ss.171–7 of that Act concerning the power of private companies to redeem or purchase their shares out of capital, whose enactment was not required by the Directive but which have often proved useful to private companies despite their complexity.

116 Note also Article 53a AktG, which provides that shareholders are to be treated equally where the same conditions are present.

117 BGBl.1 1959. Germany was the only Member State to implement the Directive on time, but the Act did not come into force until July 1979. The implementing rules for Northern Ireland are in the Companies (Northern Ireland) Order 1986, S.I. 1986 No. 1032 (N.I. 6).

118 For defects in the implementation of the Second Directive in Great Britain, see Sealy, op. cit., pp. 81–2.

119 Journal Officiel de la République Française of 31 December 1981, 3593.

120 Lovtidende A 1982, p. 649.

121 Memorial A no. 35, 16 May 1983, 864.

122 Moniteur Belge/Belgische Staatsblad of 12 December 1984.

123 Gazette Ufficiale de 18 Febbraio 1986, no. 40.

124 Greek Official Journal, FEK 191A of 28 November 1986.

CHAPTER 3: MERGERS AND DIVISIONS

1 OJ No. C89 of 14 July 1970, p. 20.

2 See COM(72) 1668 Final, dated 4 January 1973, and note also Bulletin EC Supplement 5/1970. The final version of the Directive is in OJ No. L295, 20 October 1978, p. 36.

3 OJ No. L378 of 31 December 1982, p. 47.

4 The types of merger envisaged by the Directive appear to have been unknown in the Netherlands at the time of its enactment; there was certainly no legislation regulating them. However, such legislation was introduced in 1983, after the enactment of the Directive: see Staatsblad no. 59, 1983.

5 There does not appear to be a great deal of literature on the Directive: note, however, F. Wooldridge, 'The Third Directive and the Meaning of Mergers', 1Co Law (1980) 75, and F. Barbaso, 'The Harmonization of Company Law with regard to Mergers and Divisions', JBL (1984) 176.

6 Ibid., Article 3(1).

7 Ibid., Article 4(1).

8 Ibid., Article 24. The three above-mentioned types of operation are provided for in section 427A(2) and Schedule 15A, para. 12 of the Companies Act 1985, which are incorporated therein by The Companies Mergers and Divisions Regulations 1987, S.I. No. 1991. The confirmation of the court remains necessary with regard to all these types of operations. See Companies Act 1985, s.425.

The new rules governing these operations contained in the Companies Act 1985 (as amended) remain applicable where the transferee company is a N. Ireland company: see Companies Act 1985 (as amended), s.427A(6)–(8). The transferor company must, however, be registered in Great Britain: see Companies Act 1985 (as amended), s.427A(8). Note also the French law governing commercial companies of 24 July 1966, as amended by Law No. 88–17 of 5 January 1988, Articles 371 and 375; and see also Article 339 and 352(b)(2) of the German *Aktiengesetz* as amended by the Law of 25 October 1982, BGBl.1.1425. The British Regulations of 1987 appears generally to follow the provisions of the Directive closely. However, both the German legislation of 1982 and the French legislation of 1988 contain a number of provisions governing mergers not involving public companies, which are not required by the Directive. The French legislation does not seem to implement Article 24.

9 The limitation on the amount of the cash payment occurs under French law (law governing commercial companies of 24 July 1966, as amended, Article 371), but not under German or English law.

10 For a brief account of the minor differences, see Wooldridge, op. cit., 1Co. Law (1980) 75, 78.

11 Third Directive, Articles 5, 10, 23. The minimum contents of the draft merger terms are specified by Article 5(2). See Companies Act 1985 (as amended), Sch. 15A, paras 2–4; French law governing commercial companies of 24 July 1966 (as amended), Article 374; and Articles 340 and 340a AktG.

12 Ibid., Articles 6, 23. See Companies Act 1985, Sch. 15A, para. 2(1)(b) and (c); French law governing commercial companies of 24 July 1966 (as amended), Article 374; French decree of 23 March 1967 (as amended), Article 254; Article 340d AktG.

13 Ibid., Articles 10 and 23. See Companies Act 1985 (as amended), Sch. 15A, para. 5; French law governing commercial companies of 24 July 1966, as amended, Article 377; Article 340b AktG. It should be noted that Article 10 does not specifically provide that the expert must be an accountancy firm or an industrial accountant. However, English law (Companies Act 1985 [as amended], Sch. 15A, para. 5(3)) adopts the view that the expert must be a person qualified to be an auditor. This approach is not specifically adopted under French and German law, but it appears that accountants assume the relevant function in those countries as well.

14 Articles 7, 8 and 23, ibid. See Companies Act 1985 (as amended), s.425(2) and Sch. 15A, para 1, 10(1), 12(4), 14(1). French law of 24 July 1966 governing commercial companies (as amended), Article 376; Article 340C AktG. All these enactments require separate class meetings, where relevant.

15 Article 7(1).

16 See also Article 23, which applies the same principles to mergers by the formation of a new company, Directive 77/187/EEC is set out in OJ 1977 L61/26.

17 Note, for example, Transfer of Undertakings (Protection of Employment) Regulations 1981, S.I. 1981 No. 1794; French Labour Code, Article L 122–12–1; German Civil Code, Article 613a.

18 Companies Act 1985 (as amended), section 425(1) and (2). The provisions of Article 381(2) of the French law of 24 July 1966 concerning

commercial companies (as amended) appears to reflect the requirements of the Directive more exactly; the same may be said for Article 347(1) of the German *Aktiengesetz*.

19 Under the Companies Act 1985 (as amended), section 425(1) and (2), a general meeting of the debenture-holders of the companies will be required. The position is the same under Article 380 of the French law of 1966, except where bondholders are offered redemption on simple request. In Germany, the provisions of Article 347(1) of the *Aktiengesetz* remain applicable.

20 The approval of class meetings of such holders of securities given by a three-quarters majority and the confirmation of the court are required under section 425 of the Companies Act 1985. Article 380 of the French law of 24 July 1966 concerning commercial companies (as amended) provides for repurchase on demand. Article 347a of the German *Aktiengesetz* places its emphasis on the grant of equivalent rights.

21 Ibid., Article 18.

22 No such rules have been made applicable in Great Britain, where the matter remains governed by the ordinary law. The position should be contrasted with that which obtains under Articles 349–51 AktG (as amended), which provide for the liability of the members of the managing and supervisory boards of the transferor and acquiring companies, and the institutions of actions for damages against members of the boards: see Wooldridge, 4Co.Law (1983), 232–4.

23 For a full account of these exceptions, see Wooldridge, op. cit., 1Co.Law (1980), 75, 78–9.

24 Under the Companies Act 1985 (as amended), this is fixed in the order sanctioning the compromise or arrangement or any subsequent order under section 427: Companies Act 1985 (as amended), Sch. 15A, para. 9(2). For the position in France, see Articles 372–1 and 372–2 of the law of 24 July 1966 concerning commercial companies (as amended). For that in Germany, see Articles 346(3) and (4) AktG.

25 Companies Act 1985 (as amended), Sch. 15A, para. 9(2). The court order is that sanctioning the compromise or arrangement or a subsequent one under section 427.

26 See French law of 14 July 1966 concerning commercial companies (as amended), Article 372–1; and Article 346(3) and (4) of the German *Aktiengesetz*.

27 Ibid., Article 32(1).

28 Law of 25 October 1982, BGBl.1.1425.

29 Law no. 282 of 9 June 1982, Lovtidende A 1982, 649.

30 Law of 19 January 1983, Staatsblad no. 59, 1983. The Dutch legislation also applies to mergers in which private companies [*besloten venootschappen*] are concerned.

31 Decree Law no. 262/86 of 2 September 1986.

Company Law in the UK and the EC

32 Presidential Decree no. 498/87, modifying law no. 2190/1920, JO 236 of 31 December 1987.

33 The Companies (Mergers and Divisions) Regulations 1987, S.I. No. 1991 of 1987. These Regulations amended the Companies Act 1985, and added a new Schedule 15A thereto. As already indicated, they may be applicable where any of the transferee companies is a Northern Irish company. The implementing rules for N. Ireland are contained in Companies Mergers and Division Regulations 1987, S.I. 1987 No. 442.

34 Law no. 10–17 of 5 January 1988, JO of 6 January 1988, 227. Decree No. 88–418 of 22 April 1988.

35 Law of 7 September 1987, Memorial A–77 of 15 September 1987, 1792.

36 Statutory Instrument No. 137 of 1987, Official Gazette, p. 829, 29 May 1987.

37 See Law 19/1989 of 25 July 1989, Boletín Oficial del Estado, 27 July 1989 and Decree Law 1564/1989 of 22 December 1989, Boletín Official del Estado, 27 December 1989.

38 Note in this sense J. Welch. 'Tenth Draft Directive on cross-border mergers', Co. Law (1986), 69–70.

39 OJ L378/47, 1982.

40 Sixth Directive, Articles 1(1) and 1(2). This is not the case in Germany, Denmark and the Netherlands and, as already pointed out, for this reason these countries were not required to implement the Sixth Directive. Divisions are possible in Great Britain under what is now section 425 of the Companies Act 1985: the term is not commonly used in Great Britain and is, in fact, derived from the term 'scission' used in France. The new rules contained in the Companies Act 1985 (as amended), governing division of public companies, remain applicable where any of the transferee companies is a Northern Irish company: see Ibid., section 427(6)–(8).

41 See Articles 2, 17(1)(a)–(c), 21 and 22 of the Sixth Directive; and note also the commentary on the Directive by Professor C.M. Schmitthoff in Encyclopedia of European Community Law, Sweet & Maxwell/Green, Parts C3–208 and 209.

42 Ibid., Article 24. The 10 per cent limitation does not occur under British law; see Companies Act 1985 (as amended), section 427A(2), case 3, and contrast French law governing commercial companies of 24 July 1966 (as amended), Article 371.

43 Ibid., Article 25.

44 Articles 3, 4, 7, 9 and 22, ibid. Compare Articles 5, 6, 9, 11 and 24 of the Third Directive. Note also the provisions of the Companies Act 1985, Sch. 15A, paras 2, 3, 5 and 6 (apart from para. 2(3) these are applicable to

mergers as well as to divisions) and the French law of 24 July 1966, governing commercial companies (as amended), Articles 374 and 376, and the French Decree no. 67–236 (as amended), Articles 255, 256 and 306–2.

45 Articles 8 and 22, ibid. See Companies Act 1985 (as amended), Sch. 15A, para. 5(1), and note also Articles 376 and 377 of the French law governing commercial companies of 24 July 1966, as amended. The first-mentioned provision takes advantage of the exemption for new companies contained in Article 22(5) of the Sixth Directive.

46 Articles 5 and 22, ibid. Note also the exceptions contained in Articles 6, 20 and 22(3). Compare Articles 7 and 23 and Articles 8 and 25 of the Mergers Directive. See Companies Act 1985 (as amended), s.425(2) and Sch. 15A, paras 1, 10(1) 13 and 14(2); also French law of 24 July 1966 governing commercial companies (as amended), Article 383(3).

47 Compare Articles 19 and 23 of the Third Directive. As in the case of mergers, a court order remains necessary for this to happen in Great Britain; see Companies Act 1985 (as amended), Sch. 15A para. 9. No such order is necessary in France; see law of 24 July 1966 concerning commercial companies (as amended), Articles 372–1 and 372–2.

48 Article 23, ibid.

49 The court is empowered to exclude inspection entirely in respect of any transferor company or pre-existing transferee company under para. 11(3) of Sch. 15A to the Companies Act 1985. It is not clear whether this power conforms with the requirements of the Sixth Directive.

50 Article 12(6) and 22, ibid.

51 Article 12(3) and 22, ibid. See Companies Act 1985 (as amended), Sch. 15A, para. 15, which adopts the rules stated in the above sentence and its precursor; see also French law of 24 July 1986 governing commercial companies (as amended), Articles 385, 386.

52 See Goldman Report on the Draft Convention on the international merger of public companies, Bulletin EC, Supplement 13/73, 32–4. The draft Tenth Directive may be found in OJ No. C23, 25 January 1985, p. 11.

53 See J. Welch, op. cit., 7 Co. Law (1986), 70 for a criticism of this provision.

54 COM(88) 823 Final-SYN 186, Brussels 16 Feb. 1989. A revised proposal may be anticipated in the near future: this is likely to be based to a large extent on the opinion given by the European Parliament in January 1990 on the 1989 proposal.

CHAPTER 4: THE FOURTH AND SEVENTH DIRECTIVES

1 OJ No. C7, 38 January 1972, p. 11; see also Supplement 7/71 to Bulletin EC.

2 Supplement 6/74 to Bulletin EC.

3 OJ No. L22, 14 August 1978, p. 11. The provisions of Articles 56–9 and 61 of the Fourth Directive were amended by Articles 42 and 46 of the Seventh Directive, OJ No. L193, 13 June 1983, p. 31.

4 In Great Britain it applies to public and private companies limited by shares and by guarantee, but not to banks and insurance companies. It follows from the provisions of s.745(1) of the Companies Act 1985 that the provisions of that Act relating to individual company accounts do not apply to N. Ireland.

5 Article 1(2), ibid. Now see Council Directive of 8 December 1986 (86/635/EEC) on the annual accounts and consolidated accounts on banks and other financial institutions, OJ L372/1, 31 Dec. 1986. No such Directive has yet been adopted in the field of insurance.

6 Articles 2(3)–2(5), ibid.

7 There are two formats for the balance sheet (horizontal and vertical) and four for the profit and loss account (also horizontal and vertical): see Articles 9 and 10 and 23–6, ibid.

8 See Articles 31–42, ibid.

9 See R. Pennington, *Company Law*, 5th edn, Butterworths 1985, p. 770.

10 Note, for example, Ernst and Whinney, *The Fourth Directive*, Kluwer Publishing, London 1980; T. Watts, *Handbook on the Fourth Directive*, Institute of Chartered Accountants, 1979; C.W. Nobes, 'The Harmonization of Company Law', 4 European Law Review 1980, 38; K. van Hulle, 'The EEC Accounting Directives in Perspective: Problems of Harmonization', 18CML Rev. 1981, 121; F. Wooldridge, 'The Fourth Directive on Accounts', Lloyd's Maritime and Commercial Law Quarterly 1980, 27.

11 For a detailed account of this matter, see the Commission's Report on the Implementation of the Fourth Directive of 1987. The provisions of the Fourth Directive generally apply to civil companies, partnerships, and all individuals and persons carrying on a commercial activity, as well as to commercial companies, in France. Germany has extended only certain provisions of the Directive to all companies, and individuals carrying on a commercial activity.

12 See Com(88) 292 Final-SYN 158, Brussels 14 Oct. 1988.

13 Note in this sense C.M. Schmitthoff in *Encyclopedia of European Community Law*, Sweet & Maxwell and Green, Part. C3–117.

14 OJ L314/28, 1984.

15 See Companies Act 1989, section 13(1), which inserts a new section

247(3) into the Companies Act 1985; French Commercial Code (as amended), Article 10(3) and French Decree no. 83–1020 (as amended), Articles 17 and 18; German Commercial Code (as amended), Article 267(1). By section 215(1) thereof, the relevant provisions of the Companies Act 1989 concerning individual company accounts and consolidated accounts come into force on such date as the Secretary of State may appoint by order made by Statutory Instrument.

16 See Companies Act 1989, section 13(1), which inserts a new section 247(3) into the Companies Act 1985, and French Decree no. 83–1020 of 29 December 1983 (as amended), articles 17 and 18. Note also German Commercial Code (as amended), Article 267(2). Articles 264–339 of this Commercial Code (as amended) apply only to capital companies, i.e. public and private limited companies and partnerships limited by shares.

17 Article 12, ibid. See Companies Act 1989, section 13(3), which inserts a new section 249(1) into the Companies Act 1985 and the provisions of Article 10(3) of the French Commercial Code (as amended), as well as those of Article 267(4) of the German Commercial Code (as amended).

18 The exception for financial holding companies was made at the request of Luxembourg.

19 Parent and subsidiary undertakings are defined in the Seventh, but not in the Fourth Directive. Affiliated undertakings are defined for the purposes of both instruments in Article 41 of the Seventh Directive as undertakings which are connected as described in Article 1(1)(a), 1(1)(b) and 1(1)(d)(bb) of that Directive and those other undertakings which are similarly connected with other of the affiliated undertakings. Participating interests are defined in Article 17 of the Fourth Directive. Interests in the capital of another company in excess of 20 per cent are aleays presumed to be such interests.

20 Article 46. See Companies Act 1985 (as amended by Companies Act 1989), section 234(1) and Sch. 7; French law governing commercial companies of 24 July 1966 (as amended), Article 340; German Commercial Code (as amended), Article 289 and German *Aktiengesetz* of 1965 (as amended), Article 160, and German GmbH *Gesetz* (as amended), Article 42a(1).

21 The qualifications of auditors are dealt with in the Eighth Directive, which is discussed in the next chapter.

22 The Federal Republic has taken advantage of this exemption: see German Commercial Code (as amended), Article 316(1); France has also done so in relation to small private companies: see law of 24 July 1966 governing commercial companies (as amended), Articles 17–1 and 64, and Decree no. 67–236 of 23 March 1967 (as amended), Articles 12 and 43.

23 Articles 8 and 22, ibid. The Companies Act 1985 (as amended), Sch. 4, para. 1(1) prescribes two alternative formats for a balance sheet, on

four alternative formats for a profit and loss account. French law prescribes a horizontal format for the balance sheet, and the vertical or horizontal format based upon the presentation of charges according to the type of expenditure for the profit and loss account. German public and private limited companies are required by Article 266 of the Commercial Code (as amended) to use the horizontal layout (or double-columnar) form for their balance sheet. However, it follows from Article 275 of the Commercial Code that they may use the two forms of vertical layout prescribed by the Directive for their profit and loss account.

24 It has been proposed that the exemptions granted in favour of small companies should be made mandatory. This approach is adopted in Articles 4–6, 8 and 10–12 of the proposed amending Directive of 14 October 1988, but may not be adopted in the Finalised Directive.

25 Companies Act 1989, section 13(1), which inserts a new section 247(3) into the Companies Act 1985.

26 See Companies Act 1989, section 13(1), which inserts a new section 247(3) into the Companies act 1985.

27 See Companies Act 1989, section 13(1), which inserts a new section 246(1) into the Companies Act 1985, and substitutes Schedule 6 to the former Act for the old Schedule 8 to the 1985 Act. The relevant provisions of Schedule 6 are paras 1–4.

28 Decree no. 67–236 of 23 March 1967 (as amended), Articles 293 and 293–1; Decree no. 83–1020 of 29 November 1983 (as amended), Articles 17 and 18.

29 Decree no. 67–236 of 23 March 1967 (as amended), Articles 293 and 293–1; Decree no. 83–1020 of 29 November 1983 (as amended), Article 26.

30 Commercial Code (as amended), Article 10(3).

31 Commercial Code (as amended), Article 266(1).

32 Ibid., Article 276.

33 Ibid., Article 288.

34 Ibid., Article 326.

35 Ibid., Article 276.

36 Ibid., Article 327.

37 For the present requirement of a true and fair view in Great Britain, see section 226(2)–(5) of the Companies Act 1985, which was incorporated therein by Section 4(1) of the Companies Act 1989.

38 For the implementation of the requirements of Articles 2(3)–(5) of the Directive in France and Germany, see Articles 9(5)–(7) of the French Commercial Code (as amended); and Article 264(2) of the German Commercial code (as amended). French business accounts are required to be *réguliers et sincères* (i.e. to follow accepted accounting principles), and to give a true and fair view. The same principles are applicable to consolidated accounts: see law of 24 July 1966 governing commercial companies (as amended), Article 357–6.

39 See Companies Act 1985 (as amended), Sch. 4, para. 4; French Commercial Code (as amended), Article 11; and German Commercial Code (as amended), Article 265(2).

40 See Companies Act 1985 (as amended), Sch. 4, para. 2; French Commercial Code (as amended), Article 11; German Commercial Code (as amended), Article 284(2) no. 3.

41 See Companies Act 1985 (as amended), Sch. 4, para. 1, where this principle is implicit; see also French Commercial Code (as amended), Article 13; and German Commercial Code (as amended), Article 246(2).

42 See the dictum of Swinfen Eady L.J. in *Ammonia Soda Co v. Chamberlain* [1918] 1 Ch. 266, 286–7; and Pennington, *Company Law*, 4th edn, Butterworths 1979, p. 363.

43 Note also, in the same sense, French Commercial Code (as amended), Article 14(2); German Commercial Code (as amended), Article 253(2).

44 Note, also in the same sense, French Commercial Code (as amended), Article 15; the same principle is not so clearly enshrined in the provisions of the German Commercial Code (as amended).

45 See Companies Act 1985, Sch. 4, paras 10–12 (as amended by Sch. 1, para. 5, to the Companies Act 1989); French Commercial Code (as amended), Articles 11 and 14(1); German Commercial Code (as amended), Article 252(1) nos 2, 4, 6.

46 Companies Act 1985 (as amended), Sch. 4, paras 17 and 42(3). Note also French Commercial Code (as amended), Article 14(2), and French Decree no. 83–1020 of 29 November 1983, Article 8; German Commercial Code (as amended), 253(2). The French provisions are quite similar to the British ones.

47 Articles 37(1) and 34(1), ibid.

48 Article 37(2), ibid. All Member States, other than Greece and Portugal, permit goodwill to be amortized over a period exceeding five years, subject to the above mentioned qualifications: see Commission's Report on the implementation of the Fourth Directive, 17.

49 See Pennington, *Company Law*, 5th edn, Butterworths 1985, p. 772. Note also French Decree no. 83–1020 of 29 November 1983 (as amended), Article 19, which provides that expenses incurred in the course of operations determining the existence or development of the enterprise, but whose amount is not referable to the production of goods or services, must figure in the assets shown in the balance sheet. The costs of applied research and development in respect of particular projects may be written off over a longer period, but this must be justified in the notes on the accounts.

50 Companies Act 1985 (as amended), Sch. 4, para. 21.

51 See the Companies Act 1989, Sch. 1, para. 6, which amends paragraph 34 of Sch. 4 to the Companies Act 1985 by inserting a new

clause (3A) therein limiting the circumstances in which the revaluation reserve can be reduced. It was formerly used to write off goodwill by some United Kingdom companies. See the DTI's letter of 5 July 1988, 'Accounting for Mergers and Acquisitions and the Write-Off of Goodwill, p. 7, in this sense.

52 For a detailed account of these provisions, see Pennington, *Company Law*, Butterworths 1985, pp. 773–4. See also the letter mentioned in note 51.

53 Reference should be made to Article 12(4) of the French Commercial Code (as amended), which (like the Companies Act 1985 (as amended), Sch. 4, para. 34) provides for the constitution of a revaluation reserve in appropriate circumstances; and to Article 24 of Decree no. 83–1020 (as amended), which (like Sch. 4, para. 33) requires the corresponding figures on a historic cost basis to be given in the notes on the accounts.

54 S.I. 1986 No. 1032 (N.I. 6).

55 Lovtidende A (1981) 727.

56 Lovtidende A (1981) 742.

57 Moniteur Belge, 8 July 1983.

58 Moniteur Belge, 12 December 1983.

59 The two decrees were: the decree made in application of the law of 17 July 1975 governing accounting procedures and the annual accounts of enterprises, Moniteur Belge 28 September 1983; and the decree amending the law of 17 July 1975 of 16 January 1986, Moniteur Belge 28 January 1986.

60 For these amendments, which all date from 12 September 1983 and were made applicable to the decree amending the decree of 8 October 1976 on the annual accounts of enterprises, and to the decree made in application of the law of 17 July 1975 on accounting procedures and the annual accounts; and to the decree amending the decree of 8 October 1976 on the annual accounts of enterprises see Moniteur Belge 15 October 1983, and Moniteur Belge 3 December 1983. The latter issue contains particulars of the two last-mentioned amendments.

61 Staatsblad van het Koninkrijk der Nederlanden 1983, 663.

62 Ibid., 665.

63 Ibid., 666.

64 JO 3 May 1983, 1335.

65 JO 1 December 1983, 3441.

66 JO 43/55 of 7 May 1982. The revised *plan* is, of course, based on the requirements of the Fourth Directive. See F. Choi and G. Mueller, *International Accounting*, Prentice-Hall Inc., New Jersey 1984, pp. 81–2, for a brief description of the new national chart of accounts.

67 Memorial A no. 40 of 10 May 1984.

68 BGBl. 1.2355 (1985). This statute incorporated a number of new

provisions into the Commercial Code and has also made a number of amendments to other laws, including those applicable to public and private companies of 1965 and 1982, respectively.

69 See the Presidential Decree no. 409/86, Greek Official Journal, FEK 191A of 28 November 1986, and Presidential Decree no. 419/86, Greek Official Journal, FEK 197A of 10 December.

70 Diario da Republica, 1 Serie no. 268 of 21 November 1989.

71 Boletín Oficial del Estado, 27 July 1989; see also Decree Law 1.564/1989 of 22 December 1989, Boletín Oficial del Estado, 27 December 1989.

72 [1983] OJ L193. A very abundant literature exists concerning this Directive. Note in particular T. Cook, 'The Seventh Directive: An Accountant's Perspective', 9ELR (1984) 143; M. Petite, 'The Conditions For Consolidation under the Seventh Company Law Directive', 21CMLR (1984) 81; R. Pennington, 'Consolidated Accounts: The Seventh Directive' 5Co. Law (1984) 66; S. McKinnon (ed.), *Consolidated Accounts: The Seventh Directive*, Kluwer Publishing Limited 1984; and F. Wooldridge, 'The EEC Council Seventh Directive on Consolidated Accounts', 37ICLQ (1988) 714. See also the DTI's Consultative Paper on the Implementation of the Seventh Company Law Directive on Consolidated Accounts of August 1985.

73 [1976] OJC 121/2.

74 Note in this sense Article 294 of the German Commercial Code (as amended).

75 See law no. 85–705 of 12 July 1985 and Decree no. 86–221 of 17 February 1986.

76 Law governing commercial companies of 24 July 1966 (as amended), Article 357–1.

77 See Introductory Law to the Commercial Code (as amended by the law of 24 December 1985), Article 23(2). The provisions of this law relating to individual accounts came into force at an earlier date: see Article 23(1) of the Introductory Law (as amended).

78 The Seventh Directive has been implemented without making very extensive changes to the Companies Act 1985. Many of the necessary changes had already been made before this Act was passed; see Wooldridge, op. cit., 37ICLQ (1988) 714, 716. However, additional changes were made by the Companies Act 1989. The provisions of these two Acts concerning consolidated accounts and auditors are not applicable to N. Ireland. The provisions of the 1989 Act concerning the latter matters may, however, be made so applicable by Order in Council: see Companies Act 1989, s.214.

79 Article 1(1)(a) and (b), ibid.

80 For a detailed account of these provisions, see Memorandum of the Law Society's Standing Committee on Company Law on Consolidated Accounts of February 1986, pp. 3–4; see also Wooldridge, op. cit.,

37ICLQ (1988) 714, 719; Companies Act 1985 (as amended), s.258(3) and Sch. 10A (Sch. 9 of Companies Act 1985).
  81 See Companies Act 1985 (as amended), ss.258(2)(a), (b), (c) and (d) and (4). Note also the letter of the Department of Trade and Industry of 16 August 1988 entitled 'Implementation of the EC Seventh Company Law Directive: Subsidiaries and Controlled Non-Subsidiaries' in this sense.
  82 Note in the present context D. Tweedie and J. Kellas, 'Off-Balance Sheet Accounting', Accountancy, April 1987, 91. See also the Memorandum of the Law Society's Standing Committee on Company Law, 'Implementation of the EEC Seventh Company Law Directive on Consolidated Accounts: Definition of a Subsidiary', February 1988.
  83 See Section 21(1) and Schedule 9, and section 144 of the Companies Act 1989, which provide for the definition of a subsidiary for the purposes of consolidation and for other purposes respectively. The latter section amends section 736 of the Companies Act 1985.
  84 See Article 357–1 of the law of 24 July 1966 governing commercial companies (as amended). In France, consolidated accounts must be prepared where the parent undertaking is a partnership, limited partnership, or partnership limited by shares, as well as where it is a public or private limited company.
  85 See Commercial Code (as amended), Article 290.
  86 It will be remembered that the threshold for balance sheet totals and turnover contained in the Fourth Directive were revised by Council Directive 84/569 of 27 November 1984 [1984] OJ L314/28.
  87 Seventh Directive, Article 7(1)(a) and (b). See also Companies Act 1985 (as amended), section 228(1)(a) and (b), which were incorporated therein by Section 5(3) of the Companies Act 1989. Section 228(1)(b) would seem to be based upon Article 8(1) of the Seventh Directive.
  88 Article 7(2), ibid.
  89 This committee is the same as the Contact Committee provided for under Article 52 of the Fourth Directive, and is concerned with practical problems which arise in the application of these instruments.
  90 The relevant provision of this decree is Article 1, which incorporates Article 248–13 into Directive No. 67–236 of 23 March 1967.
  91 See the law governing commercial companies of 24 July 1966 (as amended), Article 357–4.
  92 See the new forms of Articles 294–296 of the Commercial Code, which were incorporated therein by the law of 19 December 1985.
  93 Seventh Directive, Article 16(1). See French law governing commercial companies of 24 July 1966 (as amended), Article 357–5; German Commercial Code (as amended), Articles 290 and 313.
  94 Seventh Directive, Article 16(3). The true and fair requirement already existed under British law before the enactment of the Companies

Act 1989, section 5(1) of which incorporated section 227(3)–(5), which contain relevant provisions concerning it, into the Companies Act 1985. For the position under French law, see law governing commercial companies of 24 July 1966 (as amended), Article 357–6; for that in Germany, see Article 297(2) of the Commercial Code (as amended).

95 Article 16(4), ibid. See Companies Act 1985 (as amended), section 227(4); French Commercial Code (as amended), Article 9(6); German Commercial Code (as amended), Article 297(2).

96 Article 16(5), ibid. See Companies Act 1985 (as amended), section 227(5); French Commercial Code (as amended), Article 9(7).

97 Note in this sense the Department of Trade and Industry's letter of 6 August 1988 on Subsidiaries and Controlled Non-Subsidiaries, pp. 4–5.

98 Article 17, ibid. See Companies Act 1985 (as amended), section 227(1) and Sch. 4A, para. 1.

99 Article 29, ibid.

100 Articles 16(3) and 26(1), ibid.

101 Article 18, ibid.

102 Article 22, ibid.

103 By Articles 21 and 23 of the Directive, the interests of any minority shareholders in a subsidiary must be shown as a separate item in consolidated accounts.

104 The Department of Trade and Industry proposed more extensive disclosure requirements in relation both to acquisition and merger accounting: see the letter of 5 July 1988 on accounting for mergers and acquisitions and the write-off of goodwill already mentioned, at pages 4–6. These proposals resulted in the enactment of paras 12 and 13 of Schedule 4A to the Companies Act 1985, which were incorporated therein by Sch. 2 of the Companies Act 1989.

105 The corresponding provisions of French law seem less precise and detailed: see law of 24 July 1966 governing commercial companies (as amended), Article 357–3, and Decree no. 67–236 of 23 March 1966 (as amended), Article 248.

106 These are similar to, but not identical with, those of the Companies Act 1985 (as amended), s.131, and SSAP 23. See McKinnon, op. cit., pp. 78–82, for a clear account of merger or pooling of interests accounting, which is used both by the UK and the USA, but not to any significant extent by any continental country. This system of accounting has led to some unfortunate abuses in recent years.

107 Article 20(2), ibid.

108 Article 20(3).

109 See Consultative Document, pp. 19–20 and Pennington, op. cit., pp. 73–4. In pages 3–4 of the letter sent on 5 July 1988, which has already been mentioned, the DTI concluded that Article 20 should be implemented with one minor variation, and that it would be possible for

accounting standards to set conditions over and above those specified in the Directive and the implementing legislation. See Companies Act 1985 (as amended), Sch. 4A, paras 10 and 11, which implement the requirements of the Directive, perhaps not in an entirely satisfactory manner.

110 These are matters of accounting practice, and it has not been found necessary to make detailed provision for them in British legislation: see Companies Act 1985 (as amended), Sch. 4A, paras 20–22.

111 By Article 17 of the Fourth Directive, the holding of part of the capital of another company is presumed to constitute a participating interest where it exceeds a percentage fixed by the Member States which may not exceed 20 per cent.

112 This is the *mise en équivalence* method utilized in France. See Articles 248–1 and 248–2 of Decree no. 67–236 of 23 March 1966 (as amended). In accordance with what was proposed in the Consultative Document, p. 27, this method has not been prescribed for Great Britain.

113 See Pennington, op. cit., p. 75; and McKinnon, op. cit., pp. 82–6.

114 See McKinnon, p. 86.

115 For a full treatment of the notes on the accounts, see Pennington, op. cit., p. 76; McKinnon, op. cit., pp. 96–9. See also Consultative Document, pp. 29–30. Note in addition French law governing commercial companies of 1966 (as amended), Articles 357–4, 357–8 and 357–9, and French Decree no. 86–221 of 17 February 1986, Article 1 of which incorporates new Articles 248–2, 248–3, 248–6, 248–8 and 248–12 in Decree 67–236 of 23 March 1967, which contain detailed rules governing the contents of the notes to the accounts. In Germany, such rules are contained in Article 313 of the Commercial Code (as amended).

116 For the French requirements relating to the directors' report, see law governing commercial companies of 1966 (as amended), Article 357–10; for the German ones which will come into force as of 1 January 1990, see Article 315 of the Commercial Code, which was incorporated therein by the law of 19 December 1985.

117 Seventh Directive, Article 37. Auditors' qualifications will be covered by Council Directive 84/253 of 10 April 1984 on the approval of auditors [1984] OJ L126/20, when this comes into force in the Member States. Article 30 of this Directive (the so-called Eighth Company Law Directive) stipulates that Member States must make the necessary adjustments to their laws by 1 January 1988, and may provide that these adjustments shall not apply until 1 January 1990. The Eighth Directive and its implementation in Great Britain are discussed in the next chapter.

118 See Pennington, op. cit., p. 77.

119 For the French and German legislative provisions based on Article 38, see French Decree no. 86–221 of 17 February 1986, Articles 2–8, and the German Commercial Code (as amended by the law of 19 December 1985), Article 325.

120 See Pennington, op. cit., p. 77, for a fuller account of the publication requirements.

121 Implementing rules for Northern Ireland are contained in the Companies (Northern Ireland) Order 1990, S.I. 1990, no. 593 (N.I. 5).

122 Journal Officiel de la République Française (JORF) of 4 January 1985, p. 101.

123 JORF of 19 February 1986.

124 BGBl. 1.2355.

125 Decree no. 409/86, Greek Official Journal, FEFC 191A of 8 November 1986; Greek Official Journal, FEK 197A of 10 December 1986. Decree No. 419/86.

126 Memorial JO ANo 45 of 18 August 1988.

127 Staatsblad 517, 1988.

128 Moniteur Belge, 27 March 1990, 5675.

129 Boletín Oficial del Estado, 27 July 1989; Boletín Oficial del Estado, 27 December 1989.

130 OJC 144 of 11 June 1986.

131 See the Memorandum of the Law Society's Standing Committee on Company Law of December 1986 on the draft Directive in this sense.

132 See the Explanatory Memorandum on this instrument submitted by the Department of Trade and Industry on 25 November 1987 in this sense.

133 COM(88) 292 Final-SYN 158, Brussels, 14 October 1988; for the amended proposal, see COM(89)561 Final OJC 318/12, 20.12.1989.

134 Council Directive 86/635/EEC, OJL 372/1, 31 December 1986.

135 Article 2(1), ibid.

136 Council Directive 89/117/EEC, OJL 44/40, 16 February 1989.

137 Article 6(1), ibid.

138 Article 6(2), ibid.

139 Article 2, ibid.

140 Article 3, ibid.

141 Com(89) 474-Final.

142 OJL 228/3, 16 August 1973.

143 OJL 63/1, 13 March 1979.

144 Fourth Directive Article 1(2); Seventh Directive, Article 1(2).

CHAPTER 5: THE EIGHTH DIRECTIVE ON THE APPROVAL OF AUDITORS

1 OJ No. L112, 13 May 1978, p. 6.

2 OJ No. C317, 18 December 1979, p. 6.

3 OJ No. L126, 12 May 1984, p. 20. There do not appear to be a large number of articles on the Directive: see, however, P. Feuillet, *La*

Huitième Directive du Conseil des Communautés Européennes et le Commissariat aux Comptes, Revue des Sociétés (1984), 26.

4 Article 1, ibid.

5 Note in this sense Schmitthoff, in *Encyclopedia of European Community Law*, Sweet & Maxwell/Green, Part C3–280.

6 Article 30(1), ibid. The national legislation may provide that the implementing provisions do not come into force before 1 January 1990.

7 See the Department of Trade and Industry's Consultative Document, Regulation of Auditors: Implementation of the EC Eighth Company Law Directive, pub. 1986; DTI Press Notice of 10 December 1987, Regulation of Auditors: Implementation of the Eighth Directive; and TRs 650, 670 and 720, to all of which the Institute of Chartered Accountants of England and Wales was a party. The first of these Technical Releases is concerned with the implementation of the Eighth Directive; the second consists of a reply to the Consultative Document; and the third is concerned with independence and incorporation.

8 Council Directive 89/48/EEC of 21 December 1988; [1989] OJ L19/6. Implementation in the United Kingdom will take place in accordance with the provisions of s33 of the Companies Act 1989.

9 In Great Britain the right to practise as a statutory auditor will be subject to a person being a member of a recognized supervisory body, and to his or her being eligible under rules of that body for appointment as company auditor: Companies Act 1989, s.24. The Secretary of State For Trade and Industry will grant recognition of a supervisory body and of a professional qualification, and will also be empowered to revoke such grant: see Companies Act 1989, ss.30 (supervisory bodies), 32 (qualifying bodies and recognized professional qualifications), 39 (compliance order), 40 (directions to comply with international obligations) and Schedules 11 (recognition of supervisory body) and 12 (recognition of professional qualifications).

10 Member States may require that such persons should also be approved.

11 Member States are permitted to require the approval of such natural persons or firms of auditors.

12 Once again, Member States are permitted to provide for the approval of such natural persons or firms of auditors.

13 For the position in Germany, see Article 28 of the *Wirtschaftsprüferordnung* of 5 November 1975 (BGBl. 1.2803) as amended by the *Bilanzrichtliniengesetz* of 19 December 1985 (BGBl. 1.2355).

14 No such prohibition is introduced under the Companies Act 1989.

15 Article 5, ibid. For the entry requirements in Great Britain see Companies Act 1989, Sch. 12, para. 4.

16 Article 7, ibid. See Companies Act 1989, Sch. 12, para. 7(2).

17 Article 8, ibid. This period is for at least five years in Germany: see *Wirtschaftsprüferordung* (as amended), Article 8(1). It will be for three years in the United Kingdom: see Companies Act 1989, Sch. 12, para. 8(1).

18 Companies Act 1989, Sch. 12, para. 4(1) and para. 6(1) and (2).

19 The position will change when Directive 89/48/EEC on a General System for the Recognition of Higher Education Diplomas is implemented by the United Kingdom.

20 Article 12(1) has been implemented in Great Britain by Section 31(2) of the Companies Act 1989.

21 Companies Act 1989, Sch. 11, para. 7(1)–(3).

22 Note, in this sense, TR (Technical Release) 650, 20.

23 Note, for example, Companies Act 1985 (as amended), ss.385(2), 385A(2), 391(1) and (2) (appointment and removal is by the general meeting of shareholders); s.389A(1) (access of auditor at all times to books and vouchers of the company), s.389A(3) (auditors' power to obtain information regarding the company's subsidiaries); s.392A (resigning auditors' power to requisition an extraordinary general meeting); and s.394 (statement of persons ceasing to hold office as auditors). German law also contains a number of provisions designed to safeguard the independence of an auditor: note, for example, German Commercial Code (as amended by the law of 19 December 1985 1BGBl. 1.2355), paras 331(2) and (3).

24 Many of the old provisions contained in Chapter 5 of Part XI of this Act were replaced by new provisions incorporated therein by sections 119–23 of the Companies Act 1989. In addition, the 1989 Act contains certain provisions governing auditors which are relevant in the present connection and were not incorporated in the 1985 Act: one may instance ss.27–9 of that Act (ineligibility on the ground of lack of independence and its effects).

25 For the implementation of these provisions in Germany, see Article 38(1) of the *Wirtschaftsprüferordnung* (as amended by the law of 19 December 1985). Note also RT 650, 31, for a useful discussion of some of the problems concerning implementation in Great Britain which will take place in accordance with the provisions of ss.35 and 36 of the Companies Act 1989.

26 Except for the provisions of Part V, and certain other provisions which came into force on royal assent, s.215(2) of the Companies Act 1989 provides that the provisions of that Act came into force on such day as the Secretary of State may appoint by Statutory Instrument.

27 Memorial A81 of 23 August 1984.

28 Moniteur Belge of 28 February 1985.

29 BGBl., 1985, 1.2355.

30 Boletín Oficial del Estado (BOE) of 15 July 1988.

31 Greek Official Journal no. 5 of 5 January 1989, vol. A.

32 Decree 88–81 of January 1988 and Decree 88/60 of 22 January 1988. The earlier legislation comprised the law of 24 July 1966 governing commercial companies, Decree 69–810 of 12 August 1969 and Decree 81–536 of 12 May 1981.

33 See Commercial Code, Articles 446ff. and DRI no. 201 of 2 September 1986. See also Decreto Lei No. 519–L2/79 of 29 December 1989. 33A Note, for example, the Company Auditors [Examination] Regulations 1990 S.I. no. 1146.

34 These bodies are the Institute of Chartered Accountants in England and Wales: the Association of Certified Accountants; the Institute of Chartered Accountants in Scotland; and the Institute of Chartered Accountants in Ireland. Acts and omissions of such supervisory bodies are within the domain of public law and are subject to judicial review.

35 S.I. 1990, no. 593 (N.I.5).

CHAPTER 6: THE DRAFT FIFTH AND VREDELING DIRECTIVES

1 For the amended proposals see OJ No. C240 of 9 September 1983. A later text of the draft Directive appears in the Department of Trade and Industry's Consultative Document on the amended proposal of January 1990. This Document is largely concerned with the strictly company law provisions of the draft Directive, but unfortunately it betrays no evidence of a more positive attitude to employee participation. The Document gives some attention to barriers to take-overs. See also the Department of Trade and Industry's Consultative Document on Barriers to Take-overs of January 1990.

2 For the amended Vredeling proposal, see OJ No. C217/3 of 12 August 1983. The overlap is specially acute in relation to the provisions on employees' representatives, information and consultation and secret and confidential information.

3 For useful information with regard to the draft Fifth Directive, see the Commission's recent Memorandum on the European Company, COM(88) 320 Final, p. 24. See also Bull. EC Supp. 3/88.

4 COM(89) 248 Final, Brussels 30 May 1989. the Social Charter, which has no letal force, was adopted as a solemn declaration by eleven votes to one at the European Council meeting in December 1989. The Commission has proposed an action programme relating to the implementation of the Social Charter: see COM(89) 568 Final.

5 See OJC131/49 of 13 December 1972; Bull. EC Supplement 10/72.

6 Bull. EC Supplement 8/75 ('The Guertsen Report').

7 OJC 109/9, 19 September 1974.

8 OJC 149. 17, 14 June 1982.

9 OJC 240.2, 9 September 1983; Bull. EC Supplement 6/83.

10 Article 1(2), ibid.

11 See J. Pipkörn, 'Zur Entwicklung des Gesellschafts- und Unternehmensrechts', 136ZHR (1972), 499, 511ff. for the advocacy of this opinion.

12 See Daübler, 'The Employee Participation Directive' in *The Social Policy of the European Communities*, Sijthoff, Leyden 1977, pp. 83, 92, in this sense. Daübler's article contains a useful summary of the literature on the present question.

13 M. Lutter, *Europäisches Gesellschaftsrecht*, vol. 1, Walter de Gruyter, Berlin 1984, p. 40.

14 See Daübler, op. cit., p. 93, for a useful mention of the relevant literature.

15 A useful analysis of the amended draft Fifth Directive and the amended Vredeling draft Directive appears in Draft European Communities Fifth Directive on the Harmonization of Company Law. A Consultative Document, Department of Employment and Department of Trade and Industry, November 1983. The CBI published a useful paper on both instruments in February 1984 (L/75/84). A press information notice on both instruments was also published by the Institute of Directors on 27 February 1984. For other literature on the amended draft Fifth Directive, see C. Schmitthoff, [1983] JBL 456, 458 and [1984], JBL 100–02; J. Welch, 'The Fifth Directive: a False Dawn, ELR 1983, 83; F. Wooldridge, 'The Draft Fifth Directive' on the Harmonization of Company Law', 81 Law Society's Gazette 1984, 2783. See also J. Dine. 'The Draft Fifth EEC Directive on Company Law', 10 Co. Law (1989) 10 and 'Implications for the United Kingdom of the EC Fifth Directive', 38ICLQ (1989), 547.

16 Article 21a(1), ibid.

17 Article 21a(3), ibid.

18 Article 3(1) and 13(1) ibid. It should be noted that where employee participation took place otherwise than by the appointment of members of the supervisory board, or by means of objecting to the appointment of members of that board, Member States would be able to permit the memorandum of articles of association or instrument of incorporation of the company to provide that the general meeting should appoint and remove the members of the management board.

19 Article 12(1), ibid.

20 Article 12(3), ibid.

21 Article 21s, ibid.

22 Article 5(2).

23 This was contained in the old Article 3(2).

24 The need for such provision will be considered in conjunction with Article 48 of the draft Directive.

25 A subsidiary undertaking means a subsidiary undertaking for the purposes of relevant national legislation implementing Article 1 of the Seventh Directive on Group Accounts, Directive 83/349 EEC, OJ L193 1 of 18 July 1983. It should be remembered that for the purposes of the latter instrument, the concept for an undertaking is not limited to a limited company.

26 Article 63b, ibid.

27 Article 4b, ibid.

28 Article 4c, ibid. The provisions of Article 4c differ from the Dutch co-optation model in certain respects: thus the employees of the company, or its subsidiaries, or trade union officials connected with either, would not be ineligible for the supervisory board as in the Netherlands: see Dutch Civil Code, Part II, Art. 60 and J. Welch, op. cit., ELR 1983, 86.

29 Article 4d, ibid.

30 Article 4e, ibid. The restriction to the three models above may well be unfortunate.

31 Article 4h.

32 Articles 21b, 21d, 21d(a), 21e and 21f, ibid. See also 21i.

33 Articles 21b(2) and 21d, ibid.

34 Articles 4i and 21j ibid.

35 See J. Welch, op. cit., 87–8.

36 For different viewpoints see C. Schmitthoff, 'Employee Participation and the Theory of Enterprise', [1975] JBL; J.T. Lang, 'The Fifth Directive on the Harmonization of Company Law', (1975) CML Rev. 155, 345. The criticisms made of the two-tier system in the Watkinson Report, The Responsibilities of the British Public Company (CBI 1973, 37ff.), are not entirely convincing.

37 See Wooldridge, op. cit., Law Society's Gazette 1984, 2787.

38 Note in this sense, J. Welch, op. cit., 8 European Law Review 1983, 93. Article 21a(1)(b) provides that the number of executive members of the administrative organ shall be less than the number of the other members.

39 For a fuller account see J. Welch, op. cit., pp. 97–8.

40 See Articles 3(1)(b) and 13(1), and contrast Article 21t.

41 Note, for example, Articles 4(d)(2) and 12(1), ibid.

42 Article 14, ibid. The draft provision is concerned with all breaches of a director's duties, whether statutory, fiduciary or tortious.

43 Article 16, ibid. According to the latest draft, an action might be started if the holders of share of nominal value, or accounting per value, of 10 per cent of the subscribed capital so resolved. The United Kingdom government has argued that this right should be given only to minorities in

limited circumstances. For a critical account of the provisions of the draft Directive governing the liability of directors, see J. Dine, op. cit., 38ICLQ (1989), 556–8.

44 Article 31, ibid.

45 see Article 33, ibid. Certain exceptions to this provision exist.

46 Article 42, ibid. The earlier versions of this provision were criticized for their lack of clarity. The present one appears to be an improvement.

47 See J. Welch, op. cit., 97–8.

48 [1984] JBL 102.

49 OJC 297/3 of 15 November 1980; for the amended proposal, see OJC 217/3 of 12 August 1983. See also Council conclusions of 21 July 1986 on procedures for informing and consulting the employees of undertakings with complex structures, OJC 203/1 of 12 August 1986, where a rather sceptical approach towards the Vredeling proposals is manifested.

50 Note in this sense 37th Report of the House of Lords Select Committee on the European Communities on the proposed Directive of Session 1980–1. The Consultative Document published by the Department of Employment and the Department of Trade and Industry on the amended Vredeling proposal and on the revised draft Fifth Directive in 1983 contains a useful analysis of the former proposal.

51 For a critical analysis of Article 2(1), see the Memorandum of the Law Society's Standing Committee on Company Law of February 1984 on the amended proposal, p. 2.

52 Note in this sense Law Society's Memorandum of February 1984, pp. 9–10, where other defects of Article 2(2) are also discussed.

53 See Law Society's Memorandum of February 1984, p. 2, for some of these uncertainties.

54 For problems which arise in relation to Article 3, see Law Society's Memorandum, pp. 4–6, and Consultative Document of 1983, pp. 5–6.

55 See Law Society's Memorandum, pp. 6–8, 11–12; Consultative Document of 1982, pp. 6–7.

56 Article 4(2) gives five examples of decisions which may have serious consequences.

57 Note in this sense Law Society's Memorandum, p. 11; Consultative Document of 1983, p. 6.

58 See Law Society's Memorandum, pp. 10–12, in the present sense.

CHAPTER 7: MISCELLANEOUS DRAFT DIRECTIVES

1 OJL 348/62, 17 December 1988.

2 Note in the same sense, R. Buxbaum and K. J. Hopt, *Legal Harmonization and the Business Enterprise*, de Gruyter 1988, p. 256.

3 See Article 4, ibid. Article 7 treats as voting rights held by a person or entity voting rights held by nominees on his behalf, and voting rights held by an undertaking controlled by that person or entity. This provision also treats certain concert party arrangements in a similar way. Article 9 provides that an exception may be made from the requirement of declaration under Article 1 in respect of an acquisition or disposal by a professional dealer in Securities.

4 Article 3, ibid.

5 Article 16(1)(c), ibid.

6 Article 17(1), ibid.

7 British law is already stricter than the principal requirements of the Directive, and has become still more so with the enactment of the Companies Act 1989. Section 134 of this Act reduces the notifiable interest in shares from 5 per cent to 3 per cent of the nominal capital, and reduces the time for notification from 5 to 2 days.

8 For the amended proposal, see OJC 105/6, 21 April 1988. This proposal has already been subjected to minor amendments by two Council working parties. For the final version of the directive, see OJL 395/36, 30 December 1989.

9 See COM(88) 101 Final, Brussels, 18 May 1988. For the Commission proposal. For the final version of the directive, see OJL 395/40, 30 December 1989.

10 The most recent draft of the text was informally circulated in 1984, but no formal proposal for the Directive has yet been prepared.

11 A Consultative Document on the preliminary draft Directive was published by the Department of Trade and Industry in 1985. UNICE published a critical appraisal of an earlier version of the proposed Directive on 23 April 1981.

12 See section 4 (protection of a company subject to the influence of an undertaking), section 5 (the control contract instituting a vertical group) and section 6 (the unilateral declaration instituting a vertical group) of the proposed Directive.

13 See sections 5 and 6, ibid.

14 Article 9, ibid.

15 See J. Dine, 'The Eleventh Company Law Directive: a Protective Proposal', 133SJ 30, for a useful brief account of an early version of the proposed directive.

16 COM(86) 397 Final; OJ 1986 C203/12, 12 August 1986.

17 COM(88) 153 Final; OJ 1988 C105/6, 21 April 1988.

18 Article 14, ibid. the provisions of Articles 3 and 9, which govern the disclosure of accounting documents, are made inapplicable to branches opened by the former two categories of institutions. Further, Member States are not required to apply these provisions to branches opened by insurance companies.

19 See the discussion of this matter by J. Dine, op. cit., p. 30.

20 The rules and proposed rules governing disclosure in respect of branches of such companies have been discussed in an earlier chapter.

21 Note in particular Companies Act 1985, as amended, s.700; note also J. Dine, op. cit., p. 32: the required amendments will be made by secondary legislation, and no Consultative Document will be published.

22 These were discussed in some detail in Chapters 5 and 6 respectively.

23 The establishment of branches of foreign companies in Germany is largely governed by Article 44 of the *Aktiengesetz*. A branch of a foreign enterprise is required to keep within the Federal Republic complete accounting records complying with the requirements of the Commercial Code and of tax law. However, the publication of financial statements is not required.

24 see Gesetz zur Änderung des Gesetzes betreffend die Gesellschaften mit beschränkter Haftung und anderer handelsrechtlichen Vorschriften, BGBl. 1.836 (1980).

25 Danish Private Companies Act, No. 371 of 13 June 1973.

26 Law No. 85–697 of 11 July 1985, 26.

27 Law of 14 July 1987.

28 See law of 16 May 1986, which permitted the formation of single-member public and private limited liability companies.

29 Note, for example, the British Companies Act 1985, s.24.

30 COM(88) 101 Final.

31 OJ No. L395 of 30.12.1989, pp. 40–42.

32 Compare Article 11 of the Belgian law of 14 July 1987, which inserted a new provision, Article 136 *bis*, in the Co-ordinated Laws on Commercial Companies, which is in similar terms.

CHAPTER 8: SUPRANATIONAL INSTRUMENTS

1 See L. Lasok and J. Bridge, *Law and Institutions of the European Communities*, 4th edn, Butterworths 1987, p. 19.

2 No such instruments exist in the field of securities law at present. Article 100A, which was inserted in the EEC Treaty by the Single European Act and provides for the adoption of measures which have as their object the establishment or functioning of the commercial market, may also constitute a basis for the making of supranational harmonizing Regulations in the field of company and securities law by a qualified majority. However, Article 100A is limited by the fact that the Commission had to give an assurance that it would prefer Directives to Regulations if harmonization under Article 100A implied a change in the provisions of national law in one or more Member States.

3 Note, in this sense, R. Buxbaum and K.H. Hopt, *Legal Harmonization and the Business Enterprise*, de Gruyter 1988, p. 211.

4 Articles 2, 9, 12, 13, 15, 16, 17, 18, 20, 21, 22, 25, 26, 27, 29, 30, 33, 34, 41, 42 and 43 of the Regulation furnish examples of such provisions.

5 *Ordonnance* No. 67–281 of 23 September 1967, Journal Officiel of 18 September 1967.

6 OJC 14/30, 15 Feb. 1974.

7 OJC 103/4, 28 April 1978.

8 OJC 163/16, 11 July 1977.

9 OJC 108/46, 15 May 1975.

10 Council Regulation (EEC) No. 2137/85, OJL 199/1, 31 July 1985.

11 These entities are specifically mentioned because they might be excluded from the ambit of Article 58(2) by too rigid an interpretation of that text, especially where they are not profit-making.

12 The applicable system of law will be determined in accordance with the rules of private international law.

13 Thus, in some cases where it was proposed that two or more. competitors should pool research, development or manufacturing activities, the Commission should be notified with a view to obtaining negative clearance or an exemption under Article 85(3) EEC.

14 See Sch. 4 to the European Economic Interest Grouping Regulations, S.I. 1989 No. 638.

15 *EWIV-Ausführungsgesetz* of 14 April 1988, BGBl. 1.514(1988).

16 Note in particular S. Israels, 'The EEIG – A major step forward for Community Law', 9Co. Law (1988), 14 and R.M. Petriccione, 'New Forms of Organized Activity of Community Level', LIEI 1986/2, 18. R. Drury of Exeter University gave a very useful presentation of the European Economic Interest Regulations as part of the paper on the grouping which he read at the conference on the harmonization and unification of European Company Law which took place at the Churchill Hotel on 28 April 1989, organized by European Studies Conferences Ltd.

17 This might come about under a double tax treaty following the OECD model, assuming that the state of the permanent establishment, where the EEIG was taxable, was the same as that of the state of registration. The taxation of groupings in the United Kingdom is governed by s.69F and Sch. 11 to the Finance Act 1990.

18 See S. Israels, op. cit., p. 15, for an explanation of this provision. The learned author says that the case in point is the creation, in a developing country, of a joint venture contract between an EEIG and the country's government, to perform a public works contract. Note, in the same sense, R. Petriccione, op. cit., p. 39.

19 This provision was clearly much influenced by the complex provisions of the Companies Act 1980, concerning these matters. The 1980 Act did not extend to N. Ireland.

20 See fifth recital and Article 4(1)(b), which is applicable to natural persons.

21 Article 4(1)(b), ibid.

22 Articles 6 and 39(1) ibid. Where the official address of an EEIG was in Great Britain, the registry would be the registrar within the meaning of the Companies Act 1985: see European Economic Interest Grouping Regulations, Regulation 9(1).

23 Note also European Economic Interest Grouping Regulations, Regulation 9(2) and Form EEIG 1.

24 European Economic Interest Grouping Regulations, Regulation 10(1).

25 European Economic Interest Grouping Regulations, Regulation 18 and Sch. 4.

26 Thus ss.26(1)(d); (e), and (2) of the Companies Act 1985 also apply to EEIGs. It is noteworthy that, like s.26(1)(c), these provisions also apply to establishments of an EEIG: such establishments are governed by Article 10 of the Regulation. However, neither the latter instrument, nor the European Economic Interest Grouping Regulations define what is meant by an establishment. Nevertheless, a grouping which forms an establishment in a Member State other than that in which it has its official address is required to register in that State: see Article 10 of the Regulation and Regulation 12 of the Statutory Instrument.

27 See Regulation 18 and Schedule 4, which makes ss.28(2)–(6) and (7) applicable to EEIGs and their establishments for this purpose.

28 For the effects of the registration of a grouping in Great Britain, see Regulation 9(7) of the European Economic Interest Grouping Regulation.

29 Note Regulation 3 of the European Economic Interest Grouping Regulations. There is no grant of legal personality in Germany, where the grouping is treated like a commercial partnership (OHG), which does not enjoy such personality.

30 See Articles 7–9 of the Regulation, and Regulations 13 and 15 of the European Economic Interest Grouping Regulations.

31 Article 13, ibid.

32 Article 14(1)–(3), ibid.

33 See Regulation 4 of the European Economic Interest Grouping Regulations, which have effect in Great Britain only.

34 The registrar will be the competent authority in Great Britain.

35 Article 19(1), ibid. See also Regulation 20 of the European Economic Interest Grouping Regulations (application of the Company Directors Disqualification Act 1986).

36 See Regulation 5 of the European Economic Interest Grouping Regulation, which implements this provision.

37 Article 19(3), ibid.

38 Article 20(1), ibid. The above rule is, of course, the same as that contained in Article 9(1) of the First Directive.

39 Article 20(2), ibid. Such a restriction may be invoked as against third parties if it is properly published.

40 Sch. 4 to the European Economic Interest Grouping Regulations makes Part XII of the Companies Act 1985 applicable to the creation and registration of charges.

41 This was the position under draft Regulaton 6, which was deleted from the final form of the Statutory Instrument.

42 This rule may be compared with that in s.17(1) of the UK Partnership Act 1890.

43 This is applied to groupings registered in Great Britain by Regulation 6 of the European Economic Interest Grouping Regulations.

44 The Secretary of State for Trade and Industry is the competent authority for the purposes of Article 32(1), 32(3) in Great Britain: the court is the competent authority for the purposes of Article 38 in this country: see Regulation 7(1) and (3) of the Statutory Instrument.

45 Bulletin of the European Communities, Supplement 2/82.

46 See S. Israels, op. cit., 20.

47 Note the excellent treatment by S. Israels, op. cit., 20–21. Note also the helpful treatment by K. Gleichmann in his very useful article 'Europäische Wirtschaftliche Interessenvereinigung', 149 ZHR (1985) 633, 648.

48 The use of the phrase 'internal law' excludes the application of the private international law rules of member States.

49 Note, however, Article 9, which provides that the documents and particulars which must be published pursuant to the Regulation may be relied on by a grouping against third parties under the conditions laid down by the national law applicable under Articles 3(5) and 3(7) of the First Directive.

50 Note, for example, Articles 17(3), 21(2) and 27(1).

51 Article 2, ibid.

52 Note the eleventh recital as well as Article 2.

53 See S. Israels, op. cit., 21.

54 The provisions of all these recitals have been indicated or mentioned in the present chapter.

55 It may thus not always be clear whether a given matter concerns the internal organization of the grouping. Furthermore, it may sometimes be difficult to determine whether an object pursued by a particular grouping is a permissible one.

56 It should be noted, however, that the Regulation does not contain any publicity or other requirements relating to accounts; requirements concerning these may be prescribed by the contract or perhaps by national law. Note the German law of 14 April 1988, Article 6.

57 Note, for example, German law of 14 April 1988, Articles 2–4, and Regulations 9–15 of the European Economic Interest Grouping Regulations.

58 Achte Verordnung zur Änderung der Handelsregisterfügung, 19 June 1989, BGBl. 1.1113.

59 Lovtidende No. 52, 11 April 1989.

60 Lovtidende No. 80, 15 August 1989.

61 JORF 15 June 1989, 7440.

62 JO 30 June 1989, 8101.

63 See law of 28 June 1989, Staatsblad 1989, 245.

64 Law of 12 July 1989, Moniteur Belge, 22 August 1989, 14385; Law of 17 July 1989, Moniteur Belge, 22 August 1989, 14391ff.; Royal Decree of 27 July 1989, Moniteur Belge, 22 August 1989, 14400.

65 S.I. No. 191 of 1989.

66 Note, in this sense, S. Israels, op. cit., 22.

67 Bulletin of the EC, Supplement No. 4, 1975.

68 OJ C124 of 10 October 1970; Bulletin of the EC Supplement 8, 1970.

69 Completion of the first reading was made conditional upon 'seeing proposals for harmonization of Member States legislation on groups of companies'.

70 COM(88) 320 final, 15 July 1988.

71 COM(89) Final-SYN 218 and 219, 25 August 1989. See also OJ C263 of 16 October 1989, p. 41.

72 The use of Article 100A EEC is controversial, because it is arguable that as the European Company would be a new entity, no question of the harmonization of the laws of the Member States is involved. Note, however, paragraph 7 to the Preamble to the draft Regulation. Because Article 100A(2) EEC provides that matters involving the rights of workers must be decided unanimously, this provision could not be used as a basis for employee participation. It should be noted that the draft Regulation contains one fiscal provision: such provisions are also supposed to be decided unanimously.

73 There might well be some minor differences between the laws of England and Wales, Scotland and Northern Ireland concerning these matters.

74 Draft Regulation, Articles 1 and 38.

75 Draft Regulation, Article 7(4).

76 Ibid., Article 133.

77 Ibid., Article 4.

78 Ibid., Article 5.

79 Ibid., Article 16.

80 Ibid., Articles 17–30.

81 OJ No. L61, 5 March 1977, p. 26.

82 Ibid., Articles 18 and 19.

83 Ibid., Articles 20 and 21.

84 Ibid., Article 22.

85 Ibid., Article 23.

86 Ibid., Articles 24 and 25.

87 Ibid., Articles 26 and 27.

88 The rights that would be granted to the workers by Article 33 have given rise to controversy.

89 Ibid., Article 38(2).

90 Ibid., Article 38(2).

91 Ibid., Article 14.

92 Ibid., Articles 42(1) and 97(1).

93 Ibid., Article 42(1) and (5).

94 Ibid., Article 42(2).

95 Ibid., Article 42(5).

96 Ibid., Article 43. This restriction might prove to be disadvantageous: see the UNICE draft Position Paper of 26 October 1989, para. 22, in this sense.

97 Ibid., Article 44(1)–(3).

98 Ibid., Article 44(4).

99 Ibid., Article 45(1).

100 Ibid., Article 45(1).

101 Ibid., Article 46(2).

102 Ibid., Article 47.

103 Ibid., Articles 48 and 49. The definition of a controlled company contained in Article 6 is outlined below.

104 Ibid., Article 49(1). The provisions of Article 49 are somewhat more stringent than those of Article 19 of the Second Company Law Directive.

105 Ibid., Article 52(1)–(3).

106 Ibid., Article 52(5).

107 Ibid., Article 53.

108 Ibid., Article 54.

109 Ibid., Article 56.

110 Ibid., Article 53.

111 Ibid., Article 58.

112 Ibid., Article 59. The proposal does not appear to take full account of the wide variety of securities which it is now possible for a company to issue.

113 Ibid., Article 61.

114 Ibid., Article 62(2).

115 Ibid., Article 62(3).

116 Ibid., Article 63: see also draft Directive complementing the draft Regulation, Article 4.

117 Ibid., Article 64(1).

118 Ibid., Article 64(3).

119 Ibid., Article 66. The controversial nature of this proposal should require little emphasis.

120 Ibid., Article 74.

121 Ibid., Article 68.

122 Ibid., Article 71.

123 Ibid., Article 72.

124 Ibid., Article 74. As pointed out in the Consultative Document of December 1989, it is questionable whether the broad principles on fair dealing by directors contained in Articles 73 and 74 would provide adequate protection.

125 Ibid., Article 72(2).

126 Ibid., Article 77(2). UNICE has argued that this system of joint liability would place an excessive burden on companies: see draft Position Paper, para. 30.

127 Ibid., Article 81.

128 Ibid., Article 97.

129 Ibid., Article 93.

130 Ibid., Article 82.

131 Ibid., Article 84.

132 Ibid., Articles 87(1) and (2).

133 Although the wording of this provision is not clear, it is evidently intended to govern the situation where proxies are solicited by a credit institution, or by the company or a group of shareholders.

134 Ibid., Article 89.

135 Ibid., Article 90.

136 Ibid., Article 92.

137 Ibid., Article 98.

138 Ibid., Article 100.

139 Ibid., Articles 101–13.

140 For a critical treatment of them, see Consultative Document, p. 11 and Annex E.

141 OJ No. L348, 17 December 1988, p. 62.

142 Article 6 would define a controlled undertaking as one in which any natural or legal person (a) had a majority of the shareholders' or members' voting rights; or (b) had the right to appoint or remove a majority of the members of the administrative, management or supervisory board and was at the same time a shareholder in, or member of that undertaking or (c) was a shareholder or member and alone controlled, pursuant to an agreement entered into with other shareholders or members of the undertaking, a majority of the shareholders' or members' voting rights.

143 Ibid., Articles 115 and 116.

144 Ibid., Article 117.

145 It is not clear whether such a rule would apply to an SE having its

registered office anywhere in the UK by virtue of Article 129 of the draft Regulation.

146 It seems that 'continue in existence' is intended to mean the same as 'continue in business' when used in Article 119: compare section 165 of the Insolvency Act 1986.

147 Ibid., Article 122.

148 It will be noted that Article 126(1) contains no special rules governing the expenses of the liquidation, or secured or preferred creditors. The special priorities given to such creditors and expenses under English law would apply only in the case of the insolvent liquidation of an SE registered in England or Wales, to which English law would be made applicable by Article 129.

149 Ibid., Article 127. Nothing is said in this provision about the grounds on which such a challenge might be made.

150 English law is mentioned by way of example, but the provisions of Scottish law would not seem to be very different in the present regard.

151 See OJL 225/1 and OJL 225/6, 20 August 1990.

152 A Convention has recently been adopted governing the matter, see OJL 225/10, 20 August 1990.

153 Ibid., Article 6(3).

154 See the Department of Trade and Industry and the Department of Employment's Consultative Document on the proposal for a European Company Statute, December 1989, pp. 10–11, for an account of some of these apparent defects. See also the Opinion of the Economic and Social Committee on the draft Statute, OJC 124/35, 21 May 1990.

155 These objections are restated in paragraph 33 of the Consultative Document of December 1989, where this opposition is stated to be on the grounds that, in the context of the economic and social traditions of the UK, any arrangements for worker participation are best decided on a voluntary basis between employers and employees. Note also House of Lords Select Committee on the European Communities, European Commons Statute, Session 1989–90, 194, 1904, p. 20, in the same sense.

CHAPTER 9: MUTUAL RECOGNITION

1 See I. Schwarz, in Von der Groeben, von Boeckh; Thiesing and Ehlermann, *Kommentar zum EWG-Vertrag*, Nomos Verlagsgesellschaft, Baden Baden 1983, 982ff., who adopts the interesting and tenable view that Article 220 can be invoked only when no other legal basis for the enactment of a Convention, Regulation or Directive can be found. He finds that this was not the case in relation to the above Convention.

2 Note, in this sense, the works by E. Stein, *Harmonization of European Company Laws*, Bobbs-Merrill 1970, p. 44; G. Beitzke,

'Anerkennung und Sitzverlegung von Gesellschaften und juristische Personen in EWG-Bereich', 127ZHR 1, 5 (1963–4); U. Drobnig, 'Kritische Bemerkungen zum Entwurf eines EWG-Übereinkommens über die Anerkennung von Gesellschaften', 129 ZHR 91, 101 (1965–6), and C. Timmermans, 'The Convention of 29 February 1968 on the Mutual Recognition of Companies and Firms', 27 Netherlands International Law Review, 357.

3 Note also that the General Programmes for the Removal of Restrictions on the Right of Establishment and the Free Supply of Services (1962) JO 36 and 32, adopted by the Council of Ministers, provide that when the companies only have their registered office within the Community, their business activity must share a real and objective link with the economy of a Member State before they can claim the benefits of the Treaty. See Stein, op. cit., pp. 402–3.

4 See the Belgian Law of 18 May 1873, Article 196; the Luxembourg Law of 15 August 1915, Article 158; the Italian Civil Code, Article 16(2); and the Greek Civil Code, Article 19.

5 Note in this sense, Stein, op. cit., p. 44. The provisions on freedom of establishment were given a surprisingly restricted meaning in Case 81/ 87 *R v. H.M. Treasury and others, ex parte Daily Mail and General Trust plc* [1989] 1AllER 328.

6 The United Kingdom, Denmark and Ireland all adopt the incorporation rule.

7 See RGZ 7.68 and RGZ 73.76.

8 Note, for example, Italian Civil Code, Article 2505.

9 See Stein, op. cit., p. 397, note 202.

10 Such a partnership has the capacity to sue or be sued in its own name under RSC, Ord. 81. Difficulties might arise in relation to such partnerships because they do not have registered offices.

11 For the territorial scope of the Convention, see Article 12 thereof.

12 See Stein, op. cit., p. 412, and the literature cited there in this sense.

13 See C. Timmermans, 'The Convention of 29 February 1968 on the Mutual Recognition of Companies and Firms', 27 Netherlands International Law Review 357, in the present sense.

14 Note, in this sense, Stein, op. cit., p. 413.

15 This rule has been argued by some to be an improper discrimination against foreign companies. For other difficulties with Article 7, see Stein, op. cit., pp. 415–16.

16 Note, for example, U. Drobnig, op. cit., note 2, 118.

CHAPTER 10: CONCLUSION

1 There has, however, been a considerable amount of activity in the field of securities law in recent years.

2 OJL 199/1, 31.7.85.

3 Note, for example, Directive of 17 November 1986, OJL 332/22, 26 November 1986, which is concerned with the liberalization of capital movements.

4 Note, for example, Directive of 1 December 1988, OJL 348/82. 17 December 1988, which is concerned with disclosure in the case of the acquisition or sale of an important participation in a listed company.

5 Note, for example, Directive of 8 December 1986, OJL 372/1, 31 December 1986, which is concerned with the annual accounts of banks, and is closely connected with the Fourth Directive.

6 Note, for example, Oldekop, 'Die Richtlinien der Europäischen Wirtschaftsgemeinschaft', 21 JöR, n.f. 58, 92–8 (1972).

7 See R. Buxbaum, and K. Hopt, op. cit., p. 234 and M. Zuleeg, 'Die Rechtswirkung europäischer Richtlinien, 9ZGR 461, 470 (1980).

8 See A. Bleckmann, *Europarecht*, 4th edn, Cologne 1985, p. 71.

9 Op. cit., 275–80.

10 See R. Buxbaum and K. Hopt, op. cit., p. 265, in the latter sense.

11 See ibid., pp. 241–2, and the literature referred to there.

12 It is implied by ibid., n. 273, 241 that the blocking effect may result from principles stated by the European Court of Justice in such cases as Case 106/77 *Simmenthal No. II* [1978]ECR 629, 644 and Case 815/79, *Cremonini* [1980]ECR 3583, 3607. It is noteworthy, however, that these cases were concerned with directly applicable provisions of Community law. It is doubtful whether they can be interpreted in the manner suggested above. A useful account of the literature dealing with the so-called blocking effect of Directives appears in M. Zuleeg, 'Die Rechtswirkung europäischer Richtlinien, 9ZGR 466, 470(1980).

13 OJ 1985 L210/29.

14 OJC 144/10, 11 June 1986.

15 This entity consists essentially of a limited partnership between a limited company as the general partner, and its members as the limited partners.

16 See Proposal for a Thirteenth Council Directive on Company Law concerning take-over bids and other general bids, COM(88) 823 Final-SYN 196, Brussels 16 February 1989. See also the DTI's Consultative Document, 'EC Proposal for a Thirteenth Company Law Directive Concerning Take-overs', August 1989. Discussions of the draft Directive have been taking place in a Council Working Group. The European Parliament has recently given its opinion on the draft Directive, and the

final version thereof enacted by the Council will probably incorporate certain of its amendments.

17 The United Kingdom Code contains more general principles than does the draft Directive and may adopt a more flexible approach than does the latter instrument. See the Memorandum of the Law Society's Standing Committee on Company Law of September 1989 for a useful critical analysis of the provisions of the draft Directive. The Law Reform Committee of the Law Society of Scotland has adopted a more positive approach to this draft instrument.

18 Note, for example, the draft Position Paper of UNICE, and the Consultative Document on the proposed European Company Statute published by the DTI in December 1989.

Bibliography

BOOKS

Bleckmann, A., *Europarecht*, 4th edn, Cologne (1985).

Boyle, A.J. and Birds, J., *Company Law*, Jordans (1987).

Buxbaum, R. and Hopt, K., *Legal Harmonization and the Business Enterprise*, de Gruyter (1988).

Choi, F. and Mueller, G., *International Accounting*, Prentice-Hall Inc., New Jersey (1984).

Ellis, M.J. and Storm, P.M. (eds), *Business Law in Europe*, Kluwer Law and Tax Publishers (1982).

Ernst and Whinney, *The Fourth Directive*, Kluwer Publishing, London (1980).

Forde, M., *Company Law in Ireland*, The Mercier Press, Cork and Dublin (1985).

Goldman, B. and Lyon-Caen, A., *Droit commercial européen*, Dalloz, Paris (1984).

Lasok, D. and Bridge, J., *Law and Institutions of the European Communities*, 4th edn, Butterworths (1987).

Lutter, M., *Europäisches Gesellschaftsrecht*, W de Gruyter, Berlin (1984).

McKinnon, S. (ed.) *Consolidated Accounts, The Seventh Directive*, Kluwer Publishing Ltd (1984).

Palmer, *Company Law*, 24th edn (Schmitthoff and others), Stevens and Co. (1987).

Pennington, R.R., *Company Law*, 5th edn, Butterworths (1985).

Ripert, G., *Traité Elémentaire du Droit Commercial*, 12th edn, Roblot, Paris (1986).

Schmitthoff, C.M. (ed.) *The Harmonization of European Company Law*, UK NCCL, London (1973).

Sealy, L., *Company Law and Commercial Reality*, Sweet & Maxwell (1984).

Stein, E., *Harmonization of European Company Laws*, Bobbs-Merrill Company, Indianopolis (1970).

Von der Groeben, H., von Boeckh, H., Thiesing, J. and Ehlermann, C.D., *Kommentar zum EWG-Vertrag*, 3rd edn, Nomos Verlagsgesellschaft, Baden-Baden (1983).

ARTICLES

Ault, A.J., 'Harmonization of Company Law in the European Economic Community', 20 Hastings Law Journal (1968) 77.

Barbaso, F., 'The Harmonization of Company Law with regard to Mergers and Divisions', JBL (1984) 176.

Beitzke, G., 'Anerkennung and Sitzverlegung von Gesellschaften und juristischen Personen im EWG-Bereich, 127ZHR 1.

Cook, T., 'The Seventh Directive: An Accountant's Perspective, 9 European Law Review (1984) 43.

Daübler, W., 'The Employee Participation Directive', in *The Social Policy of the European Communities*, issued by the Common Market Law Review, Sijthoff, Leyden (1977), 83.

Dine, J., 'Implications for the United Kingdom of the EC Fifth Directive' 38ICLQ (1989) 547.

Dine, J., 'The Draft Fifth EEC Directive on Company Law', 10Co. Law (1989) 10.

Dine, J., 'The Eleventh Company Law Directive: A Protective Proposal' 133SJ 30.

Drobnig, U., Kritische Bemerkungen zum Vorentwurf eines EWG-Übereinkommens über die Anerkennung von Gesellschaften', 129ZHR 93.

Ehlermann, C.D., 'The Internal Market following the Single European Act', 24CMLR 361.

Farrar, J.H. and Powles, D.G., 'The effect of section 9, of the European Communities Act 1972 on English Company Law', 36MLR (1973) 270.

Feuillet, P., 'La Huitième Directive du Conseil des Communautés Européennes et le Commissariat aux Comptes', Revue des Sociétés (1984) 26.

Ficker, H.C., 'The EEC Directives on Company Law Harmonization', in *The Harmonization of European Company Law*, ed. C.M. Schmitthoff, UKNCCL (1973), 68.

Fikentscher, W. and Grossfeld, B., 'The Proposed Directive on Company Law', 2CMLRev. (1964, 65) 259.

Frommel, S.N., 'EEC Companies and migration – a setback for Europe', [1988] Intertax 409.

Glaesner, H.J., 'Die Einheitliche Europäische Akte', 21 Europarecht 1986, 119.

Gleichmann, K., 'Europäische Wirtschaftliche Interessenvereinigung', 149ZHR (1985) 633.

Houin, R., 'La régime juridique des sociétés dans la CEE', 1RTDE (1965) 11.

Houin, R., 'Les pouvoirs des dirigeants dans la CEE', 2RTDE 1966, 307.

Israels, S., 'The EEIG – A major step forward for Community Law', 9Co. Law (1988) 14.

Kuetgen, R., 'La Deuxième Directive en Matière des Sociétés', Revue Pratique des Sociétés (1977) 1.

Lang, J.T., 'The Fifth Directive on the Harmonization of Company Law' (1975) CMLRev. 155 and 345.

Lang, J.T., 'The Second EEC Company Law Directive', Irish Jurist 1976, 37.

Lutter, M., 'Die erste Angleichungs-Richtlinie zum Art 54 Abs 3(g) ENGW und ihre Bedeutung für das geltende deutsche Unternehmensrecht', 4 Europarecht (1969) 1.

Lutter, M., 'Die Entwicklung des Gesellschaftsrechts in Europa, 10 Europarecht 1975, 44.

Morse, G., 'The Second Directive: raising and maintenance of capital' (1977) 2 European Law Review 126.

Nobes, C.W., 'The Harmonization of Company Law Relating to the Published Accounts of Companies', 5 European Law Review 1980, 38.

Oldekop, K., 'Die Richtlinien der Europäischen Wirtschaftsgemeinschaft, 21JöR n.f. 58.

Pennington, R., 'Consolidated Accounts: The Seventh Directive', 5Co. Law (1984) 66.

Petite, M., 'The Conditions for Consolidation under the Seventh Company Law Directive', 21 CMLR (1984) 81.

Petriccione, R.M., 'New Forms of Organized Activity at Community Level', LIEI 1986/2, 17.

Pipkörn, J., 'Zur Entwicklung des europäischer Gesellschaftsrechts-und Unternehmensrechts', 136ZHR (1972) 499.

Prentice, D., 'Section 9 of the European Communities Act 1972', 89LQR.

Rodière, R., 'L'harmonisation des législations européenes dans le cadre de la CEE', IRTDE (1965) 336.

Schmitthoff, C.M., 'Amendments to the Fifth Draft Directive and to Vredeling', [1983]JBL 456.

Schmitthoff, C.M., 'Employee Participation and the Theory of Enterprise', [1975]JBL 265.

Schmitthoff, C.M., in *Encyclopedia of European Community Law*, Sweet & Maxwell/W. Green & Son, Part B10-135, C3-006, C3-117, and C3-280.

Schmitthoff, C.M., 'The *Daily Mail* Case in the European Court', [1988]JBL 454.

Schmitthoff, C.M., 'The board structure', [1984]JBL 100.

Schmitthoff, C.M., 'The Future of the European Company Law Scene', in *The Harmonization of European Company Law*, ed. Schmitthoff, UKNCCL, London (1973), 3.

Scholten, V., 'Company Law in Europe', 4CMLRev. (1966–7) 377.

Storm, P., 'European Company Law', in *Business Law in Europe*, ed. M.J. Ellis and P.M. Storm, Kluwer Law and Tax Publishers (1982), 13.

Timmermans, C., 'The Convention of 29 February 1968 on the Mutual Recognition of Companies and Firms', 27 Netherlands International Law Review 347.

Tweedie, D. and Kellas, J., 'Off-Balance Sheet Accounting', Accountancy, April 1987, 91.

van Hulle, K., 'The EEC Accounting Directives in Perspective: Problems of Harmonization', 18CMLRev. 121.

van Ommerschlage, P., 'La première directive du Conseil du 9 mars 1968 en Matière des sociétés', CDE 1969, 495 and 619.

Welch, J., 'Tenth Draft Directive on cross-border mergers', 7Co. Law (1986) 69.

Welch, J., 'The Fifth Directive: a False Dawn', 8ELR (1983).

Wooldridge, F., 'Harmonization of Company Law in the European Economic Community', Acta Juridica 1978, 327.

Wooldridge, F., 'The Draft Fifth Directive on the Harmonization of Company Law', 81 Law Society's Gazette (1984) 2783.

Wooldridge, F., 'The EEC Council Seventh Directive on Consolidated Accounts' 371.CLQ (1988) 714.

Wooldridge, F., 'The Fourth Directive on Accounts', Lloyd's Maritime and Commercial Law Quarterly 1980, 27.

Wooldridge, F., 'The Implementation of the Third Directive in Germany' 4Co. Law (1983) 232.

Wooldridge, F., 'The Third Directive and the Meaning of Mergers', 1Co. Law (1980) 75.

Zuleeg, M., 'Die Rechtswirkung europäischer Richtlinien', 9ZGR 4616 (1980).

OFFICIAL PUBLICATIONS

Commission of the European Communities
Amended Proposal for a Council Directive amending Directive 78/660 on annual accounts and Directive 83/349/EEC on consolidated accounts with respect to the exemptions for small and medium-sized companies and to the drawing up and publication of accounts in ECU, Doc COM(89) 561 Final-SYN158.

Amended proposal for a Council Directive on the annual accounts and consolidated accounts of insurance undertakings, Doc COM(89) 474-Final.

Amended proposal for an Eleventh Council Directive on company law concerning disclosure requirements in respect of branches, Doc COM(88) 153 Final.

Communication from the Commission concerning its action programme relating to the implementation of the Community Charter of Basic Social Rights of workers, Doc COM(89) 568 Final.

Completing the Internal Market – White Paper from the Commission to the European Council, Doc COM(85) 310.

Conventions concluded by the Member States of the European Communities Pursuant to EEC Treaty. Article 220, Bull. EC, Supp. 2/1969.

Cross-border Mergers of Public Limited Companies – Proposal for a Tenth Directive, Bull. EC, Supp. 3/1985.

Draft Convention and Report on bankruptcy, winding up arrangements, compositions and similar proceedings Bull. EC, Supp. 2/87.

Draft Convention on the International Merger of Sociétés Anonymes and Report (the so-called Goldman Report) on the Draft, Bull. EC Supp. 13/1973.

Employee participation and company structure in the European Community, Bull. EC, Supp. 8/75 (Guertsen Report).

Internal market and industrial co-operation, Doc COM(88) 320 Final, Bull. EC Supp. 3/88.

Preliminary draft of a Community Charter of Fundamental Social Rights, Doc COM(89) 248 Final.

Proposal for a Council Directive amending Directive 78/360/EEC on annual accounts and Directive 83/349 EEC Consolidated accounts, Doc COM(88) 292 Final-SYN 158.

Proposal for a Council Regulation embodying a Statute for European Companies, Bull. EC, Supp. 8/70.

Proposal for a Council Regulation on the Statute for European Companies, Bull. EC, Supp. 4/75.

Proposal for a Council Regulation on the Statute for a European Company, Doc COM(89) 268 Final, OJ C263/41, 16 October 1989.

Proposal for a Thirteenth Council Directive on Company Law on take-over bids and other general bids, Doc COM(88) 823 Final.

Proposal for a Twelfth Council Directive on company law on single-member private companies, Doc COM(88) 101 Final.

Proposal for a Eleventh Council Directive based on Article 54(3)(g) EEC concerning disclosure requirements in respect of branches, Doc COM(86) 397 Final.

The Fourth Company Law Directive: implementation by Member States (Doc, Luxembourg 1987).

United Kingdom

House of Lords, Select Comittee on the European Communities, Employee Consultation (House of Lords, Session 1980/81, 37th Report, 14 July 1981).

House of Lords, Select Committee on the European Communities, European Company Statute (House of Lords, Session 1989/90, 19th Report, 10 July 1990).

Parliamentary Debates, House of Lords, Official Report, 8 November 1989, cols 676ff.

Department of Employment and Department of Trade and Industry: Consultative Document on the Draft European Communities Fifth Directive on the Harmonization of Company Law, November 1983.

Department of Trade and Industry: Consultative Document on the Amended Proposal for a Fifth Directive on the Harmonization of Company Law in the European Community, January 1990.

Department of Trade and Industry: Consultative Document on Barriers to Take-overs in the European Community, January 1990.

Department of Trade and Industry: Consultative Document on the European Communities draft Ninth Directive on a Conduct of Groups containing a Public Limited Company as a Subsidiary, February 1985.

Department of Trade and Industry: Consultative Document on the EC Proposal for a Thirteenth Company Law Directive concerning Take-overs, August 1989.

Department of Trade and Industry: Consultative Document on the Proposal for a European Company Statute, December 1989.

Department of Trade and Industry: Consultative Document on the EC Regulation on the European Economic Interest Grouping, May 1986.

Department of Trade and Industry: Consultative Document, Regulation of Auditors, Implementation of the EC Eighth Company Law Directive, 1986.

Department of Trade and Industry: Consultative Paper on the Implementation of the Seventh Company Law Directive, August 1985.

Department of Trade and Industry: letter on Accounting for Mergers and Acquisitions and the Write-Off of Goodwill, 5 July 1988.

Department of Trade and Industry: letter on the Implementation of the EC Seventh Company Law Directive, Subsidiaries and controlled Non-Subsidiaries, 16 August 1988.

MEMORANDA OF THE LAW SOCIETY'S STANDING COMMITTEE ON COMPANY LAW

Memorandum on the Amended Proposal for a Council Directive on Procedures for informing and consulting employees, (OJ NoC 217, 12.8.83, p. 3), February 1984.

Memorandum on the Draft EC Directive amending the Fourth and Seventh Directives (OJC 144, 11.6.1986), December 1986.

Memorandum on the Implementation of the EEC Seventh Company Law Directive on Consolidated Accounts Definition of a Subsidiary, February 1988.

Memorandum on the Proposal for a Ninth Directive on the Conduct of Groups, July 1982.

Memorandum on the Proposal for a Thirteenth Directive on Take-overs and Other General Bids, September 1989.

OTHER DOCUMENTS

Confederation of British Industry: Memorandum to the Council for the meeting on 11 October 1989 on the European Company Statute.

UNICE: draft Position Paper on the European Company Statute, 25 October 1989.

Table of Cases

Decisions of the European Court of Justice

Amministrazione delle Finanze dello Stato v. Simmenthal S.p.A. [1978]ECR 629: 106/77.

Commission v. Belgium [1983]ECR 467: 301/81.

Cremonini [1980]ECR 3583: 815/79.

Friedrich Haaga GmbH [1974]ECR 1201: 32/74.

Insurance Services, Re: Commission v. Germany [1987]2CMLR 69: 205/84.

Nederlandse Ondernemingen v. Inspecteur der Invoerrechten [1977]ECR 113: 51/76.

R v. HM Treasury and others, ex parte Daily Mail and General Trust plc [1989]1AllER 328: 81/87.

Von Colson and Kamann v. Land Nordrhein – Westfalen [1984]ECR 1891: 14/83.

Decisions of United Kingdom Courts

Ammonia Soda Co v. Chamberlain [1918]1Ch 266.

Barclays Bank Ltd v. TOSG Trust Fund Ltd [1984]BCLC1.

Hopkinson v. Mortimer, Harley & Co. [1917]1Ch 646.

International Sales and Agencies Ltd v. Marcus [1982]2AllER 551.

Phonogram Ltd v. Lane [1982]2AllER 182.

Royal British Bank v. Turquand Ltd (1856)6E and B327.

Index